The Evolution of the American Academic Library Building

David Kaser

The Scarecrow Press, Inc.
Lanham, Md., & London
1997

SCARECROW PRESS, INC.

Published in the United States of America
by Scarecrow Press, Inc.
4720 Boston Way
Lanham, Maryland 20706

4 Pleydell Gardens, Folkestone
Kent CT20 2DN, England

Copyright © 1997 by David Kaser

British Library Cataloging-in-Publication Information Available

Library of Congress Cataloging-in-Publication Data
Kaser, David, 1924–
    The evolution of the American academic library building / David
Kaser.
      p. cm.
    Includes bibliographical references and index.
    ISBN 0-8108-3219-4 (alk. paper)
    1. Library architecture—United States—History. 2. Academic
libraries—United States—History. I. Title.
  Z679.2.U54K37   1997
    727'.8'0973—dc20   96-36032
                                      CIP

ISBN 0-8108-3219-4 (cloth: alk. paper)

∞ ™ The paper used in this publication meets the minimum requirements
of American National Standard for Information Sciences—Permanence of
Paper for Printed Library Materials, ANSI Z39.48—1984.
Manufactured in the United States of America.

To My Students
I learned more from them than they did from me.

Contents

List of Figures vii

List of Tables viii

List of Plates ix

Preface xi

Chapter 1. In the Beginning 1
 A. *Background*
 B. *American Academic Life at Mid-century*

Chapter 2. Academic Library Buildings, 1840–1875 13
 A. *Antebellum Library Buildings*
 B. *New Libraries, 1864–1875*

Chapter 3. New Directions and Partitioning, 1875–1890 29
 A. *New Directions*
 B. *Partitioning*
 C. *Briefer Mention of the Others*

Chapter 4. Consolidation without Innovation, 1890–1900 45
 A. *Controversy between Architects and Librarians*
 B. *Preferences in Architectural Style*
 C. *. . . and Some Others*

Chapter 5. Andrew Carnegie and the Period, 1900–1910 63
 A. *Carnegie and the Black Colleges*
 B. *Carnegie Buildings on Other College Campuses*
 C. *Other Building Donors of the Period*
 D. *Publicly Funded Buildings*

Chapter 6. Enter the Behemoths, 1910–1945 85
 A. *Radical Departures*
 B. *More Conventional Solutions*
 C. *A Stereotyped Pattern, 1920–1945*
 D. *Booms and Busts in Library Construction*
 E. *A Single Innovation*

Chapter 7. Changes in Design, Structure, and Style 107
 A. *The Era of the Structural Stack*
 B. *Advent of the Modular Building*

C. *The Need for Building Expertise*
D. *Innovations and Improvements*

Chapter 8. The Contemporary Modular Building   129
    A. *The Classic Module*
    B. *. . . and the Romantic Module*
    C. *Problem Areas*
    D. *Architects*
    E. *New Directions*

Chapter 9. The Rise of the Anti-Building   155

Appendix 1. List of Library Buildings, 1840–1994   165

Sources   185

Index   197

About the Author   207

List of Figures

Fig. 1.   Rectangular Library with Perimeter Shelves   3
Fig. 2.   Transverse Shelving in Classical Revival Building   4
Fig. 3.   Transverse Shelving in Gothic Revival Building   4
Fig. 4.   Sectional View Showing Shelving in . . . Gothic
           Revival Building   5
Fig. 5.   Radial Shelving in Round Building   6
Fig. 6.   Locations of Antebellum College Library
           Buildings   15
Fig. 7.   Floor Plan of the Library at Princeton, 1873
           (*Library Journal* 2 (Oct. 1877): facing p. 54)   25
Fig. 8.   Richardson's Plan for Vermont's Billings Hall,
           1886   33
Fig. 9.   Miller's Library for Cornell, 1890
           (*Library Journal* 14 (Apr. 1889): 122)   37
Fig. 10.   Number of College . . . Library Buildings
           Built . . . , 1840–1899   46
Fig. 11.   Plan of the Northwestern University Library, 1894
           (*Library Journal* 19 (Oct. 1894): 338)   56
Fig. 12.   McKim's Library for Columbia University, 1897
           (*New England Magazine* ns17 (Dec. 1897): 436)   58
Fig. 13.   Number of New Academic Library Buildings
           Constructed, 1900–1915   79
Fig. 14.   Funding Sources of Academic Libraries
           Constructed, 1900–1910   81
Fig. 15.   Entry Level of Johns Hopkins University Library,
           1916
           (*Library Association Record* 3d ser II (1932): 284) 90
Fig. 16.   Second Floor of the University of Michigan
           Library, 1920
           (E. H. Hanley, *College and University Library
           Buildings*, 1939, p. 33)   98
Fig. 17.   Common Stack Locations in Academic Libraries,
           1910–1945   99
Fig. 18.   Bluffton College Library, 1930
           (E. H. Hanley, *College and University Library
           Buildings*, 1939, p. 89)   100
Fig. 19.   Fluctuations in the Number of New . . . Library
           Buildings Opened, 1916–1950   105
Fig. 20.   Typical Stack Deck in a Small Academic Library   109

Fig. 21.   Typical Fixed-Function Library Building with . . .
Stack Tower   111

Fig. 22.   . . . Bailey's Modular Plan for the Meredith College
Library Building, 1969   117

Fig. 23.   New Academic Library Buildings Opened . . . ,
1951–1970   119

Fig. 24.   Number of New Libraries Built . . . , 1971–1990   156

Fig. 25.   Number of New Libraries and Library Additions
Constructed, 1980–1994   157

List of Tables

Table 1.   Antebellum College Library Buildings Showing
Year of Completion   9

Table 2.   American Academic Libraries Built, 1840–1875   19

Table 3.   Institutions Receiving Buildings from Donors
Other than Carnegie, 1900–1910   80

Table 4.   Enrollment and Library Collection Growth in
Selected Universities, 1890–1920   87

Table 5.   Some Large Libraries Constructed, 1920–1945   101

Table 6.   Ten Largest Libraries Built in the United States,
1964–1984   148

List of Plates

Plate 1—The Styles of Early American Library Buildings Tended to Be Classical Revival in the South, Shown on the Left, and Gothic Revival in the North, Shown on the Right: a) University of South Carolina, b) University of North Carolina, c) Yale University, d) Haverford College.

Plate 2—During the 1870s and Early 1880s, College and University Libraries in the United States Were of Varied Styles and Designs: a) Saint Lawrence University, b) Union College, c) Brown University, d) Washington and Lee University.

Plate 3—Romanesque-style Library Buildings Were Popular for about a Decade Beginning in 1885: a) University of Vermont, b) Colgate University, c) Wittenberg College, d) Carleton College.

Plate 4—The Adoption of Classical Revival Architecture for the Columbian Exposition in 1892 Resulted in a Resurgence in Its Popularity for Most Public Buildings, Including Libraries, for Many Years Thereafter: a) Columbia University, b) Emory University, c) Grinnell College, d) Livingstone College.

Plate 5—Interior Views of Selected Academic Libraries, 1856–1912: a) Main Library Hall, College of Charleston, b) Rotunda, Lehigh University, c) Reading Room, Cornell University, d) Main Library Hall, Union College, e) Main Reading Room, University of California, f) Main Reading Room, University of Texas.

Plate 6—A Stereotyped Pattern for Academic Libraries from 1911 to 1946 Featured a Large Reading Room on the Second-floor Front and Multitier Stacks to the Rear: a) University of California, b) University of Texas, c) University of Kansas, d) University of Oklahoma.

Plate 7—Early Modular Academic Library Buildings in the 1950s Tended to Take on a Boxlike Appearance that Many Felt Was Dull: a) University of Iowa, b) LaSalle University, c) University of Louisville, d) Saint Louis University.

Plate 8—Attempts of Many Kinds Were Made in the 1960s and 1970s to Disguise the Boxy Appearance of the Modular Library Building: a) Washington University, b) Butler University, c) Heidelberg College, d) Clark University.

Plate 9—In the Last Third of the Century Some Libraries Took Modest Forms While Others Were Extreme: a) Indiana University, b) University of California—San Diego, c) Tougaloo College, d) Macalester College.

Plate 10—Interior Views of Selected Academic Library Buildings, 1965–1982: a) Main Lobby, Scarritt College, b) Current Periodicals Area, University of South Carolina, c) Shelf and Study Area, University of Minnesota, d) Shelf and Study Area, Vassar College, e) Below-grade Shelf and Study Area, University of Illinois, f) Reading Room, Colgate University.

Preface

Many years ago a wise man suggested to me that whenever I was unsuccessful in a search for published information on a subject, I should consider writing a book or paper on that subject. Presumably if I had wanted the information, someone else was likely someday to want the same information. That advice has stimulated me to write many monographs throughout my life, including the present one. In my consulting on academic library buildings over the past thirty-five years I have often wanted to know why certain early libraries, or even recent libraries, were designed as they were. When I would go to the record to learn why, however, I uniformly found the record to be nonexistent at its worst and very scanty or even inaccurate at its best. In the mid-1980s Dr. Sang Chul Lee, a knowledgeable scholar on this topic, wrote of it: "The literature on this subject is not rich. The investigation of the vast number of academic library buildings and the attempt to form a systematic view on their development are yet to be done."[1] About that same time I concluded that surely here was a book just waiting to be written, and I began working on it.

I soon discovered what was doubtless a principal reason for the absence of an intensive literature on the subject. It was that no record had ever been compiled of the many hundreds of academic library buildings that had been constructed in the United States. A remarkably few had ever been documented at all, but that few understandably had been cited over and over, creating the often inaccurate assumption that they were landmark or watershed buildings that warranted being generalized from to account for the whole. In some cases, that assumption was at least partially warranted, but in many others it was not. Instead, innovations and influences often originated in buildings that were known only in their day, having long since been forgotten.

First, therefore, I had to compile as complete a record as I could of the buildings that had been built. That was the purpose of the list of 1,526 structures that I include herein as Appendix 1. I certainly do not claim that it is complete, or perhaps even totally accurate, although I will be surprised if it proves to be less than 90 percent complete for nineteenth-century buildings or less than 85 percent complete for twentieth-century buildings.[2] It was teased out of a wide range of sources, including published documents (institutional histories as well as the library, architectural, and educational literature), personal visits to more than six hundred of the buildings, exploitation of numerous institutional archives, telephone and mail polling of many libraries, and even the scanning of myriad picture postcards. Nonetheless I consider Appendix 1 to be at best a "preliminary checklist" and invite interested readers to inform me of additions that should be made to it. The list is limited to complete buildings (not additions) constructed initially to be used either totally or primarily as central academic libraries on four-year college or university campuses. Wherever possible I have used the date a library was first opened for use, although this datum often proved to be quite elusive. Understandably institutional archives were more often able to provide the date a cornerstone was laid, a groundbreaking occurred, or a dedication ceremony took place. Once this "database" began to approach completion, the monograph itself could proceed apace.

Only a small selection of the total, of course, could even be mentioned here. The selection of libraries to be discussed or mentioned here, as well as the pictures and sketches to be displayed, was a highly personal matter. In some cases they represent value judgments on my part of the significance or influence of certain buildings, either temporal or lasting. In most cases, however, they were chosen because I felt that they were typical of what was being done in an era or in a region or in a particular environment. Except where otherwise indicated, I made the illustrations and photographs.

I must express my appreciation to the Indiana University Research and Graduate Development Office for financial assistance and to my many graduate assistants, especially Steven Kirby, who were of immeasurable help in searching the literature. I am grateful also to several publishers who granted me kind permission to reuse blocks of material here that I had published previously with them; they are acknowledged individually with the material quoted. Host institutions were invariably gracious in response to my requests for aid in tracking down obscure information about their libraries. I am especially appreciative to those archives that I enumerate in my discussion of sources at the end of the book, not only for their assistance in finding relevant matter but also for their willingness to permit me to publish from it. The unsung heroes of this exercise, however, were my many students throughout the years who waited patiently whenever I permitted my personal hobbyhorse to run roughshod over a prepared syllabus. All of my files, including a slide collection of more than eight hundred building facades, have been deposited in the Library Building Archive in the School of Library and Information Studies at Florida State University in Tallahassee. I am grateful to the university for providing the files a home.

Bloomington, Indiana

Notes to Preface

1. Sang Chul Lee, "Planning and Design of Academic Library Buildings." DLS dissertation, Columbia University, 1985, p. 23.

2. If that estimate should prove to be accurate, it suggests that the total number constructed during the 155-year period that fit the criteria of this study would approach 1,800.

Chapter One

In the Beginning . . .

A. Background

The exterior form and interior layout of any good building must be determined by its purpose. This truism is as applicable to academic library buildings as it is to any other kind of structure. Yet the purpose (or purposes) of a library building may depend upon one's point of view. Unique among all buildings, libraries must obviously meet their societal responsibilities as repositories for acquiring, organizing, and preserving, as well as laboratories for utilizing, the human record. Along with other buildings, however, libraries may also serve as monuments to a spirit, an idea, or an individual. Also like other kinds of buildings, libraries will usually attempt to fulfill an aesthetic role by gracing a site or adorning a prospect.

Considered in another way, it might be said that buildings of all kinds, including libraries, ought to fulfill at least three purposes. All buildings must shelter their contents, they should facilitate the functions that they house, and they may enhance aesthetics.[1] Many of the academic libraries that have been constructed in the United States have addressed all three of these roles with some success.

Indeed, except in cases of external cataclysms such as fire or earthquake, few if any of the 1,800 academic libraries estimated to have been built in this nation to date have failed in the fulfillment of at least their primary obligation to shelter their contents and activities. Many have also been remarkably helpful in assisting the libraries they contain to perform their functions effectively. Some have proved to be strikingly handsome in appearance. And a very few have done all three.

Historically, American academic library buildings can be studied from several different perspectives. First, library historians would probably prefer to view them as through the eyes of the classical archaeologist—in other words, as artifacts that reflect and elucidate

1

a functional requirement of their times. Second, historians of education might find it most useful to look at their evolution almost in a Darwinian sense—as it helps them to understand the shaping influences of modifications in American university pedagogy. Third, changes in library structures can be examined as the results of new building materials or innovative construction techniques. And fourth, of course, the topic can be approached as the history of an art form. No doubt there are other possible perspectives for such a study, but in the belief that at least these four will be instructive, this monograph will give some attention to each of them in developing its theses.

Just as nothing ever really ends, neither does anything ever truly begin. Thus it is not wholly defensible to try to isolate American library buildings from others in the world, or to begin this study suddenly when the first was built here in 1840, as though there had been no academic library buildings anywhere prior to that time. That would be starting in medias res, as it were. There had, of course, been many noble university library buildings in Europe and elsewhere before the nineteenth century, and some contemporary American scholars and architects were well acquainted with them. Boll's excellent study of early academic library buildings in New England contains an admirable review of the evidence for transatlantic influence in their design.[2]

The best of those earlier European library buildings took one of three fundamental patterns. The first of the three European models available to American library building planners in the early decades of the nineteenth century was a simple rectangular room with single-faced book presses arrayed along its perimeter walls between the window lights as shown in Figure 1. Where ceiling heights permitted, these perimeter bookshelves sometimes had galleries of additional shelves above them, with their weight usually supported by the wall structure itself. Among the many European examples of this layout for library buildings were the Arts End of the Bodleian Library at Oxford, dating from the early seventeenth century, Louis Le Vau's design of the Bibliothèque Mazarine in Paris, dating from the middle of the seventeenth century, and Sir Christopher Wren's library in Saint Paul's Cathedral in London, dating from the early eighteenth century.

One would expect that the stark simplicity of this pattern would have made it a very attractive option for Americans to adopt, but surprisingly few of this nation's early colleges employed it. It was used in some of the early public library buildings in the United States, that of the Library Company of Philadelphia (1791) being

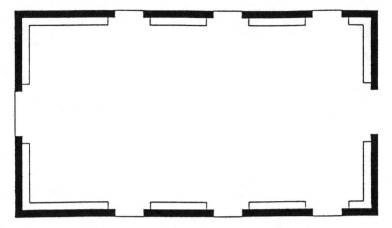

Figure 1. Rectangular Library with Perimeter Shelves

the most notable, but among academic institutions before the Civil War it was utilized only at Amherst. The failure of this concept to attract imitators on college campuses may have resulted from its very limited book storage capability in relation to the floor area it required.

Easily the most popular European model to be adopted on this continent in the middle decades of the nineteenth century was the alcoved hall with double-faced book presses extending inward between the windows in the two longer walls. Two variations of this scheme are shown in Figures 2 and 3. No doubt the best example of this layout in Europe at the time was Thomas Burgh's magnificent Long Room in the Library of Trinity College Dublin, which, except for its gallery and barrel vault, had been completed in 1732. There were several advantages to this transverse configuration of shelving, including the facts that: (1) it permitted more books to be shelved in the same amount of floor area; (2) it allowed daylight to play upon the faces of the bookshelves; (3) it could accept upper galleries; and (4) if needed, the resulting alcoves could accommodate carrels, although reading desks were seldom an important consideration in American libraries until well after the Civil War.

Not only was this interior layout efficient in terms of the very limited academic library functional requirements of the time, but also its simple rectangle could be fitted with equal facility into either of the two dominant architectural forms of the era. Both the Classical Revival and Gothic Revival architecture that were then in vogue lent themselves to this internal arrangement. Figure 2 shows how this stack layout could be, and often was, superimposed upon the

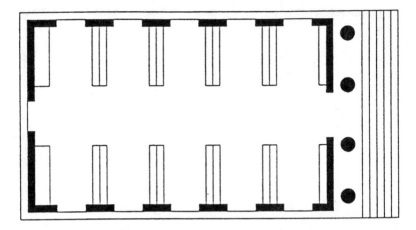

Figure 2. Transverse Shelving in Classical Revival Building

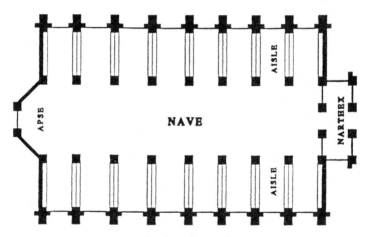

Figure 3. Transverse Shelving in Gothic Revival Building
(as used at Yale, 1846)

cella of a typical prostyle Greek or Roman temple, with its entry through a portico at one end, which served as a vestibule.

But as may be seen in Figures 3 and 4, this stack layout could be even better fitted into a traditional basilica, most often adapted as a Gothic chapel. Here the narthex served as the vestibule, book shelves ranged between the piers and the columns creating alcoves in the aisles, while the nave functioned for purposes of general circulation and for reading space as necessary. Lancet windows between

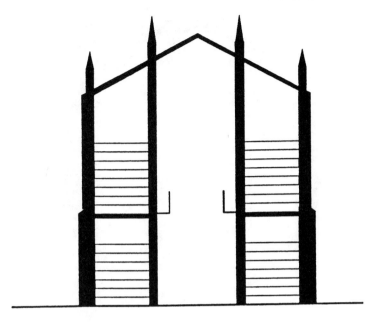

Figure 4. Sectional View Showing Shelving in Aisles and Galleries in Gothic Revival Building (as used at Wesleyan, 1868)

the buttresses lighted the book shelves on the main floor and gallery, while clerestory windows lighted the nave. Given these two very felicitous possibilities, it remained only for an architect or the officers of an American university to determine whether a Classical or a Gothic exterior treatment best suited its site and fashion.

There was still a third model that has beguiled American library designers from the beginning. This was a round, or more commonly a polygonal, plan. A recent European example of such a library was James Gibbs's Radcliffe Camera at Oxford University, which had been opened in 1749. In conceptualizing the University of Virginia's Rotunda in 1826, however, which was to house the institution's library for more than a century, Thomas Jefferson went to a much earlier model and drew directly and faithfully from the Pantheon in Rome.[3] Figure 5 demonstrates how architects have normally utilized its radial potential. As in the rectangular plan, alcoves were created by double-faced ranges of shelves extending inward between buttresses and columns, but with the columns here deployed in a circular line to support a dome rather than linearly to support a barrel vault. Just as in Figures 3 and 4, side windows lighted the alcoves,

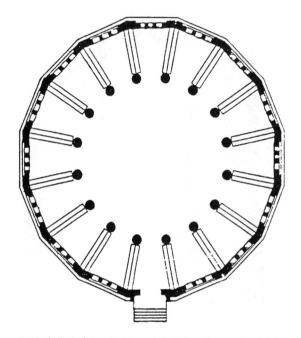

Figure 5. Radial Shelving in Round Building (as used at Union, 1877)

lantern windows lighted the clerestory, and if ceiling heights were adequate, galleries could be added.

In the last analysis, of course, this third pattern may be viewed simply as a curvilinear representation of the rectangular basilica discussed earlier. It was brought to its ultimate level, in theory although never in practice, in 1835 by the French botanist Benjamin Delessert in his *Mémoire sur la Bibliothèque Royale*.[4] As will be seen later in this study, subsequent library designers in both the nineteenth and the twentieth centuries have continued on occasion to lay out round, semicircular, or polygonal book stacks. The potential visualized for them, however, has never been fulfilled, primarily because of their inefficient use of floor area. Maximum utilization of floor space is lost as soon as the radiating ranges become farther apart than the functional minimum distance required for passage between their hub ends.

Beginning then in 1840 with these three fundamental floor patterns—perimeter shelving, transverse shelving (in two styles of wrapping), and radial shelving—American academic libraries proceeded for the next one hundred fifty years to perform increasingly complicated functions and, as a result, to require increasingly complex building forms. Library building planning during that century and a half went through four clearly distinctive and easily differentiated functional stages, the first three of which each required almost exactly equal time periods to run their courses. These four stages, and the periods in which they dominated, were as follows:

First Period (1840–1875)—Single-function book halls

Second Period (1875–1910)—Multi-partitioned structures

Third Period (1910–1945)—Fixed-function buildings with multi-tier stacks

Fourth Period (1945-date)—Modular integration of book and reader spaces

This study will be organized around these four stages, and the meaning and significance of their delineations will be explained as it advances.

Several delimitations will be imposed upon this study. First, this study will deal only with buildings originally designed and constructed either solely or primarily to serve library purposes; rooms outfitted as libraries in multipurpose buildings will not be discussed except in passing. Second, it will address only central library buildings in colleges and universities, forgoing satellite, departmental, or school libraries, as well as libraries in academies, theological seminaries, or other freestanding professional schools. Third, it will discuss only buildings constructed de novo rather than wings added to previously existing library structures. And fourth, it will concern only library buildings in the United States. All four of these delimitations can be challenged as somewhat arbitrary, but in total they were felt to constitute the most tolerable expedient for keeping the study to reasonable length. In keeping with the practice of the times, the two nouns "college" and "university" will be used almost synonymously until the end of the nineteenth century. As far as possible, however, today's names of institutions will be used.

Given these constraints then, this study cannot begin until more than two hundred years after Harvard University acquired the first academic library book collection in British North America in 1638. Indeed, of the ninety-five colleges listed in the United States on January 1, 1840, none had yet attained book collections of sizes large enough to justify the erection of separate structures dedicated solely to library purposes.[5] Along with other requirements of college operations—enrollment, administration, professoriate, even housing and dining—libraries to that time had been so small in size and so limited in scope that they had all been able to cohabit buildings containing other college functions.

Indeed it was not uncommon among the smaller or younger institutions of the time for an entire college operation to be of such a size that it could be housed within a single structure. In larger, older, or more firmly established institutions, however, a library might share a building with only one other major function, perhaps the chapel or a suite of classrooms.

At Yale, for example, the library had been housed above the college chapel before 1846 when it was removed into its own first free-standing building. Brown, on the other hand, located its library beneath Manning Chapel from the time the chapel was constructed in 1835 until the institution erected its first separate library building forty-three years later. Modeled by architect James C. Bucklin on the Temple of Diana Propylea in Eleusis, the library shelves on the lower level of Manning Hall were laid out to create a dozen alcoves in the manner described earlier. Likewise, from 1766 onward the library at Harvard, then as now comprising the country's largest academic book collection, occupied "a large room on the upper floor [of Harvard Hall], arranged in ten alcoves,"[6] until its first separate library building was opened in 1841. Mention has already been made of Thomas Jefferson's Rotunda at the University of Virginia, which was cohabited by the library and other university functions from the time it was built in 1826 until its reconstruction seventy years later following a disastrous fire that nearly destroyed it completely.

Few institutions, however, were fortunate enough to enjoy even this quality of library space. The library at the United States Military Academy was housed for a time in the Observatory. That at Louisiana State University languished until the present century in an abandoned powder magazine. And at the University of North Carolina the library was shelved for many years in a bedroom in the president's residence.

B. American Academic Life at Midcentury

Until the latter half of the nineteenth century, American academic library buildings could be small and simple because the colleges themselves were small and simple. In 1840 the average enrollment in the colleges of New England, which were then the largest in the nation, was only 166, whereas in the Trans-Allegheny West, where colleges were smallest, average enrollment was a meager seventy-two. Almost until the time of the Civil War all study in the nation was at the undergraduate level and was available only to men. Curricula were severely restricted and were intended only to build upon the instruction given in the Latin schools of the land. The only mode of learning was the continuing and largely sterile cycle of lecture and recitation. Overworked and underpaid professors were drawn predominantly from the clergy rather than from fields of productive scholarship. Except for the very few wealthier institutions, the entire college operation tended to be largely a shabby, impoverished, hand-to-mouth affair.[7] In retrospect it seems remarkable indeed that this lugubrious state of affairs nonetheless resulted somehow in producing the leaders needed to bring the nation through one of its most vigorous periods of growth.

Given this very circumscribed purpose of American higher education at the time, it is not surprising that college libraries were of very limited importance and consequently of very infrequent use. Again, in 1840 the average sizes of college-owned library book collections were 8,002 volumes in New England, 4,023 in the Middle Atlantic states, 3,477 in the South, and only 2,516 above the Ohio River. In most cases these libraries operated totally without book funds—the University of North Carolina appears not to have purchased a single library book for thirty-five years following 1824—but rather they accreted only occasional gifts of charity to their meager collections. Administered uniformly by a lone professor assigned parttime to be library custodian, unheated and unlighted library rooms were usually open only one or two hours a week for use by members of the college community. Table 1 shows the sizes

TABLE 1
Antebellum College Library Buildings Showing Year of Completion,
Number of Volumes Owned by the Library, and the Number of Hours
Weekly the Library Was Open for Service in 1857.[9]

Name of Institution	Year Library Was Opened	Volumes in the Library, 1857	No. of Hours Open Weekly
South Carolina	1840	25,000	20
Harvard	1841	74,000	28
Yale	1846	36,000	30
Williams	1847	7,200	2
North Carolina	1851	3,500	5
Amherst	1853	12,000	3
Charleston	1856	7,000	?
Ohio Wesleyan	1856	6,300	?
Centre	1862	5,100	2

of the college-owned book collections, as well as the numbers of hours weekly that the libraries were open, at the nine institutions that erected separate library buildings prior to the Civil War. Operated under the most restrictive of policies, these libraries were even less stimulating of intellectual vigor than were their parent institutions.[8]

Understandably libraries with such limited obligations could operate in very small amounts of space laid out in very simple designs. Almost the sole function of college libraries prior to the Civil War was to house and protect the books owned by the college. Then as now, the library was usually also the repository of the college's "nonbook media", comprising in the nineteenth century collections of portraiture, globes, and marble statuary, of which there always seemed to be some. Busts of Classical-period authors and philosophers were usually conveniently situated at the inner ends of stack ranges, and portraits of past presidents of the college or bishops in the church were hung on the gallery front, both sometimes serving as location symbols for the books in the adjacent ranges.

Sometimes, but not always, a few tables and chairs were provided in case someone wished to consult a reference on-site, but more often so that the librarian would have a place to sit while he (and they were always men) inscribed new acquisitions into the manuscript catalogue of the library's holdings or added a name to its donor list. But those few tables and chairs, if indeed they were needed at all, could be fitted in almost anywhere, most easily into the aisle alcoves or in the nave. The infrequency of their use meant that they did not require any particular location or configuration. Rather, the single function of providing most effective book storage dictated the simple arrangement of space within all library buildings of the time.

Although there was little disagreement as to the appropriate interior layout of American library buildings when they first began to appear in 1840, preference regarding exterior design treatment was about equally divided between two styles, largely determined by the region of the country. In the Southland, popular taste still favored the severe, restrained lines of Classical Revival architecture that had been rediscovered and adapted by Palladio in the sixteenth century and had flourished so long in harmony with the spirits of both the Renaissance and the Enlightenment. Elsewhere in the Union, however, especially in New England, the Romantic Movement was in full sway, bringing with it a growing partiality for the more effusive and elaborate motifs of Gothic Revival buildings.[10] This was the pedagogical and bibliothecal environment in the United States when the first separate college library building was built at the beginning of the fourth decade of the nineteenth century.

Notes

1. In his excellent early study of library function entitled *Etude sur la Construction des Bibliothèques*, Léon de LaBorde proposed that a good library building should be planned on three principles, namely: ". . . la conservation des livres, la facilité des recherches, [et] la tranquillité des études." (Paris: A. Franck, 1845), p. 8.

2. John J. Boll, "Library Architecture: A Comparison of Theory and Buildings, with Emphasis on New England College Libraries." Ph.D. dissertation, University of Illinois, 1961, pp. 23–113.

3. Lewis Mumford, *The South in Architecture* (N.Y.: Harcourt Brace, 1941), pp. 62–78.

4. (Paris: H. Dupuy, 1835).

5. *American Almanac and Repository of Useful Knowledge for the Year 1840* (Boston: David H. Williams, 1840), pp. 186–89.

6. *Harvard University Library, 1638–1938* (Cambridge, Mass.: Harvard University Library, 1969), p. 11.

7. Frederick Rudolph, *The American College and University; A History* (N.Y.: Vintage, 1968); D. G. Tewksbury, *The Founding of American Colleges and Universities before the Civil War* (Hamden, Conn.: Archon, 1965).

8. Howard Clayton, "The American College Library, 1800–1860," *Journal of Library History* 3 (1968), 120–137. See also Arthur T. Hamlin, *The University Library in the United States* (Philadelphia: University of Pennsylvania Press, 1981), and Orvin L. Shiflett, *Origins of American Academic Librarianship* (Norwood, N.J.: Ablex, 1981).

9. These data are gleaned from William J. Rhees, *Manual of Public Libraries, Institutions, and Societies in the United States and British Provinces of North America* (Philadelphia: J. B. Lippincott, 1859), passim.

10. James M. Fitch, *American Building* (Boston: Houghton Mifflin, 1948), p. 55. By mid-century this transition was well-nigh complete, at least insofar as academic library buildings were concerned, and all but one or two of those constructed in the subsequent twenty years were wrapped in Gothic exteriors.

Chapter Two

Academic Library Buildings, 1840–1875

The first period in American academic library building design—that of single-function book halls—began with the first building in 1840 and continued for thirty-five years thereafter.

A. Antebellum Library Buildings

Nine college and university libraries were constructed in the United States prior to the Civil War. Five of them were in the north and four were in the south. Each of them will be discussed here.

South Carolina. The first completely freestanding academic library building constructed in the United States was opened for use at the University of South Carolina, then called the South Carolina College, in Columbia sometime before May 6, 1840. Prior to the opening of this building, the institution's library had languished for a while in a room above the College chapel and, after 1817, on the floor above the chemistry laboratory where a leaky roof had damaged its books and rotting floors had threatened its collapse entirely. In the late 1830s, however, South Carolina College was becoming one of the nation's strongest antebellum institutions, due largely to the presence on its faculty of the erudite and stimulating German-American scholar Dr. Francis Lieber. Himself the product of the German seminar, a style of instruction emphasizing research, about which more will be said later, Lieber began insisting immediately upon his arrival in Columbia in 1836 that the College needed a stronger library. Here he found a willing ally and resourceful proponent in the institution's president, Robert W. Barnwell. As a result, not only was the construction of a new building soon authorized, but also annual book funds (an extreme rarity in those days) were appropriated, improved custody of the books was mandated, and new policies for their generous use were drawn up. As a consequence, by the time of the Civil War, South Carolina College had the fourth largest academic library book collection in the nation, following only Harvard, Yale, and Brown.

With the school located in the South, it should be no surprise that the style of building chosen by the Columbia institution for its library building was Classical Revival (Plate 1a). It is probably more accurate to say that it should be no surprise that the institution selected as its architect a man already widely known for his designs in the Classical medium. Robert Mills had apprenticed with both Thomas Jefferson and Benjamin Latrobe before designing on his own account a number of notable Classical-style buildings in Pennsylvania, Maryland, and especially the District of Columbia. He is best known today for the Washington Monument, a commission that he had won in competition in 1836. Moreover, Mills was a South Carolinian by birth and had even won a competition for the College's Rutledge Hall as early as 1801.

Mills intentionally patterned the interior of the College library on that of the Library of Congress, which had been redesigned by Charles Bulfinch following its burning by British troops in the War of 1812. Since the Library of Congress was again destroyed by fire in 1851, and since Bulfinch's plan for it no longer exists, Mills's library at South Carolina probably provides our best source of information on Bulfinch's plan for the Congressional Library. Mills located two rows of fluted Corinthian columns and engaged columns along the length of the hall, creating seven arched alcoves on both the front and the rear walls. A gallery rose above the arcade, and alternate alcoves were fenestrated with high arched windows. The entry was centered on the long front wall, rather than at the end as was more common, and access to it was gained through a stately portico with four Doric columns.[1]

In its early decades this structure was used primarily for book storage, but it took on additional functions later, serving for more than a century as the University's only library building until its main collections were removed to the new McKissick Library in 1941. Mills's building remains a library even today, now housing the University's special collections of South Caroliniana.

All told, sixteen library buildings were built in the United States during the thirty-five-year period under discussion in this chapter. As was seen in Table 1, nine of them were constructed before the end of the Civil War, five in the North and four in the South; two were in the Trans-Allegheny West, one above the Ohio River, and one below the Ohio. Of those nine, four each were built in the 1840s and in the 1850s, and one was built in the early 1860s. The locations of these nine are shown in Figure 6. Six of the nine were based upon Classical models, two were faithful copies of Gothic chapels, and the architecture of one has been called "Tuscan Villa" in style.

Harvard. After South Carolina College, the second and third library buildings erected in the nation were pure Gothic. These were Gore Hall, which was opened at Harvard in July of 1841, and Yale's "Old Library," which was completed five years later.[2] In conceptu-

Figure 6. Locations of Antebellum College Library Buildings

alizing the exterior for Gore Hall, architect Richard Bond took as his fifteenth-century model the chapel at King's College, Cambridge. Except for reducing the size of the building by more than half and adding a transept to form a Latin cross[3], Bond followed his prototype faithfully. He even took care to mock up lath and plaster imitations of King's Chapel's cut stone groin vaults that sprang from the ribs of the columns in its nave. In Gore Hall these columns, arrayed in two rows of ten, set off the nave from the aisles, where double-faced ranges of bookshelves created alcoves both on the main floor and in the gallery above. On the exterior, four towers marked the corners of the main hall, and twenty pinnacles set off the roofline. One end of the transept accommodated the building's main entry hall, and the other contained three book rooms.[4]

As with its contemporary library buildings, Gore Hall was used effectively, and almost entirely, as book storage space during its first three decades of existence. A single exception to that generalization was that its entry hall was also available for study purposes when needed, although students are reported to have groused often about not being allowed to proceed farther into the building. A stack wing was added in 1877, about which more will be said later, and the nave was completely revamped in 1895 to accommodate more books. Gore Hall was razed in 1912 to make room for Widener Library, which was then erected on the site.

Yale. Yale's first library (Plate 1d), completed five years after Gore Hall, really began as four separate libraries accommodated in a single interconnected structural complex. As was common on American campuses at the time, there were not only a College-owned book collection at Yale but also three other libraries owned by student societies,[5] and the new building was planned to house all four collections although in separate apartments. In order to accomplish this purpose, the building's central hall was designed as was Harvard's to resemble a small King's College Chapel. At Yale, however, this main hall was then connected by recessed wings on both flanks to two smaller chapellike halls right and left. The large central hall contained the College-owned library, and the two smaller halls and one wing were occupied by the three student society libraries.

On the interior, all three parallel halls were laid out in similar fashion, with traditional central naves, transverse bookshelves creating alcoves in the aisles, and galleries above. The central hall especially was quite elegant with a nave arcade of clustered stone columns rising to support a high timbered groin vault. The nave itself was lighted by tall arched windows in its two ends and in the clerestory, but because of the flanking wings, side windows were located in only four aisle alcoves at the gallery level, and none at the main level. With such limited fenestration, the library's interior was always quite dark. On the exterior, the central hall was marked by four prominent towers capped by finials, two in front and two in back, while stubbed pinnacles terminated the twelve buttresses.

A small reading room for the College library was located at the entry through one wing, but again by far the greater area was planned from the beginning to be used solely for book storage. No additional library space became available to the University until 1890, when the Chittenden Library was opened for use. The 1846 building, however, continued to serve as a library until the Sterling Memorial was completed in 1932. Since that time it has fulfilled handsomely its current function as the University's Dwight Chapel.

Williams. When Williams College set out to plan the fourth academic library building in the United States, it retained Thomas A. Tefft of Providence, then only twenty years of age, to be its architect. In conceptualizing this building, which came to be named Lawrence Hall, Tefft benefited greatly from the expertise of his fellow townsman, Charles Coffin Jewett, then librarian of Brown University. Jewett had just returned from an extended visit to the libraries and universities of Europe and was unquestionably the most knowledgeable librarian in the Western Hemisphere at the time. Lawrence Hall, therefore, is the only antebellum library in the nation for which a librarian played a substantial planning role.

As a result of Jewett's contributions, the design of Lawrence Hall was fully three decades ahead of its time in terms of its response to the needs of library functions. Jewett alone among American scholars and librarians in 1846 knew that, just as had occurred in Europe, especially in Germany, libraries on this continent would soon be called upon to perform many functions beyond simply keeping books sheltered from the weather. In addition, therefore, to providing only bookshelves as other American libraries were doing, Jewett and Tefft created dedicated spaces for other bibliothecal activities: periodical reading, for example, special collections, and what is today called technical services, as well as ample study space. Ironically, however, the plan was so far ahead of its time that no one then at Williams, or perhaps anywhere else in the country, fully comprehended the designers' intentions in having it so constructed. As a result, several of its carefully crafted innovations, primarily in the internal use of space, were never implemented.

The plan for Lawrence Hall at Williams College came quite close to one of the European models described in the previous chapter. Octagonal in shape and two levels in height, rather like the Tower of the Winds in Athens, its original intention was to house most of the aforementioned new services in separate rooms on the lower level. The upper level was to have double-faced bookshelves seven feet high extending from its eight corners inward to a circle of Ionic columns supporting an entablature, which in turn sustained a dome and an octagonal lantern. This allowed an open rotunda to serve as study space with a raised platform at its center for the library attendant in the manner envisioned by Delessert twelve years earlier. The upper level also had adequate ceiling height to permit the future addition of two seven-foot galleries when needed, thereby creating an ultimate book capacity for the hall of an estimated 30,000 volumes.

Although Williams College constructed the building largely as Tefft had designed it on the outside, it did not see fit to follow Jewett's scheme for using the space inside, choosing instead to mount single-faced bookshelves twelve feet high along the interior faces of the perimeter walls between the windows. Unable to perceive Jewett's vision of a library of the future, Williams built a library for its present in 1847 when Lawrence Hall was completed. By the time the College came to feel the need for Jewett's innovations, it was no longer possible to adopt them. Nonetheless, Lawrence Hall served as the library of Williams College until its Stetson Library was built in 1922.[6]

North Carolina. Meanwhile back in the South, another rectangular alcoved library was being planned, this one for the University of North Carolina (Plate 1b). Although UNC, the oldest state university in the land, would be able to boast the nation's second largest college enrollment prior to the Civil War, it had not been similarly successful in developing strong academic and library programs. Nonetheless, by 1850 the University had retained noted New York architect Alexander Jackson Davis to design its first library building.

Davis, who had done fine work in both the Gothic and the Classical genres, understood that the latter would be the more appropriate choice for the Chapel Hill institution. His eighty-four-by-thirty-two-foot rectangular library, first named Smith Hall, rested on a podium, with its entry at one end through a pedimented portico graced by four fluted Corinthian pillars. In designing the capitals for the pillars, Davis followed Latrobe in an unsuccessful attempt to establish an "American Order" by substituting sheaves of wheat and ears of corn for Hellenic acanthus leaves, but in every other detail the building's exterior was pure Greek. There is little indication today as to how the interior was first arranged, but its dimensions suggest that it was laid out, as one would expect, in alcoves created by transverse shelves. If that assumption be correct, it is likely that the building's sole function was to serve for book storage.

Smith Hall was opened as a library in 1851, but it suffered vicissi-

TABLE 2
American Academic Libraries Built, 1840–1875

Date*	Institution	State	Architect	Style
1840	South Carolina	SC	Robert Mills	Classical
1841	Harvard	MA	Richard Bond	Gothic
1846	Yale	CT	Henry Austin	Gothic
1847	Williams	MA	Thomas A. Tefft	Classical
1851	North Carolina	NC	Alexander J. Davis	Classical
1853	Amherst	MA	Henry A. Sykes	Tuscan
1856	Charleston	SC	George C. Walker	Classical
1856	Ohio Wesleyan	OH	Morris Cadwallader	Classical
1862	Centre	KY		Classical
1864	Haverford	PA		Gothic
1868	Wesleyan	CT	Henry Austin	Gothic
1870	Marietta	OH		Classical
1870	Mount Holyoke	MA	Hammett Billings	Classical
1871	Saint Lawrence	NY		Romanesque
1872	Hamilton	NY	Ryder & Harris	Classical
1873	Princeton	NJ	William A. Potter	Gothic

*Years indicate when these library buildings were opened to the public.

tudes of several kinds in its early life. Federal troops occupied the campus during the Civil War, and legend has it that the Michigan Ninth Cavalry, while billeted in the town, stabled its mounts in the building, substituting stalls for the bookshelves in its alcoves.[7] Whether true or not, Smith Hall was the University of North Carolina's only library building until 1907, when its Carnegie Library was opened. The building still stands, however, serving today as the Carolina Playmakers Theater.[8]

Amherst. There would be little value in describing here in this much detail all of the academic library buildings constructed in the United States during this first, "single-function" period before

1875. Yet some brief observations about several of them would be useful. Mention has already been made of Amherst College's Morgan Library, which was the only additional antebellum library to be built in New England. In both its exterior appearance (neither Classical nor Gothic but Italianate) and its internal use of space (perimeter wall shelves), Morgan Library differed from its contemporaries. Superseded as the College library when the Converse Memorial building was opened in 1917, Morgan Hall today houses College offices.

College of Charleston. As would be expected, the first library built for the College of Charleston in South Carolina in 1856 was also done in the Classical Revival mode (Plate 5a). Narrow wings flanked the central part of its facade, through which entry was gained and which comprised four pilasters supporting an entablature and pediment. On the inside, short transverse ranges of bookshelves created seven small alcoves, front and back, each six feet by eight feet, which were surmounted by a gallery with arched windows.[9] Small, compact, and very neat, this building of some sixty-four by thirty-six feet, following its restoration after an earthquake in 1886, was the home of the College library until the opening of the Robert Scott Small Library in 1972. Today it houses the Office of Admissions.

Ohio Wesleyan. Little is known about the interiors of the two prewar libraries constructed west of the Alleghenies. Sturges Library at Ohio Wesleyan University was opened in 1856. It was described the following year as having an alcoved and galleried upper hall, seventy by sixty feet in size and twenty-five feet high, where the institution-owned collection was located. Four rooms on the floor below were occupied by student society libraries.[10] Sturges Hall is a classroom building today, but its interior was so completely altered when Ohio Wesleyan constructed its new Slocum Library in 1898 that, in the absence of further documentation, it is no longer possible to visualize its original use with clarity or confidence.

Centre. The first Sayre Library (its replacement bore the same name) opened at Centre College in Kentucky in 1862 and burned down less than two decades later, leaving only one document of its existence. That single document is a photograph of the building, which is preserved in the College Archives. It shows an octagonal, two-story structure with a lantern, strongly reminiscent of Lawrence Hall at Williams and very likely influenced by it. The Kentucky building, however, is taller and of more graceful proportions. It may be assumed to have had an internal circular colonnade similar to Lawrence Hall, but whether the bookshelves were laid out radially as Jewett intended at Williams or peripherally as was actually done there can no longer be ascertained.

B. New Libraries, 1864–1875[11]

Seven new academic library buildings were built during the decade immediately following the Civil War. They will be discussed in less detail than were the antebellum structures.

Haverford. Haverford College opened its small but beautiful Gothic Revival library late in the Civil War. Notwithstanding its very simple design, it was criticized in the Quaker mentality of the area for looking too much like either a "pagan structure" or an "Episcopal chapel."[12] Fifty by thirty feet in size, it had three lancet windows on each side opening into alcoves on both the main floor and its narrow gallery. This library has been added to several times and still comprises the Philips Wing of Haverford's Magill Library.

Wesleyan. The plan for Wesleyan University's Rich Hall Library, now its "92 Theatre," is ascribed to architect Henry Austin, who had designed Yale's first library building two decades earlier. Completed in 1868, Rich Hall is also Gothic Revival in style and was laid out with six alcoves on each flank of the nave. As Wesleyan's library collections grew, first one gallery and then a second were added above, bringing the ultimate capacity of the structure to some 80,000 volumes. During the period under discussion in this chapter the building was used solely for book storage.

Marietta and Mount Holyoke. Marietta College in Ohio and Mount Holyoke College in Massachusetts both opened library buildings in 1870. The former housed student society libraries and a chapel on the ground floor, while the upper floor and its gallery were occupied by the College-owned collections.[13] A Carnegie-funded building replaced it as the College library in 1907, and it was razed threescore years later. Mount Holyoke's first freestanding library building meanwhile was a single room, forty by thirty-five feet, which was outfitted with bookcases arranged in "cozy nooks" around the perimeter and with reader tables in the center. Lacking the usual gallery, the entire space was lighted with arched windows, five to each side and one in the end. From early in its life, this library appears to have been more easily accessible to students than had been common in American libraries to that time. The building still stands.

Saint Lawrence. Meanwhile, in upstate New York both Saint Lawrence University and Hamilton College were also building libraries. Opened in 1871, the Herring Library at Saint Lawrence was

Plate 1. The Styles of Early American Library Buildings Tended to Be Classical Revival in the South, Shown on the Left, and Gothic Revival in the North, Shown on the Right.

a) University of South Carolina (SC), 1840. Robert Mills, Architect.

b) University of North Carolina (NC), 1851. Alexander J. Davis, Architect.

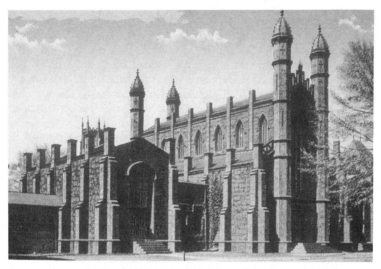

c) Yale University (CT), 1846. Henry Austin, Architect.

d) Haverford College (PA), 1864. Architect not known.

the first academic library building in the United States to be patterned upon Romanesque models. It would not be the last. Built of rough-cut stones of varied sizes and set in random patterns with a massive chimney, Herring Library had round-arched windows, originally in stained glass, centered in each of its four facades (Plate 2a). On the interior its small single hall comprised five alcoves to the rear and four alcoves and entry to the front, both with galleries above. Added to and reoriented to its rear in 1902, it continued to serve as the campus library until the Owen D. Young Library was opened in 1959. It is still standing but does not today have a specific purpose.[14]

Hamilton. In Clinton, New York, in the following year Hamilton College opened its T-shaped, two-story Perry H. Smith Library, with its entry centered below a gable in a hipped roof. Plate tracery windows on the upper level lighted a museum and art gallery, while arched windows below lighted a librarian's office. The bottom of the T to the rear of the building constituted the library hall, with three tiers of alcoves right and left. Decommissioned when the James Library was opened in 1914, the building is now Hamilton's Clark H. Minor Theater.[15]

Princeton. Completed in 1873, the Chancellor Green building at the College of New Jersey, soon to become Princeton University, is the last to fit the scope of this chapter. As a transition building, however, it also comes close, for reasons to be discussed in the next chapter, to transcending those delimitations. As Lawrence Hall at Williams College was the first American academic library building to benefit from a librarian's involvement in its planning, the Chancellor Green building was the second. Princeton librarian Frederic Vinton had worked for nine years with Charles Coffin Jewett at the Boston Public Library, and he had been eight years at the Library of Congress prior to coming to his position in the New Jersey institution in 1873, so he knew what he wanted. Although Vinton's appointment at Princeton became effective concurrent with the opening of its library building, it seems that he must have exerted considerable influence upon its design, since it evinces all of his expressed principles and preferences.

Growing from his conviction, a somewhat radical one for the time, that a college library "should be accessible in the highest degree," Vinton concluded that a "circular form seems most convenient" for its building.[16] Reminiscent of Jewett's concept for Williams College, architect William A. Potter now planned a similar but larger octagonal building for Princeton. This one, however, was actually constructed as designed (Figure 7), complete with radial stacks and an upper gallery, both of which had been planned but forgone in the earlier building at Williams. A central dais here pro-

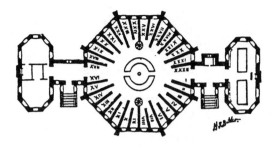

Figure 7. Floor Plan of the Library at Princeton, 1873

vided a station for the librarian, and some study tables could be fitted into the space between it and the hub ends of the stack ranges. Inner ends of alternate ranges were shortened to ease access to the alcoves, bringing this plan very close to Delessert's aforementioned theoretical scheme than had been attempted at Williams. Also borrowing a concept from Yale's library, Potter added a small octagonal pavilion to each flank of the main hall, but rather than using them for student society libraries as at the New Haven institution, the rooms here served administrative purposes.

The exterior of the Chancellor Green building bespeaks clearly the Victorian America in which it was built. "Ruskinian Gothic" almost to the extreme, it elaborates upon motifs drawn from a variety of sources but its overall appearance leaves an impression that is decidedly Byzantine. Four lofty, narrow, arched windows in six of its eight sides brought daylight to most of its thirty-two alcoves on both main and gallery levels, and large cinquefoil windows in each of its eight pediments lighted the clerestory. Four smaller windows on each side of a large octagonal lantern at the top helped to light the whole.

Given its interior layout, Vinton was able to implement his liberal goal of "accessibility" by allowing students to consult the shelves directly rather than having books fetched to them by members of the library staff. Iron railings on the gallery front and perforated iron grates in the gallery floor enabled a library attendant on his elevated central platform to see everyone in the library domain simply by pivoting 360 degrees. It was, he observed "a perfect panopticon,"[17] a quality that would no doubt have pleased Jeremy Bentham, who had advocated the same design for prisons. The Chancellor Green building is used for student activities today.

Notes

1. Daniel W. Hollis, *South Carolina College* (Columbia: University of South Carolina Press, 1951), pp. 135, 296; John Morrill Bryan, *Architectural*

History of the South Carolina College, 1801–1855 (Columbia: University of South Carolina Press, 1976), pp. 87–95.

2. Technically, the third "academic" library building to be constructed in the United States was not at Yale but rather at the Princeton Theological Seminary in 1843. A handsome Gothic structure with five alcoves on each side, the building is no longer standing. It is not treated here because of the decision, recorded in the opening section of this study, to exclude seminaries and other professional school libraries from its purview.

3. It has been suggested that Bond added a transept at Harvard to eliminate any possibility that the building's appearance might be described, as had its model at Kings College, as "a brood sow lying on her back."

4. John Burchard, *The Architecture of America* (Boston: Little Brown, 1966), p. 50. I gratefully acknowledge, however, that my treatment herein of the first library buildings constructed at Harvard, Yale, Williams, Amherst, Wesleyan, and Mt. Holyoke is heavily indebted to John J. Boll's thorough study, "Library Architecture: A Comparison of Theory and Buildings, with Emphasis on New England College Libraries." Ph.D. dissertation, University of Illinois, 1961, passim.

5. For a full treatment of the interesting phenomenon of student society libraries, see Thomas S. Harding, *College Society Libraries* (Brooklyn, N.Y.: Pageant Press, 1971).

6. R. E. Malmstrom, *Lawrence Hall at Williams College* (Williamstown, Mass.: Williams College Museum of Art, n.d.).

7. David Kaser, *Books and Libraries in Camp and Battle* (Westport, Conn.: Greenwood Press, 1984), p. 90.

8. Louis R. Wilson, *Library of the First State University* (Chapel Hill: University of North Carolina Library, 1960), pp. 14–16.

9. J. H. Easterby, *A History of the College of Charleston* (N.Y.: Scribner, 1935), pp. 116–117; William J. Rhees, *Manual of Public Libraries . . . in the United States* (Philadelphia, Pa.: Lippincott, 1858), pp. 448–450; College of Charleston Board of Trustees Minute Books, 1851–1857, III/1, pp. 162, 204, 220, 332, in the College Archives.

10. Henry C. Hubbart, *Ohio Wesleyan's First Hundred Years* (Delaware, Ohio: Ohio Wesleyan University, 1943), pp. 301–303.

11. It is ironic that one of the best designed, and certainly the best preserved, of the single-function book halls still in use as a library today does not quite fit the constraints of this study. Perhaps the Gardner A. Sage Library of the New Brunswick Theological Seminary adapted the interior of the Gothic basilica to library purposes better than any other academic library ever built in this country. See Edward T. Corbin, *A Manual of the Reformed Church in America* (N.Y.: Board of Publication of the Reformed Church, 1902), pp. 175–176.

12. Rufus M. Jones, *Haverford College; A History and an Interpretation*. (N.Y.: Macmillan, 1933), p. 54.

13. Arthur G. Beach, *A Pioneer College: The History of Marietta* (np, np, 1935), p. 159; "History of Marietta College Library," *Marietta College Olio* 33 (March, April 1905): 81–84, 99–100.

14. Paul Malo, "The Herring-Cole Library," unpublished paper dated

January 22, 1968, in the Special Collections of the Owen D. Young Library, St. Lawrence University.

15. Walter Pilkington, *Hamilton College, 1812–1962* (Clinton, N.Y.: Hamilton College, 1962), pp. 200–201; J. M. Allan, "The Library of Hamilton College, Clinton, NY, from January 1793 to January 1963," London: Library Association unpublished fellowship thesis, 1968, pp. 159–208.

16. Frederic Vinton, "Hints for Improved Library Economy," *Library Journal* 2 (October 1877): 53–54.

17. Ibid., 55.

Chapter Three

New Directions and Partitioning, 1875–1890[1]

The second main period of American academic library building design—namely that of "multifunction" buildings—began in 1875 and continued for the next thirty-five years. By this time, new directions of several kinds were establishing themselves in the American psyche, all of which would lead to changes in academic library buildings.

A. New Directions

Perhaps the three new directions that played the most significant roles in eliciting changes in college and university library buildings were in the areas of: (1) changes in higher education; (2) changes in construction materials and techniques; and (3) the rise of professional consciousness of two groups, namely of librarians and of architects. They will be discussed here briefly in that order.

In Higher Education. In the United States, professional education was becoming more generally available.[2] Also technical education was being increasingly accepted as a valid academic pursuit, hastened by the passage in 1862 of the first Morrill Act establishing land-grant colleges. In addition, attention was being given in the college curriculum to such new fields of study as the sciences, political economy, modern languages, modern history, and geography. Graduate work was becoming available, and college educational opportunities were opening up to women. Perhaps the most significant change to occur, however, was that the preferred style of instruction was shifting rapidly away from the traditional lecture to a new teaching method involving investigation and problem-solving as its principal goal. Already this seminar style of instruction, recently imported from the German universities, was being used by a number of professors in established institutions, and it was destined to become the full commitment of the new Johns Hopkins University in 1876.[3]

These developments had massive impact upon library operations. Small collections of a few good books were no longer enough; large collections, embracing poor books as well as good books, were now required. For the first time, pamphlets and periodicals became important to higher education, as did also newspapers, documents, primary sources, and unpublished manuscripts. Also for the first time, libraries had to be open many hours daily, and their new and more extensive responsibilities required much larger and better trained staffs.[4]

It was soon apparent that the simple, single-function buildings that had previously housed academic libraries would no longer be adequate. For the first time, large amounts of book storage space were now needed, and extensive accommodations were required for numerous readers. Special rooms were now needed that could be devoted to special reader activities, such as consulting periodicals or manuscripts, or that could be used by staff for library administration, or that could house reserve books or rare books or seminar collections. None of the pre-1875 buildings had these capabilities.

In Construction Techniques and Materials. By 1875 the use of iron in library building construction had become quite widespread. Its use made possible the ultimate completion in 1877 of the round library building at Union College, which was initiated decades earlier but had languished unfinished because of structural inadequacy. The first structural book stack used in the United States was made of iron and installed in a new wing on Gore Hall at Harvard, also completed in 1877. Already, however, the age of steel in building construction was making its presence felt, and in 1884 the nation's first steel skeleton office building, the Home Insurance Building, was opened in Chicago. Thereafter steel structural members and steel components, including stacks, came quickly into use in academic library buildings, resulting in their greater fire resistance and eventually permitting the erection of high-rise libraries.

The illumination of academic libraries was also in a period of rapid change. The gas lighting that had been installed in some libraries in recent years left much to be desired. Although better than the oil lamps that had preceded them, many worried about gas lights as a fire hazard, and they were widely recognized as a major cause of disintegration of book paper, especially in the upper reaches of book stacks where heat buildup and concentrations of gaseous impurities resulted. Fully three years before Thomas Edison produced the first successful electric light bulb in 1879, librarians at the first meeting of the American Library Association (ALA) speculated upon the eventual use of electricity to light libraries, and a committee was appointed to monitor and report developments.[5] By 1886, however, both Columbia and Cornell and perhaps other institutions as well were already using electric lights to illuminate their libraries, and others would be quick to follow. In 1887 Melvil Dewey issued a complete report to the ALA on the library use of electric lights in which he reported that the only disadvantage he had been able to identify in them was that they caused freckles!

Still other innovations came into use in the libraries built during this period. Telephones were introduced to aid in communication. An automatic book delivery system was installed in the addition to Harvard's library in 1877, and they eventually came to be used elsewhere as well.[6] Hydraulic, and later electric, book lifts and elevators also came slowly to be installed in academic library buildings in the subsequent years.

In the Professional Consciousness of Architects and Librarians. Concurrent with these changing capabilities came an awakening of the professional consciousness of both architects and librarians that would result in changes in the nature of academic library buildings. Clearly bespeaking this development on the part of librarians, of course, was the founding of the American Library Association and the establishment of the first library periodical, both in 1876. Both provided channels through which librarians could exchange views, experiences, opinions, and lore to their mutual benefit. Much of this early exchange concerned the new kinds of buildings that were needed.

Their experience was matched by a similar professional awakening on the part of architects. Through the entire second half of the century, most of the leading American architects were trained at the École des Beaux-Arts in Paris, and its influence on architectural style, practice, and education in this country was substantial. Its impact upon public library design in the United States has been well documented by Oehlerts,[7] but its impact was equally great upon academic library building design. The American Institute of Architects was established in 1857, and this nation's first school of architecture was opened at the Massachusetts Institute of Technology in 1866. Library buildings would no longer be allowed just to happen; instead they would reflect hereafter a merging of the professional tenets of two distinct vocations: librarianship and architecture.

B. Partitioning

This brief but significant period from 1875 to 1890 in academic library building design can be divided almost equally into two parts. During its first half, efforts were made to meet the new functional needs of libraries by what has been called tri-partitioning—that is, by the allocation of interior space to three separate library purposes: book storage, reader accommodations, and staff work areas. It quickly became obvious, however, that tri-partitioning would not be adequate, and in the second half of the period, buildings were multi-partitioned into more complex spatial arrangements that have a decidedly twentieth-century character about them.

Tri-Partitioning. Some modest concessions had been made even before 1875 to the need to divide up library space rather than simply assign it all to the single function of book storage. As was mentioned in Chapter 2, the original concept for Lawrence Hall at Williams College in 1846 had allocated some of the ground floor to staff activities and to a periodical facility, doubtless reflecting the prescient counsel of Charles Coffin Jewett. The recently built Chancellor Green building at Princeton had been tri-partitioned in a sense, with the center of its octagon occupied by the librarian's station, reading tables arrayed in a concentric circle around it, and radial stacks extending thence to the building's perimeter. Here again it was a librarian's involvement, in this case that of Frederic Vinton, that gained this improvement. Neither of these buildings, however, fully attained the degree of separation needed for these distinct functions.

Lehigh. The first completely tri-partitioned academic library in this country, and the first to make a frank separation of books from readers, was constructed at Lehigh University in 1876. This so-called Venetian-style structure was designed by Addison Hutton of Philadelphia. It located its reader tables in a rectangular space at one end of the building and its books in a three-level, semicircular stack, comprising iron columns and wooden shelves and floors (Plate 5b), at the other end.[8] Some space was also designated for library staff, completing its tri-partitioning. This building, twice enlarged, still serves Lehigh as its Linderman Library.

Brown. At almost the same time, 1878, Brown University opened its first separate library building, and it also represented a completely tri-partitioned plan. Although technically this Venetian Gothic building was designed by architect William A. Walker of Providence, his plans were based almost entirely upon sketches prepared by librarian Reuben Guild. Guild had long been a protégé of Charles Coffin Jewett, and he made his sketches after carefully studying the new Chancellor Green library at Princeton. In the form of a Greek cross, Brown's building placed its reader stations in a central rotunda that was lighted from clerestory windows in the lantern above, while its galleries of bookstacks occupied semi-octagonal termini in three of the arms. (Plate 2c)[9] It thus preserved the panoptic principle that had been used at Princeton. Lehigh and Brown represented innovations only in their tri-partitioning, however; the strong influence of the alcoved book room may still be seen in them.

Vermont. Two other simply tri-partitioned buildings of this era were those at the University of Vermont and at Dartmouth, both opened in 1886. Billings Hall at Vermont was the only academic library building designed by the great innovator Henry Hobson Richardson. One of the last buildings he designed before his untimely death, Richardson once wrote that "it is the best thing I have yet done."[10] Typical of his candid Romanesque style, its several separate gross functions are clearly adumbrated in its massive facade, with book room to the left, reading room ahead, special collection added later to the right, and staff space in one of the two towers.[11] In detailing the interior, however, Richardson appears to have been largely oblivious of the rapidly changing functional requirements of libraries. Both the rectangular book room and a special collection room were simply traditional galleried alcoves, heavily imitative of the earlier period (Figure 8). Billings has now been renovated to serve as a student center (Plate 3a).

Dartmouth. The exterior of Dartmouth's library, Wilson Hall, is clearly influenced by Richardson's Romanesque style. In its interior appointments, however, this building, which was designed by Samuel J. F. Thayer of Boston, displays greater sensitivity to changing library function than did Richardson's building at Vermont. Rather than copying the earlier alcove arrangement, this three-level book

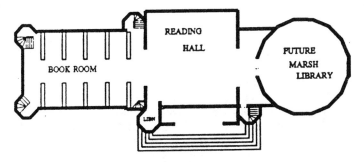

Figure 8. Richardson's Plan for Vermont's Billings Hall, 1886

room was clearly patterned upon the recent multitier structural stack that had been introduced to this continent eight years earlier in the wing added to Gore Hall at Harvard.[12]

Featuring floors, stairs, uprights, and shelves all made entirely of iron, this kind of book storage space had been invented near mid-century by Henri LaBrouste for use in the Bibliothèque Nationale and was about to become a standard feature of American academic libraries right up until the second World War. More will be said of it later. Meanwhile Wilson Hall served as Dartmouth's library until 1928, when the Baker building was built, and today it is the home of the University's drama and film studies department.

Multi-Partitioning.

Michigan. As was said above, however, tri-partitioning did not take library building planning far enough to meet their rapidly evolving functional requirements. This was abundantly evident at the University of Michigan as it began in the early 1880s to plan its first library building. Michigan President Charles Kendall Adams retained Boston architect Henry Van Brunt, friend and neighbor of Harvard librarian Justin Winsor, to design his building. Van Brunt had recently designed the 1877 stack wing on Gore Hall and, with Winsor to guide him, was probably the best informed academic library architect in the country. The resulting building at Michigan—which merged the academic concerns of President Adams, the library acumen of both Justin Winsor and Michigan's librarian Raymond Cazallis Davis, and the architectural expertise of Henry Van Brunt—represented the current state of the art when it was opened in 1883.

This library at Michigan contained a large reading room and administrative areas at its entry level; seminar, reference, and research facilities at the second level; an art gallery on the third level; and a three-level multitier structural stack to its rear. There was also a lecture hall. This building therefore was the first to incorporate all or most of the special as well as general facilities requisite to good twentieth-century university library service.[13]

It appears that Van Brunt was influenced in massing the building at Michigan by the library opened seven years earlier at Lehigh, although he reversed its principal elements, using a rectangular stack and semicircular reading room rather than Lehigh's rectangular reading room and semicircular stack. He also borrowed the twin towers from Lehigh but, since Michigan was a coeducational institution (the first to construct a library), he used them to provide separate entrances for men and women. Regrettably, however, these alterations diminished the building's grace, making it look faintly like a sitting hen with two heads. Van Brunt himself said that the "apse-like form [of the reading room] suggests a rear and not a front." It was also difficult to designate it as of any particular architectural style; President Adams called it Norman Gothic, but library histo-rian Jackson Towne perhaps more appropriately denominated it "Ann Arbor Victorian."[14] At any rate, all but its stack tower was razed in 1918 so that Michigan's present Harlan Hatcher Library could be built on the site.

Syracuse. In 1889 Syracuse University opened its Von Ranke Li-brary, a Romanesque design fashioned by local architect Archi-medes Russell. While this building contained all of the elements of a modern university library, they were less well articulated than they had been at Michigan or than they would be in the remaining three buildings of the decade. The principal novelty of the Von Ranke building was that its three-level structural stack was erected in two sections, one on each side of a large room, with reading tables ar-rayed between them, resulting in a configuration quite similar to the earlier alcoved book room.[15] This building served only briefly as a library. In 1907 its services and contents were removed to the Uni-versity's new Carnegie Library, and the structure was remodeled as an administration building, a function that it still serves today.

Three more academic libraries were constructed in this country in the closing years of the decade, and all three were good, serviceable, carefully planned, multifunctional designs. Each of the three was conceptualized sufficiently in tune with modern library and educa-tional needs so that it was able to serve adequately for some three-score years and ten as its parent institution's only central library building. These buildings were at Pennsylvania, Colgate, and Cor-nell, all three of which were dedicated within a few months of each other in 1890.

Pennsylvania. The library at the University of Pennsylvania was the work of the somewhat eccentric but brilliant architect Frank Furness. Called French Gothic in style, its exterior incorporated both military components, such as its crenelated tower, and ecclesi-astical elements, such as its apsidal northern terminus. Its square tower housed the stair, and the apse or ambulatory created six curvi-linear chapellike alcoves in which were located subject reference or reserve collections. The building contained a large reading room, ample staff work space, seminar and lecture rooms, map and file room, and a three-level stack constructed entirely of fireproof mate-rials, all configured in a manner consistent with library operations. In distributing these many functional spaces, the architect benefited from extensive advice received from Justin Winsor of Harvard and Melvil Dewey of the Albany Library School.[16] Much of the building was roofed entirely of glass, especially above the stack and the apse, and the stack floors were also of glass, all used to increase natural illumination in these areas.[17] The Furness building remained the University's central library until the construction of the Van Pelt building in 1962, and today it houses the School of Architecture.

Colgate. In Hamilton, New York, meanwhile, philanthropist James B. Colgate had committed himself to providing a library building for the institution that now bears his name. After reviewing several schemes that had been submitted in a competition, however, he rejected them all because, in his words, "there was too much architect, and but little library." Working thereafter with his next-door neighbor in Yonkers, architect Edwin A. Quick, Colgate set out to acquaint himself with contemporary library needs. He wrote:

> With him [i.e., Quick], I began a course of inquiry. We consulted librarians, and visited libraries. When we commenced, our conception of a library was an immense building arranged with galleries and step ladders, and with books piled to the third heaven. That was our idea; but it ended in something very different. We went on consulting librarians, and found it was necessary to have a stack room, so arranged that the books should not be exposed to either heat or dampness, for these destroy bindings. Then it was necessary to have a good reading-room, librarian's room, a cataloguing room, a repairing room, and a reception room. Mr. Quick pursued this idea with a great deal of pertinacity, and after writing, consulting, and seeing plans innumerable, we at last produced something.[18]

Colgate might have added that the building also had reference, periodical, documents, and seminar rooms, for so it did. He denominated its architectural style "Romanesque American"—presumably meaning that it was not simply a slavish copy of an eleventh-century original—and that is perhaps as good a description as any. Cruciform in shape, it featured a three-level fireproof bookstack with a reading room above,[19] faintly reminiscent of the Bibliothèque Ste. Geneviève and anticipating the New York Public Library of later date (Plate 3b). The institution finally moved its library out of this building in 1958, and since that time it has been occupied by Colgate's central administration.

Cornell. In 1884 President Andrew Dickson White of Cornell University seemingly favored Henry H. Richardson as an architect, but at the same time he greatly admired the library building that Henry Van Brunt had just designed for the University of Michigan. White even made a sketch of what he felt would be an appropriate library structure for Cornell, and its facade is clearly copied from that of the Ann Arbor building. In the following year, moreover, after White's resignation, Charles Kendall Adams left the presidency at Michigan to assume that office at Cornell, and his new appointment seemed to assure Van Brunt's appointment as the architect for Cornell's new library. Adams, White, and Van Brunt proceeded in the subsequent two years to make many studies and sketches preparatory to the actual designing of the building, and as a result more scholarly thought and architectural deliberation probably went into this library than had gone into any that had been built previous to that time.[20]

Finally, however, when the donor demurred, the architectural contract for Cornell's library went not to Van Brunt but to William H. Miller. Miller followed faithfully all of the functional requirements identified by Presidents White and Adams, and he used much of the massing of the building as sketched by Van Brunt. With a cruciform basilica reminiscent of, but not at all copied from, the earlier alcoved book rooms, the new library featured a large reading room in the nave and in one aisle, while periodical and entry rooms occupied the other aisle, a five-level structural stack in one transept

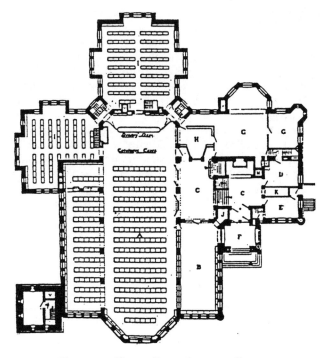

Figure 9. Miller's Library for Cornell, 1890

and a seven-level stack in a rectangular apse, with fully seven seminar rooms, staff work space, separate cloak rooms for men and women, and special facilities for the new Andrew Dickson White collection in the other transept. This was Cornell's only library building until the Olin Library was occupied in 1961, and it is today the University's Uris Undergraduate Library. Called "Square Romanesque" by some,[21] this building was probably the best academic library built to that time (Plate 5c).

C. Briefer Mention of the Others

The rate at which new college library buildings were constructed gained speed throughout this period. As a result only a few can be singled out for extended discussion here, but this is not to say that the others were unimportant. Other institutions that built libraries between 1875 and 1890 were the following:

- 1876 *University of Rochester.* Construction of its first library, Sibley Hall, was overseen by donor Hiram Sibley, who even insisted that the windows be made larger than the architect had designed them so that the building would be adequately lighted; this change, however, resulted in its remaining very cold through the winter months. It was razed in 1968.[22]
- 1877 *Union College.* Already mentioned, Joseph Jacques Ramée's round Classical Revival structure was begun very early for an unspecified purpose and was completed by architect Edward T. Potter as the Nott Memorial Library, a function it served until 1961. It remains standing today (Plates 2b, 5d).[23]
- 1878 *Denison University.* Doane Hall, a fifty-by-sixty-foot structure in the form of a Greek cross somewhat similar to Brown University's library completed in the same year, contained one room with a gallery and was topped by a cupola. It served as a library until 1937 and was later taken down.[24]
- 1878 *University of the South.* The Gothic-style Hodgson Library, the first permanent stone building built at Sewanee, was added to in 1900 and converted to an infirmary, which stands today.[25]
- 1879 *Roanoke College.* Bittle Library, a small but handsome Gothic structure, was added to in 1894 and served as a library until 1962. It is still standing.
- 1881 *University of California.* Brown Library, eclectic in style, contained a semicircular, three-level, radial stack to the rear,

rather similar to Lehigh's; it served until 1911 and was demolished in 1961.[26]

- 1882 *Washington and Lee University.* Designed by J. Crawford Neilson of Baltimore, Newcomb Hall served as the institution's library until the Carnegie building on that campus was opened in 1908 (Plate 2d).[27]

- 1883 *Centre College.* Centre's second "Sayre Library" was built when its first one burned down in 1880. This new Romanesque structure, containing a loft interior with two galleries of shelves, then housed the library until Centre's Carnegie building was opened in 1914.

- 1884 *Mills College.* This cottage-style structure, the Sage Library, was decommissioned for library purposes in 1906 when Carnegie provided a new one. Although it is still standing, it has now been almost completely wrapped into another College building with only a portion of its original mansard roof remaining identifiable.

- 1885 *Oberlin College.* The Rev. Charles V. Spear of Pittsfield, Massachusetts, gave $30,000 for the construction of the Gothic-style Spear Library. This two-story building, with a handsome reading room on the upper floor, was converted to other purposes when Carnegie provided a new library in 1908. It was subsequently torn down.[28]

- 1885 *Hobart and William Smith Colleges.* This small Gothic structure, Demarest Hall, overlooks the north end of Seneca Lake. With additions, it served as the College Library until 1976 when the present Smith Library was constructed. Today it constitutes a wing on the Chapel building.

- 1886 *Dickinson College.* Designed by Charles L. Carson, a student of H. H. Richardson, the James Williamson Bosler Memorial Library originally bespoke its Romanesque roots, with tower and arched portal and windows, but it was later given a more Georgian appearance. Its original function was taken over by the Spahr Library in 1968, although the building still exists.[29]

- 1887 *Grinnell College.* The Goodnow Library was early described as having "a high hall with galleries for 50,000 volumes, besides a spacious reading room, two apartments for art, and a tower for an astronomical observatory." It was replaced as a library in 1906 by a Carnegie building, but it still stands.[30]

- 1887 *Kenyon College.* Hubbard Hall, Kenyon's first library building, was a stone structure with shelves and alcoves at the entry level and a large reading room above. It was destroyed by fire on January 1, 1910.[31]

Plate 2. During the 1870s and Early 1880s, College and University Libraries in the United States Were of Varied Designs and Styles.

a) Saint Lawrence University (NY), 1871. Architect not known.

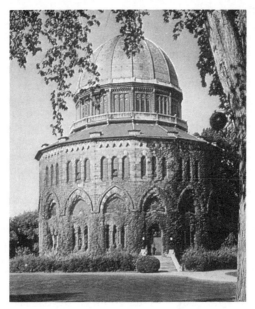

b) Union College (NY), 1877. Edward T. Potter, Architect.

c) Brown University (RI), 1878. Walker & Gould, Architects.

d) Washington and Lee University (VA), 1882. J. Crawford Neilson, Architect.

- 1888 *Drew University.* The "Cornell" Library, costing $80,000, was designed primarily in the Romanesque style. It featured a traditional book hall with transverse shelving creating six alcoves on each side of a nave at both the entry and the gallery levels. Roofed completely with glass so as to provide more light, the Cornell Library was razed in 1938.[32]
- 1889 *University of Mississippi.* This Romanesque building of two and one-half floors with a round tower was constructed with a $10,000 appropriation from the University trustees. Its role was later taken over by a Carnegie library.[33] [34]

Thus during the brief decade and a half covered by this chapter, librarians for the first time began to rationalize their recently enlarged responsibilities in an attempt to conceptualize proper spatial requirements and layouts to meet these new needs. Architects sought new construction materials, techniques, and forms, and they imported the multitier structural stack from Europe in order to meet these new expectations. Both worked together, and in concert with the professoriate, to effect a new kind of library building, one with a functional integrity of its own, a library qua library, capable of fulfilling the multiplicity of book- and study-related requirements of modern higher education. As a result of this cooperation, several good new functional buildings were built by 1890 that were destined to meet effectively the library purposes of their parent institutions well into the middle years of the present century and to serve as models for American academic library buildings right up to the second World War.

Notes

1. Portions of this chapter are reproduced here almost verbatim from their first appearance in the author's "The American Academic Library Building, 1870–1890," *Journal of Library History* 21 (Winter 1986): 60–71, by permission of the University of Texas Press.

2. Magali S. Larson, *The Rise of Professionalism* (Berkeley: University of California Press, 1979).

3. See Carl Diehl, *Americans and German Scholarship* (New Haven, Conn.: Yale University Press, 1978).

4. Edward G. Holley, "Academic Libraries in 1876," *College & Research Libraries* 37 (January 1976): 15–47.

5. *Library Journal* 1 (November 30, 1876): 124; 3 (April 1878): 64.

6. Ibid., 1 (November 30, 1876): 22.

7. Donald E. Oehlerts, *Books and Blueprints; Building America's Public Libraries* (N.Y.: Greenwood, 1991), pp. 10–11 and passim.

8. *Harper's Weekly* 32 (September 1, 1888): 657–58.

9. Boll, "Library Architecture . . . ," pp. 379–97; William Jordy and Christopher Monkhouse, *Buildings on Paper; Rhode Island Architectural Drawings, 1825–1945. Catalogue of an Exhibit* (Providence: Rhode Island School of Design, 1982), pp. 188–189.

10. Ashton R. Willard, "College Libraries in the United States," *New England Magazine* ns17 (December 1897): 433.

11. Jeffrey K. Ochsner, *H. H. Richardson: Complete Architectural Works* (Cambridge, Mass.: Massachusetts Institute of Technology, 1983), pp. 300–305; Laurel Ginter, "Building Billings," *Vermont* (Winter 1984), pp. 2–7.

12. Willard, "College Libraries . . . ," pp. 434–35.

13. John C. Abbott, "Raymond Cazallis Davis and the University of Michigan Library 1877–1905." Ph.D. dissertation, University of Michigan, 1957, pp. 96–134.

14. Jackson E. Towne, "Charles Kendall Adams and the First University Library Building," *Michigan History* 37 (1953): 140.

15. Addison Van Name, "Report on Architecture," *Library Journal* 14 (January 1889): 173: W. Freeman Galpin, *Syracuse University: The Pioneer Days* (Syracuse, N.Y.: Syracuse University Press, 1952), p. 95.

16. Talcott Williams, "Plans for the Library Building of the University of Pennsylvania," *Library Journal* 13 (August 1888): 237–42; 14 (May–June 1889): 171.

17. James F. O'Gorman, *The Architecture of Frank Furness* (Philadelphia: Museum of Art, 1973), pp. 164–67.

18. Arthur Meggett, "The James B. Colgate Library," *Philobiblon* (February 1964) pp. 1–9; Howard D. Williams, *History of Colgate University 1819–1969* (N.Y.: Van Nostrand, 1969), pp. 184–86.

19. F. S. Retan, "Colgate Library Building," *Madisonensis* 21 (May 18, 1889): 209–212.

20. Kermit C. Parsons, *The Cornell Campus: A History of Its Planning and Development* (Ithaca, N.Y.: Cornell University Press, 1968) pp. 152–72.

21. George W. Harris, "The New Library Building of Cornell University," *Library Journal* 14 (April 1889): 121–24.

22. Herman K. Phinney, "Rah for Sibley!" *Rochester Alumni Review* 11 (February–March 1933): 55–57; (April–May 1933): 78–80.

23. Mendel, Mesick, Cohen, firm, *The Nott Memorial: A Historic Structure Report* (Albany, N.Y.: Prepared for the Trustees and Alumni Council of Union College, 1973).

24. G. Wallace Chessman, *Denison: The Story of an Ohio College* (Granville, Ohio: Denison University, 1957), pp. 356–357.

25. George R. Fairbanks, *History of the University of the South* (Jacksonville, Fla.: H. & W. B. Drew, 1905), pp. 166–67, 186, 358.

26. Kenneth G. Peterson, "The History of the University of California Library at Berkeley." Ph.D. dissertation, University of California, 1968, pp. 170–177.

27. Betty R. Kondayan, *Historical Sketch of the Library of Washington and Lee University* (Lexington, Va.: Washington and Lee University, 1980), pp. 26–28.

28. Ohio Library Commission, *Sketches of Ohio Libraries* (Columbus, Ohio: F. J. Heer, 1902), p. 230–233.

29. Charles C. Sellers, *Dickinson College: A History* (Middletown, Conn.: Wesleyan University Press, 1973), pp. 281–83, 583.

30. John S. Nollen, *Grinnell College* (Iowa City: State Historical Society of Iowa, 1953), pp. 184–87.

31. George F. Smythe, *Kenyon College; Its First Century* (New Haven, Conn.: Yale University Press, 1924), pp. 225–26, 260.

32. Addison Van Name, "Report on Library Architecture," *Library Journal* 14 (Nos. 5–6 May–June 1889): 167–68.

33. Allen Cabaniss, *The University of Mississippi; Its First Hundred Years* 2d ed. (Hattiesburg: University and College Press of Mississippi, 1971), pp. 103–04; James B. Lloyd, *The University of Mississippi; The Formative Years* (University: University of Mississippi, 1979), pp. 69–70.

34. Other libraries indeed may also have been built, but the author has made a comprehensive search for nineteenth-century academic library buildings, and these are all that have come into his ken. See his preliminary checklist of "19th-Century Academic Library Buildings," *College & Research Libraries News* 48 (September 1987): 476–78.

Chapter Four

Consolidation without Innovation, 1890–1900

Insofar as academic library buildings were concerned, the terminal decade of the nineteenth century was a period of consolidation rather than of additional innovations. New departures of a number of kinds, some prudent and some ill-advised, had been made during the 1880s. Now all of those earlier innovations needed to be tested against experience, debated, modified and adapted, and then either scrapped or assimilated, depending upon the results.

To be sure, the number of new academic library buildings being erected continued to rise, especially in the North, although less rapidly in the states formerly comprised within the Confederacy. Whereas fully 45 percent of the academic libraries constructed in the nation prior to the Civil War were in the South, the ratio plummeted during the balance of the century to less than 16 percent. The psyche, economy, and will of the region had simply been too desolated by the conflict to permit more.[1] Nonetheless nationwide twenty-eight new academic libraries were built in the 1890s, almost doubling the sixteen constructed in the previous decade. The experience of the entire threescore years is shown in the accompanying graph in Figure 10.

A. Controversy Between Librarians and Architects

The growing number of library buildings being constructed led understandably to increased amounts both of literature devoted to them and of time spent discussing them in professional forums. As early as 1876, at the first conference of the American Library Association (ALA), William Frederick Poole, then librarian of the Chicago Public Library, had criticized the current "passion for producing architectural effects, rather than meeting the legitimate wants of

College Libraries Constructed
By Decade, 1840-1899

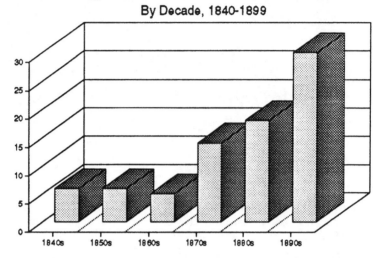

Figure 10. Number of College and University Library Buildings Built in the United States, 1840–1899, by Decade

a library,"[2] although his remarks provided only sketchy details of what he meant by either "architectural effects" or "legitimate wants."

Five years later, however, Poole produced an extended attack upon library architecture in a paper entitled "The Construction of Library Buildings," which he delivered at the Washington Conference of the ALA in February 1881 and which was subsequently published in the *Library Journal*.[3] In it Poole, who probably knew more about buildings than any other American librarian at that time, animadverted upon their "lofty rooms, and large open space[s] surrounded with alcoves and galleries . . . for the storage of books." Poole had not worked in an academic library since his own graduation from Yale College in 1849, so he understandably cited as his examples such public libraries as those of Bates Hall and the Athenæum in Boston, the Astor in New York, and the Peabody in Baltimore. He could, of course, as easily have cited the pre-1875 academic libraries at Yale, the University of South Carolina, Harvard, Wesleyan, and elsewhere, which had similar features. Poole seemed unaware, however, of some of the departures that had been made during the previous five years in the design of such recent academic library buildings as those at Lehigh and Brown, where tripartitioning had been initiated.

In his 1881 paper Poole delineated his eight "objections" to the style of library design then prevalent. They included the wastefulness of space in the central portion of such buildings, the difficulty of moving from one gallery portion of the building to another, their insecurity from fire, the difficulty of enlarging them, their exorbitant construction cost, the fact that they were noisy, the expense of heating such large loft spaces, and the problems presented by upper galleries, which were difficult for attendants to serve and where books and bindings disintegrated from the excessive heat.

Immediately following Poole's litany of objections to past library buildings, architect J. L. Smithmeyer presented a paper describing his plan for the new Library of Congress building that, Poole quickly noted with some pique, would contain virtually all of the features that he himself had so strenuously eschewed only a few minutes before.[4] Nonetheless he was gratified that following the ensuing discussion, the assembled delegates unanimously adopted the following resolution supporting the basic principle that Poole had advocated:

> *Resolved,* That, in the opinion of the Association, the time has come for a radical modification of the prevailing typical style of library building, and the adoption of a style of construction better suited to economy and practical utility.[5]

He was also pleased that his paper would soon be reprinted in the *American Architect*, where the entire architectural community could see it and where its appearance could be salutary.[6]

Poole's paper had contained not only criticism of what had gone before but also his suggestions for the future. He had explained why his ideal of a serviceable new-style library building would require multi-partitioning of space, although he had not called it that. He had also described his new concept of individual subject-divisional shelf-and-study rooms, a plan that would soon become widely used in large public library buildings throughout the nation and would eventually be adopted in some academic libraries as well. In another paper presented a year later, Poole developed these innovative concepts more fully, as well as repeating and expanding upon some of his criticisms of what had gone before.[7] Three years thereafter, he published a third paper applying his principles to small rather than large library buildings.[8]

Poole's recurring criticisms eventually began to have an effect on the planning of new buildings. In a report presented in 1887 on library architecture during the previous biennium, Joseph N. Larned, superintendent of the Buffalo Library, was able to state that "the old type of library building which Mr. Poole has denominated the Cathedral or Gothic Church type. . . has nearly disappeared," and "that American library architecture has distinctly taken a new departure." He specifically attributed these improvements to the "remarkable influence" of Poole's paper read at the Washington Conference in 1881.[9]

If continued long enough, of course, criticism will elicit not only change but also counter-criticism, and such was the result here. Ironically, however, the particular spark that ignited the eventual blowup was not something said by the often testy William Frederick Poole, but rather a seemingly off-the-cuff comment by the normally circumspect and tactful new president of the ALA, Charles Ammi Cutter of the Boston Athenæum. At the ALA conference in the Catskill Mountains in 1888, discussion of library buildings featured a presentation of Henry H. Richardson's plans, completed shortly prior to his death, for the Howard Memorial Library near Richardson's hometown in New Orleans. Although the subsequent discussion was not unduly critical, it contained an unfortunate remark by Cutter opining that "the architect is the natural enemy of the librarian."[10] Coincidentally Cutter was then also editor of the *Library Journal*.

Response from the architectural profession was immediate. The next issue of the *American Architect* contained an anonymous defense of Richardson and a hard-hitting, slashing attack upon librarians who seemed unable, in the mind of the author, to agree upon "where book-shelves and reading-halls and work-rooms ought to go for the highest efficiency."[11] If librarians could not see eye-to-eye among themselves on such matters, it asked, how could architects be expected to satisfy them?

The writer's point was not wholly without merit. Within the library community there had indeed been a long-standing disagreement primarily between Poole, who felt ardently that books should be stored on freestanding shelves eight feet high in subject-oriented rooms with fifteen- or sixteen-foot ceilings, and most other librarians, who felt strongly but less passionately that they were better stored in multitiered structural stacks, about which more will be said later. To this time, however, this colloquy had been playing itself out largely within the relative privacy of the ALA conferences and the pages of the *Library Journal*. It now became clear that this seeming absence of a consensus among librarians themselves threatened to damage the value of their testimony among the architects who were to be so important to their futures.

It fell to William Isaac Fletcher, librarian of Amherst College, to play the role of peacemaker. He immediately extended an olive branch in the form of an essay, or what he entitled an "Irenicon," that was published in the *American Architect* on October 27, 1888. In it he allowed that some librarians were "perhaps a trifle long-haired," but that the cause of the new controversy between architects and librarians lay elsewhere than in their supposed "crankiness." He explained that, despite some debate among librarians in camera, there was a very high level of unanimity among them regarding certain principal issues, such as:

> the abandonment of lofty interiors with fixed alcoves and galleries, and the substitution of iron stacks or portable wooden cases placed near together in plain rectangular interiors; the demand for an abundance of light, preferably from the higher part of the walls, and not from the roof; and use of small tables and light chairs, instead of the large heavy tables and the artistic chairs . . . [which were, in the judgment of librarians] awkward in use.[12]

He went on to add his opinion that many poor library buildings resulted from architects getting their directions not from librarians but from lay building committees, trustees, and donors who had little if any understanding of how libraries really functioned. Regarding Richardson, he felt that

> had he lived but a few years longer, he would have come to build libraries no less beautiful and appropriate in general effect than he left, but better fitted to meet the wants of the modern library.

Fletcher's "irenecon" had its calculated effect. The editor of the *American Architect* promptly invited him to prepare a second article for an early issue of his magazine detailing some additional observations and suggestions that would help architects better understand what it was that librarians felt they needed in their buildings. Fletcher accepted the invitation with alacrity and supplied a fuller piece shortly thereafter.[13]

As this new dialogue between librarians and architects continued to develop, criticism began to decline. Architect Normand S. Patton of Chicago was invited to speak on "Architects and Librarians" at the next conference of the ALA. In his remarks he punctuated Fletcher's statement of a few months earlier that librarians should indeed be involved in the planning of library buildings. He observed that:

> It would be a singular mistake to plan a church and forget the convenience of the minister; and yet many a library has been planned, and apparently the librarian has been left out of the calculation. . . . A

library cannot be arranged properly unless the librarian has an important if not a controlling part.[14]

The assembled delegates understandably agreed, and their assent earned Patton several subsequent commissions from them. Among academic libraries that he would later be called upon to design would be those at Carleton (1896), Beloit (1905), Marietta (1906), Indiana University (1907), Heidelberg College and the University of Tennessee (1911), and Purdue University (1913).

Two years later another significant service was performed for the future of library buildings when a trustee of the Brookline, Massachusetts, Public Library and frequent ALA conference attendee, Charles C. Soule, prepared a paper entitled "Points of Agreement among Librarians as to Library Architecture."[15] This document proposed nineteen basic common-sense principles upon which librarians believed sound library building planning had to take place. They included such simple axioms as: "a library building should be planned for library work"; and "no convenience of arrangement should ever be sacrificed for mere architectural effect"; and "a library should be planned with a view to economical administration." Soule read his paper at the ALA Conference in San Francisco in 1891, and it received the instant approbation of the delegates present. It also earned quickly the concurrence of the architectural profession and in effect spelled the end of the controversy. Thus opened a long period of harmony and close cooperation between the two professions. Soule meanwhile continued to revise and republish his "Points. . ." for the next twenty years, and they remained very influential.[16]

B. Preferences in Architectural Style

Several developments in architectural style in the 1890s affected especially the external appearance of academic library buildings. Principal among them were Romanesque and Renaissance.

Romanesque. In his "Report on Library Architecture" in 1890, H. M. Utley noted that Gothic designs were no longer in style. Rather, he reported, "the current idea as to style of architecture for libraries of moderate dimension is the Romanesque."[17] Bonk has noted accurately, however, that "the 1880s and 1890s were bumper years for imitation of Richardson exteriors, but the interiors followed the new plans being recommended by the librarians."[18]

The early popularity of the Romanesque designs of Henry Hobson Richardson has already been discussed in the previous chapter, where it was noted that he died in 1886, a few months after the completion of his only academic library, Billings Hall at the University of Vermont. It was also mentioned there that even before the end of that decade four other university libraries had, to a greater or lesser degree, emulated his use of Romanesque motifs, namely those at Dartmouth, Syracuse, Colgate, and Cornell.

In the next seven years four more large institutions and five smaller ones, all west of the Alleghenies, followed with Romanesque structures of their own. The first of the larger institutions was Indiana University in 1890. The center portion of its new library building was planned for bookshelves, with narrow window openings between all ranges. This room also served from the start as a reference/reading room, although the ceiling was high enough to accept an upper tier of shelves at a later time. Indiana had only a small number of books in 1890, its collections having twice been totally destroyed by fire, once in 1854 and again in 1883. Understandably the new 1890 building was fireproof, but it was also so small that it was able to accommodate the University's needs only until 1907, when the University constructed a much more ample library building that served until 1970.[19]

In 1893 Ohio State University opened its Orton Hall Library, which was designed by Columbus architects Yost and Packard. On the interior it featured a large room on the entry level, seventy by forty feet in size with a ceiling thirty feet high. Although only one tier of shelving was installed at the time of its first opening, it was originally planned that a three-level stack would be erected at the north end of this room, and the floor was engineered to support this added weight. Instead, however, a gallery was later constructed around the perimeter of the room in order to provide for collection growth until the structure was abandoned as a library in favor of the University's present library building almost two decades later. It is currently the University's Geology Building.[20]

In the following year the University of Kansas opened its new Spooner Library designed by Henry Van Brunt. Van Brunt had already planned the library wing on Gore Hall at Harvard in 1877 and the library at the University of Michigan in 1883 as well as several public library buildings. Thus when he removed his office from Boston to Kansas City in 1885, he was probably the best informed architect of his time regarding the needs of academic libraries. Van Brunt said later that, consistent with the newly developed precepts of library building planning, he had attempted at the University of Kansas to let the interior needs of the Spooner Library determine its exterior appearance, free of unnatural architectural effects or any "fictitious aspect of academical symmetry."[21] Function-

Plate 3. Romanesque-style Library Buildings Were Popular for about a Decade Beginning in 1885.

a) University of Vermont (VT), 1886. Henry Hobson Richardson, Architect.

b) Colgate University (NY), 1890. Edwin A. Quick, Architect.

c) Wittenberg College (OH), 1892. Architect not known.

d) Carleton College (MN), 1896. Patton & Miller, Architects.

ally this was quite a successful library, with the entry on the middle level that contained a large reference/reading room, administrative areas, periodical room, delivery desk, and access to a five-tier book stack to the rear. The building contained five seminar rooms, and the entire third floor was "taken up with a banqueting-hall with the necessary adjuncts."[22] Spooner Hall still stands, having served as the University's library building until the Watson Library was opened in 1924.

The University of Illinois moved its library activities into its first freestanding library building in September 1897. This building, which was trefoil in concept with a five-tier stack tower planned for the rear, was designed by Nathan C. Ricker of the University's Department of Architecture. It was 167 by 113 feet in size and contained on its entry level a reference/reading room and a periodical room in its two wings. In its center portion was a grand entry hall and delivery room in a skylighted rotunda, as well as access to the second tier of the book stack. Seminar rooms, administrative space, and library school quarters occupied the upper and lower floors. This building, now Altgeld Hall, served as the main University library until the present structure was opened in 1926.[23]

The exteriors of five smaller academic libraries of the 1890s were also very reminiscent of Richardson's work. In 1890 Olivet College in Michigan opened that state's second academic library building, following only the 1883 building at Ann Arbor. Faithfully Richardsonian on the exterior, although with its interior featuring a two-tier bookstack in its nave and a separate reading room in its apse, it was designed by New York City architect Arthur B. Jennings.[24] It was added to a century after its original construction and is still in use as Olivet's Burrage Library. Also Richardsonian, the exterior of the 1892 Zimmerman Library at Wittenberg College in Ohio mirrored Richardson's public library in Quincy, Massachusetts, although its interior offered a reading room to the right and a separate stack room to the left (Plate 3c). It was the home of the College Library until 1955, and it now houses the Psychology Department.[25]

In 1894 Colorado College opened its Slocum Library, the first freestanding library building in that state. Designed by Andrews, Jacques & Rantoul of Boston, it was constructed of native "Peach Blow" sandstone and featured six high arched windows on each of its long sides and a red tile roof. It was razed in 1962 following completion of the College's Tutt Library.[26] In 1896 Carleton College opened its Scoville Library, which was destined to be the College Library for a half century before being converted to its present use as administrative space. Designed by Normand S. Patton of Chicago, this building also had a separate reading room and three-tier stack on the inside but was wrapped in a Romanesque exterior (Plate 3d).[27]

In 1898 Saint Augustine's College in Raleigh, North Carolina, constructed a library building that was made possible by a donation of $1,600 from Mary Benson of Brooklyn, New York. Inspired by this relatively modest gift, the College added to it $1,100 that it had received as a gift earlier and constructed its "Benson Library." Avowedly designed as a miniature copy of Richardson's Ames Library in North Easton, Massachusetts, and constructed largely by students from the College's masonry class and under the supervision of its instructor, it was dedicated on March 18, 1898. This Benson Library was decommissioned as a library when a new Benson Library was opened in 1930, but it remains standing today, now conjoined to an adjacent structure as part of Taylor Hall.[28]

None of these nine buildings featured Richardsonian interiors, but all were Romanesque in style, and all of their exteriors, save perhaps that of the Spooner Library, displayed distinctly the strong influence of Richardson. All employed the massive rough-hewn polychrome stone accents, round-arched entries and window caps, and, except for Kansas, the bold, unbalanced facades and stair towers that Richardson had so favored. A few other academic library buildings built in the 1890s displayed some Romanesque elements in their exterior treatments—primarily Baldwin-Wallace College in 1893, the University of Nebraska in 1895, and Franklin and Marshall College in 1898—but for the most part the great fervor for Richardsonian library buildings on the nation's college and university campuses concluded with the end of the century.

Renaissance. The Classical style had never really departed from the American academic library scene during the Richardsonian ascendency. Indeed in 1894 Saint Stephen's College [now Bard] built for its library a faithful replica of the Parthenon itself forty feet by seventy feet that, although added to seventy years later, still serves as the College library. For the most part, however, the decline in use of the Romanesque style as the 1890s passed was accompanied by a rise in the use of classical elements as handed on during the Renaissance.

Architectural historians have long recognized the major role of the World's Columbian Exposition in Chicago in 1893 as the causal factor of the rapid transition in popularity from the Romanesque to the Renaissance architectural styles during the later 1890s. Beaux Arts-trained Charles Follen McKim was coordinating architect for the Exposition buildings. Under his direction and with the designs of other architects who were also either trained at or strongly influenced by the École des Beaux-Arts, the principal pavilions erected to house the World's Columbian Exposition displayed the unrelenting ostentation and unmitigated formalism of the Renaissance buildings of imperial France. More than 27 million visitors to the Columbian Exposition saw these buildings personally, and millions more saw them in pictures. As a result, they immediately became the dominant model for new public buildings in myriad hamlets and towns throughout the United States and remained so for a quarter of a century thereafter.[29]

A year later, for example, the opulent Orrington Lunt Library was opened at Northwestern University. Designed by Chicago architect William A. Otis in the manner of the Italian Renaissance, its semicircular portico gave entry into a general reading room with adjacent delivery desk in front of a large book room. The Lunt building was used as a library until the Charles Deering Library was opened in 1932.[30] In 1894 Doane College in Iowa opened a vastly simpler and somewhat prim thirty-three- by sixty-foot brick structure also of Renaissance design, and in 1898 three more Renaissance buildings were put into use. The first was at Lincoln University near Oxford, Pennsylvania, the second was at Ohio Wesleyan University in Delaware, Ohio, and the third was at Emory University, then located in Oxford, Georgia.

Lincoln first announced the opening of its new Vail Library in its *Catalogue* for 1899/1900. Designed by Addison Hutton, who had been the architect for the Lehigh building twenty-four years earlier,

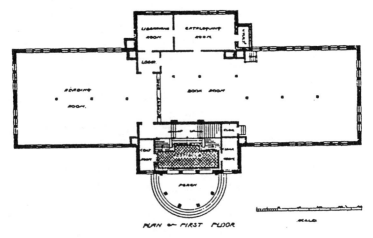

Figure 11. Plan of the Northwestern University Library, 1894

this ninety- by thirty-three-foot Renaissance two-story brick structure featured "massive steps [that] support a system of columns and pilasters, which form an imposing entrance to the building." The rotunda was in turn surmounted by a dome. It was constructed with a gift of $20,000 from University Trustee William H. Vail, a physical education enthusiast of Blairstown, New Jersey, who originally requested that the building contain in its basement a bowling alley for students, a wish that fortunately never came to pass. Vail Memorial served as the institution's library for three-quarters of a century before it was converted to an administration building,[31] and it remains standing today.

It will be recalled that Ohio Wesleyan University built its first library, Sturgis Hall, in 1856. In 1898 Ohio Wesleyan removed all library materials and services from the Sturgis building to the new Charles Elihu Slocum Library, a three-story rough-hewn stone structure with four Doric columns and two engaged columns supporting a pediment to form a centered portico. The reading room on the second floor featured a magnificent oval skylight with stained-glass portraits of eighteen personages from various learned callings. Slocum Hall served as the University Library building until construction of its L. A. Beeghley Library in 1966, and it remains in use for other academic purposes today.[32]

In a somewhat similiar idiom, Emory University's Candler Library was a white stone structure designed by architect S. M. Patton of Chattanooga. Its service rooms extended to the right and left of its recessed central entry, and the books were housed in a two-level semicircular stack extending to the building's rear, somewhat reminiscent of Lehigh's library built in 1876. Following Emory's removal to its present location in Atlanta, the building continued until 1970 to be used as the library for the University's Oxford College. Today it is a student center (Plate 4b).[33]

Although it was clearly the World's Columbian Exposition of 1893 that provided the big stimulus to adopt Renaissance models for American public buildings, a lesser event in October 1895 also hastened their advent in libraries particularly. That event was the nearly total destruction by fire of Thomas Jefferson's 1826 Rotunda, which contained the Library at the University of Virginia. As has been mentioned, Jefferson had faithfully patterned the Rotunda on the Pantheon in Rome.[34] Immediately following the fire, the University of Virginia retained the principal American proponents of Classical Revival architecture, the Boston firm of McKim, Mead & White, to restore the landmark structure. Working with Jefferson's Rotunda so impressed Charles Follen McKim and Stanford White with the architectural potential of round buildings for libraries that, by the end of the decade, each had produced a new round university library on his own account.[35]

In point of time, the first of the two round libraries to be finished and occupied was the Low Library at Columbia University, which was opened on its new Morningside Heights campus late in 1897. Columbia appears, however, to have been in touch with McKim, Mead & White about its need for a new library at least four years earlier than that, and many of its features were determined prior to the fire at Charlottesville. Built in the form of a Greek cross, the four story Low Library had a huge circular reading room capped

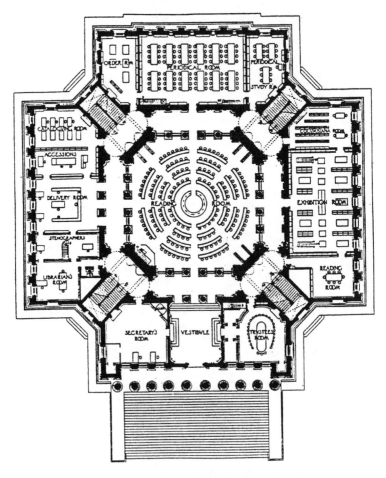

Figure 12. McKim's Library for Columbia University, 1897

by a dome rising 106 feet above its center, with large semicircular clerestory windows on each of its four sides. The forward wing contained a massive vestibule, a boardroom, and office space, and the other three wings contained an admixture of study areas and bookshelves, as well as considerable administrative space that was assigned to nonlibrary purposes (Plate 4a). Principal book storage was in the center of the building below the reading room.

Despite its palatial qualities, or perhaps because of them, the Low Library was fraught with problems. Its vast open spaces, its hard marble surfaces, and the use of such large portions of the building for nonlibrary purposes all worked together to generate an acoustical ambience not conducive to study and contemplation. Nonetheless, the Low Library was the first truly sumptuous academic library building constructed in the nation, costing well over a million dollars. It served as the University's main library building until the opening of Columbia's Butler Library building in 1933.[36]

A similarly imposing round structure was given to New York University by the family of Jay Gould and constructed in 1899. Designed by the flamboyant Stanford White, the "Gould Library" was erected on NYU's University College campus in the Bronx. A contemporary description of the building reads in part as follows:

> The proportions are very noble, and in entire harmony with the commanding character of the site. The outside walls are Perth Amboy brick, which gives a general tone of warm buff to the exterior. Combined with the brick are Medford granite and Indiana limestone.
>
> The main entry is from the east front. Opposite the door is the broad marble stairway leading to the reading-room, while other stairways to the right and left of the entrance go down to the auditorium. The only ornament to the fine main stairway are four huge bronze torches supporting electric globes.
>
> These somewhat austere approaches make the warmth and color of the reading-room a surprise as well as a delight. In form it is circular, and open clear to the top of the dome, which is supported by 16 massive columns of green Conemara marble. The color of these columns has been made the keynote of the decorative work, which was done under the direction of Louis C. Tiffany of the Tiffany studios. The color scheme is green and gold, warmed by dashes of crimson in the stained glass. A band of glass mosaic encircles the room at the base of the dome.[37]

Although thankfully these two buildings did not inspire a resurgence of round library buildings, they did help to anchor in place the rapidly rising preference for Renaissance models. They also helped to establish the public perception that, just as imperial palaces were appropriate for housing such recent public libraries as the

Boston Public Library (1896) and the Library of Congress (1897), they were also appropriate for libraries on college and university campuses. This legacy would burden academic library building planning for many decades to come.

C. . . . And Some Others.

There are always a few aberrations. Peru State College in Nebraska constructed an unusual library building in 1890. It was a gabled frame structure with a surrounding veranda in the fashion of the fine Victorian farmhouses that were coming to dot the plains states in that era. It was replaced in 1906. In 1898 Claflin University in Orangeburg, South Carolina, opened its new Lee Library building. This tiny but graceful one-story structure was built of red brick, in a manner that can perhaps best be described as "cottage style," with a small porch entering into an L-shaped service area. It still stands on the edge of the campus and has served varied purposes in recent years, especially since the construction of Claflin's Hubert Vernon Manning Library in 1967.

Neither of these two buildings, however, was influential insofar as library functional layout or architectural style were concerned. The century ended with a decided preference for the Renaissance mode in its academic library buildings, best bespoken by two recent palatial edifices in New York City to turn the heads of the envious.

Notes

1. Of the 729 attendees at the conferences of the American Library Association between 1876 and 1886, only forty-six were from the South. It should be pointed out, however, that during the period, no conferences were held south of the District of Columbia. As regards library buildings, Charles Ammi Cutter observed in 1888 that "the establishment of libraries stops with the line of the terminal moraine." *Library Journal* 13 (September- October 1888): 318.

2. Ibid., 1 (November 30, 1876): 125.

3. Ibid., 6 (April 1881): 69–77.

4. "The National-Library Building.—The Proposed Plan," *Library Journal* 6 (April 1881): 77–81.

5. Ibid., 7 (July-August 1882): 131.

6. *American Architect* 10 (September 17, 1881): 131.

7. "Progress of Library Architecture," *Library Journal* 7 (July-August 1882): 130–136.

8. "Small Library Buildings," *Library Journal* 10 (September-October 1885): 250–256.

9. "Report on Library Architecture," *Library Journal* 12 (September–October 1887): 379.

10. Ibid., 13 (September–October 1888): 318.

11. Quoted ibid., 13 (November 1888): 339–340. Although the Howard Memorial building that brought on this tempest was a public library and seemingly outside the scope of this treatise, Richardson's plans for it were almost exactly a mirror image of the building he had designed earlier for the University of Vermont. For a thorough account of Richardson's library impact and for additional light on this controversy, see Sharon C. Bonk, "Temples of Knowledge," *Milestones to the Present; Papers from Library History Seminar V*, ed. by Harold Goldstein (Syracuse, N.Y.: Gaylord Professional Publications, 1978), pp. 53–72.

12. Reprinted in *Library Journal* 13 (November 1888): 338–339. The same issue of the *Library Journal* also contained an editorial (pp. 331–332), gracious but less apologetic, and some anonymous doggerel entitled "Ye Architect and Ye Librarian," which included the following lines, hardly calculated to smooth the way to an amicable conclusion (p. 338):

> An architect sat in an office so high,
> Genius lighted his forehead, ambition his eye;
> "Oh, I'm planning a library wondrous to see, And its praises
> shall ring the world round," quoth he.
> Then he flourished his pencil, and quickly up grew
> A building the public all hastened to view.
> The walls they were arched in the true gothic style,
> And tinted soft colors the eyes to beguile;
> The windows were oval and lozenge and square,
> Some cut to the flooring, some high in the air.
> The glass mediæval admitted dim rays
> That artists and poets united to praise.
> There were nice little corners to lounge in at ease,
> And dusky recesses the æsthetes to please,
> And corridors quaint, where the shaded light fell
> And dados and friezes too lovely to tell.
> There were bookcases? Yes, I was going to say
> These were hid in odd corners quite out of the way,
> So that nobody heeded, except to exclaim
> At the wonderful carving of bracket and frame.
> And the public remarked, as in rapture they gazed:
> "Too highly this architect cannot be praised!"

13. Reprinted as "Library Buildings," *Library Journal* 14 (January–February 1889): 39- 40.

14. Ibid., 14 (May-June 1889): 159–161.

15. Ibid., 16 (December 1891): 17–19.

16. They were last revised and incorporated into Soule's book, *How to Plan a Library Building for Library Work* (Boston, Mass: Boston Book Company, 1912).

17. *Library Journal* 15 (December 1890): 12–14.

18. Op. cit., p. 64.

19. Mildred H. Lowell, "Indiana University Libraries, 1829–1942." Ph.D. dissertation, University of Chicago, 1957, pp. 108–113.

20. Ohio Library Commission, *Sketches of Ohio Libraries* (Columbus, Ohio: F. J. Heer, 1902), pp. 133–129.

21. Quoted in Clifford S. Griffin, *The University of Kansas: A History* (Lawrence: University Press of Kansas, 1974), p. 182.

22. *Library Journal* 20 (January 1895): 30.

23. Katherine L. Sharp, *Illinois Libraries, Part III; College, Institutional and Special Libraries* (Urbana, Ill.: University of Illinois, 1907), pp. 60–63; Thomas E. Ratcliffe, "Development of the Buildings, Policy and Collection of the University of Illinois Library in Urbana, 1897–1940." MSLS thesis, University of Illinois, 1949, pp. 1–16, 100–104.

24. *Olivet Optic*, August 17, 1889.

25. C. W. Anschutz, "Library of Wittenberg College," *The Cycle, Published by the Junior Class of Wittenberg College* 1 (June 1892): 31–32.

26. Barbara M. Arnest, "Historic Coburn Library Still Serves CC," *Colorado College Magazine*, Winter 1960.

27. *Library Journal* 22 (January 1897): 17–18.

28. Cecil D. Halliburton, *History of St. Augustine's College* ([Raleigh, NC], Saint Augustine's College, 1937), pp. 23, 26, 60, 68.

29. Donald E. Oehlerts, "American Library Architecture and the World's Columbian Exposition," in *Milestones to the Present; Papers from Library History Seminar V*, ed. by Harold Goldstein (Syracuse, N.Y.: Gaylord Professional Publications, 1978), pp. 73–79. See also John Burchard and Albert Bush-Brown *The Architecture of America* (Boston, Mass.: Little Brown and Company, 1961), pp. 250–281.

30. *The American Architect and Building News* 41 (July 22, 1893): 59; Lodilla Ambrose, "The Orrington Lunt Library," *Library Journal* 19 (October 1894): 338–340.

31. Horace Mann Bond, *Education for Freedom: A History of Lincoln University* (Lincoln University, 1976), pp. 410–411, 461; *Library Journal* 23 (May 1898): 209.

32. Ohio Library Commission, *Sketches of Ohio Libraries* (Columbus, Ohio: F. J. Heer, 1902), pp. 182–184.

33. Henry M. Bullock, *A History of Emory University* (Nashville, Tenn.: Parthenon Press, 1936), pp. 114–115, 189–192; *Library Journal* 21 (November 1896): 517.

34. Lewis Mumford, *The South in Architecture* (N.Y.: Harcourt Brace, 1941), pp. 62- 78.

35. Harry Clemons, *The University of Virginia Library, 1825–1950* (Charlottesville: University of Virginia Library, 1954); *Library Journal* 21 (July 1896): 339–340; ibid., 23 (September 1898): 544.

36. Winifred B. Linderman, "History of the Columbia University Library, 1876–1926." DLS dissertation, Columbia University, 1959, pp. 207–223.

37. *Public Libraries* 6 (April 1901): 239. This piece is accompanied by several interior and exterior photographs of the library. Its facade was featured on a United States postage stamp in 1980.

Chapter Five

Andrew Carnegie and the Period 1900–1910

During the decade from 1900 to 1910 the college library scene in the United States changed very profoundly, due substantially to the benefactions of Andrew Carnegie. Although Carnegie's elaborate giving of public library buildings to local communities is legendary and well documented,[1] his many contributions to academic institutions for the construction of libraries are less well known. During this period alone some 130 academic library buildings were built in the United States, and Carnegie provided the funds for almost two-thirds of them. In fact, by 1910, he had funded the construction of just over half of all of the college libraries ever built in the United States.

Contrary to popular assumption, Carnegie does not appear to have favored any particular architectural style for the buildings he funded, nor did he ever suggest or expect that his name would grace those buildings. Sometimes the recipients chose to name them for him, and sometimes they named them for others. Carnegie did, however, involve himself seriously in assuring that they be economical to construct and that they function effectively as libraries, and here his influence was substantial and salutary. In the first place, no Carnegie buildings were intended to memorialize anyone so there was no need for them to be grand or imposing, a fact that diminished the immediate influence of the sumptuous recent buildings at Columbia and New York University. In the second place, and in the long run this was a more significant factor, Andrew Carnegie was himself both a product and a producer of the fin de siècle emphasis upon efficiency and economy in industrial operations. He therefore felt strongly that public buildings, including the libraries that he funded, be similarly utilitarian and modest in both their design and their accoutrements befitting the era and purpose that they were intended to serve.[2] Indeed his influence in this regard would be felt on American library building planning for at least threescore years thereafter.

It was simple fortuity that the most efficient functional layout of library operations during this period could be accomplished best in structures designed in the Renaissance style that was then in vogue for public buildings. Elevated podiums permitted access of natural light and fresh air into their basements as well as their upper floors. Entry was thus gained most often at the middle level of three-floor buildings allowing for the most economical administration of their entire interiors. A centered entry positioned the circulation desk felicitously facing the door, with multitiered book stacks to its rear, again for greatest simplicity of use and operation. Reading and reference rooms were situated handily to the right and left.

A. Carnegie and the Black Colleges[3]

Since it is not possible to discuss here all eighty-four academic library buildings that Carnegie funded during this decade, this study will concentrate only upon those he provided to the colleges that served predominantly black students. The experience of these institutions is largely typical of the rest.

When the century began only three predominantly black colleges had freestanding library buildings—Lincoln in Pennsylvania, Saint Augustine's, and Claflin—all of which have already been mentioned in the previous chapter. The rest of the nation's black colleges shared the fate of the large majority of their contemporary institutions in lacking such facilities. By the end of the first decade of the twentieth century, however, new library buildings had been funded on fifteen additional black college campuses, and all but one of the new ones had received their funding from Andrew Carnegie.

Only Hampton University obtained its funds elsewhere. The railroad magnate, Collis P. Huntington, had been a trustee of Hampton for ten years prior to his death in 1900. When he died, his widow gave then Hampton Institute $100,000 for the construction of a "Collis P. Huntington Memorial Library," and the building, which was designed by Washington, D.C. architect Alexander B. Trowbridge, was dedicated on April 28, 1903. Speakers at the dedication ceremony included Hampton alumnus Booker T. Washington and Yale University president Arthur T. Hadley.[4] The Huntington Memorial remained the Library for Hampton University until the opening of the William R. and Norma B. Harvey Library in 1992.

1. Carnegie's First College Libary, 1900

Tuskegee. It is no surprise that Booker T. Washington was one of the first college presidents anywhere, and perhaps *the* first to get to Andrew Carnegie. Although Carnegie had funded thirty-five American public libraries in the 1800s,[5] the Carnegie archives show that he did not make any library building grants to colleges until the year 1900 when he suddenly funded three, one of which was at Tuskegee Institute.[6] Yet even this grant may have been agreed to orally in the previous year, if Washington's later recollections can be relied upon. "You gave us $20,000," he wrote to Carnegie on November 26, 1913, "for the [Library] in 1899."[7]

The whole project at Tuskegee as proposed by Washington would appeal greatly to Carnegie. The architect who was to design the building was Tuskegee's own director of industries, R. R. Taylor, who was the first black graduate of the Massachusetts Institute of Technology. The building was to be constructed by the hands of Tuskegee's own students working under Taylor's tutelage and from bricks again made by Tuskegee's own students at Tuskegee's own kilns. Washington moreover knew whereof he spoke, having himself been trained as a brick mason at Hampton Institute. It is easy to see why the self-made industrial magnate may have chosen to accede to this proposal as his first academic library building.

The library at Tuskegee opened in 1901. Taylor had designed a stiffly dignified building in the best Classical Revival tradition, with four Ionic columns supporting a pediment to form a portico in its center front, with wings thirty feet by forty feet extending in both directions from the main entrance. At its entry level it had a reading room with a delivery desk, separate rooms for newspapers and for other periodicals, a stack room, and the librarian's office. On the floor above there was an assembly room, three study rooms, a museum, and another stack room.[8] The following year Principal Washington wrote to Carnegie's private secretary to inquire where the Institute might obtain a good portrait of Carnegie to hang in the building, because on February 27, 1903, the donor himself planned to visit the campus to see the new building in person.[9] This structure remained the institution's Library until the construction of the Hollis Burke Frissell Library in 1932. It still graces the campus and continues to serve it in several capacities.

Carnegie's subsequent relations with Tuskegee are mute testimony that he was eminently pleased with what he saw there during his visit. Only six weeks after Carnegie's visit, on April 14, 1903, Washington gave an address at Madison Square Garden in New York City, and three days later Carnegie gave an astounding $600,000 worth of U. S. Steel Corporation bonds to the Tuskegee Institute endowment, with the stipulation that $150,000 of the amount be put aside for the personal use of Booker T. Washington and his family for as long as they should need it.[10] In his autobiography published seventeen years later, however, Carnegie reported that immediately upon Washington's receipt of the letter announcing the gift, the Tuskegee Principal came to see him and requested that the unusual stipulation be eliminated in favor of wording to the effect that the Tuskegee Trustees be requested to make "suitable provision" for Washington. Carnegie wrote a new letter in accord with Washington's wishes, and both versions of the letter are included in the published edition of Washington's letters. There is no question but that the industrialist held Washington in very high regard.[11]

2. Buildings Offered in 1904

After a little spurt of three grants to colleges in 1900, however— Grove City College and the College of Emporia, in addition to Tuskegee—Carnegie inexplicably and almost entirely discontinued his interest in academic institutions for more than three years. He gave one library building to Upper Iowa College in 1901, another to Pennsylvania State University in 1902, and four additional ones [Beloit, Mount Holyoke, and Cornell Colleges, as well as the University of Oklahoma] in 1903. When he finally did take up the cause again in 1904, however, he did it with his usual unbridled relish, giving grants in that year to twelve institutions, of which five were for black students. A clue to this hiatus in his giving may be found in a letter from Carnegie's private secretary, James Bertram, to President J. G. Merrill of Fisk University when the latter wrote in December 1902 seeking to gain the philanthropist's interest in his institution. Bertram replied that

> Mr. Carnegie has re-iterated within the last few days that his time is fully taken up with the [Public] Library business, and that he cannot give any attention to colleges, large or small, at present. Some day he will probably take them up.[12]

Talladega. Chronologically, the second black school to be offered a library building grant following Tuskegee's success in 1900 was its sister institution founded in Talladega, Alabama, in 1867, Talladega College. In December 1903 Carnegie received a letter from one B. F. Stewart, a black barber from Norwalk, Ohio, to whom the industrialist had allegedly once promised "any favor."[13] On December 4, Stewart wrote to him that Talladega College "had nearly 8,000 Vols.

scattered through several Class rooms," which it needed to gather into a proper library building. Six weeks later Bertram wrote to Talladega President G. W. Andrews offering $15,000 for such a building,[14] and construction was begun almost immediately. Due reportedly to unanticipated price increases, however, it languished for a time unfinished. The College's subsequent petitions to Carnegie for supplemental funds to complete the building were unsuccessful, as was almost always the case, although he did later give $1,000 for an organ for the College Chapel. The Carnegie Library served Talladega until the dedication of its present Savery Library building on March 1, 1939, after which time it was razed.

Wilberforce. The next black college to receive a Carnegie grant had first requested one somewhat earlier than Talladega. Secretary Horace Talbert of Wilberforce University, established in western Ohio in 1856, first approached Carnegie in a letter dated April 16, 1903. Obviously emulating the successful Tuskegee petition, Talbert specified that "all of the work for the building such as brick-making, brick masonry, carpentering, blacksmithing, etc., would be done by the students," and on the following day the institution got Booker T. Washington to write a letter in support of its appeal. This was, however, apparently before Carnegie had decided to initiate a program of giving academic library buildings, and the project was delayed for several months until that was accomplished. Asked by Bertram for particulars later, Talbert painted a grim picture of the library situation at Wilberforce.

> In Shorter Hall we have the University Library, [he wrote on February 2, 1904] a room fifteen by sixteen by fourteen, shelves all packed in double rows. In same hall we have the Payne Library, a room sixteen by twenty four by fourteen. This room is also packed from floor to ceiling, and the books are doubled on the shelves. In O'Neil Hall the Library room is nine by fourteen by fourteen. In Seminary there are two Library rooms filled with books. No. One is twelve by twenty by fourteen. No. Two is ten by twelve by fourteen.

This lugubrious situation elicited an immediate positive response, and Bertram wrote on February 15 announcing Carnegie's willingness to provide $15,000, an amount that was later increased to $17,950.[15]

The Library building at Wilberforce was dedicated at Commencement in June 1907.[16] Containing some 9,000 square feet of floor space, the simple brick structure comprised a main floor and basement. Classical Revival in style, it featured a central pedimented entry up a flight of ten steps with three windows in each of the two balancing wings. Later added to with a similar wing rearward, the building served as the University Library until the institution moved to a new campus in the 1980s.

Alabama A. & M. On December 3, 1903, Alabama A. & M. University president W. H. Councill, himself a former slave, wrote to Carnegie requesting a grant for a library building. In a subsequent letter he explained that his institution was then maintaining an inadequately housed operation out of two or three small rooms in Palmer Hall, and the donor responded on March 10, 1904, that he would provide $10,000 for the purpose. The amount was later increased to $12,000, and the building was built. Regrettably, however, this new building burned to the ground less than a year after its opening. Carnegie immediately provided another $4,540 to be added to the insurance proceeds so that the building could be replaced, and the second building was occupied by October 31, 1906.[17] The nature of the ill-fated first building can no longer be determined, but its successor is still standing and in a good state of repair. It is a stately brick building of neo-Classical design, with four round columns supporting a pediment, which is flanked on either side by four windows on each of its two floors. It served for more than forty years before it was decommissioned as a library.

Benedict. Benedict College, founded in Columbia, South Carolina, in 1870, had also solicited Carnegie's assistance during the hiatus of his giving to colleges, first seeking him out unsuccessfully in January 1902 and then again in January 1903. Persistence, however, was eventually rewarded, and when President A. C. Osburn wrote a third time on December 8, 1903, he hit pay dirt. Supplying the increasingly ubiquitous letter of support from Booker T. Washington, he requested $5,000 for library construction, $1,000 for library equipment, and another $5,000 for library endowment. Carnegie acceded to the first two parts of his appeal, and $6,000 was tendered to the College in Bertram's letter of March 15, 1904. With this sum Benedict was able to erect and furnish a ten-room brick and stone structure fifty-three feet square with a main floor and a basement. The building was taken down more than three decades later following the opening of the institution's J. J. Starks Library in 1937.[18]

Atlanta. President Horace Bumstead of Atlanta University approached Andrew Carnegie on February 4, 1904, requesting $50,000 for a library building because the institution's library had "already outgrown its present quarters in Stone Hall, our central building." When Bertram responded that the amount requested was too high, President Bumstead acknowledged that his estimate of the cost had perhaps been too much influenced by the recent $100,000 expenditure on the aforementioned somewhat palatial Huntington Memorial Library at Hampton Institute. Upon reflection, however, he had concluded that $30,000 was perhaps a more appropriate figure. Carnegie gave $25,000, construction commenced, and the building was occupied in January 1906.[19]

The new Library building at Atlanta had a main floor, a basement, and a fireproof three-level structural stack. Constructed of red brick trimmed in stone, this simple rectangular Colonial-style structure featured a delivery room opposite its centered entry with a reference room to its left and a reading room and art alcove to its right. There was a 150-seat public meeting room in the basement. The building still stands on the campus of Morris Brown College, one of the constituent colleges of Atlanta University, although it is no longer used as a library.[20]

3. Buildings Funded in 1905

Fisk. As he had done in 1904, Carnegie again in 1905 offered funds for library buildings for five black colleges. The first of these five offers was to Fisk University, which had been chartered in 1866 in Nashville, Tennessee. As was said earlier, Fisk President J. G. Merrill first approached Carnegie in 1900 and again in 1902 before the philanthropist had taken up any real program of giving to academic institutions. When President Merrill approached him a third time in 1905 it appears that he really wanted money to construct a music building, but Bertram replied that the only thing Carnegie might be persuaded to build was a library, so Merrill changed his request. On March 15, 1905, Fisk was offered $20,000 for a library building provided the University would raise a matching amount in new endowment.

It had long been Carnegie's practice in his program of funding public library buildings to require a recipient community to pledge to support the operation of the library with no less than 10 percent of the gift amount per year for ten years, and the proviso now exacted from Fisk was intended to accomplish the same goal but adapted to the academic environment. At first the Fisk board of trustees simply put aside $20,000 from its unappropriated funds as a separate endowment for the purpose, but Bertram rejected this arrangement, insisting that the money had to be *new* endowment. During these negotiations, Paul D. Cravath, representing Fisk, wrote on April 4, 1905, suggesting that the University might use its own money to build a library, if "Mr. Carnegie might be willing in lieu of giving a library, to provide for the erection of a building" to house the applied sciences. This upset Bertram, who tended to be abrupt and cantankerous under the best of circumstances, and he immediately wrote a curt note enquiring if Fisk really wanted a library building at all. He then sat back and waited for the new endowment to be raised, a stalemate that lasted for more than two years.

Again it was through the good offices of Booker T. Washington, whose third wife was an alumna of Fisk, that the project got back on track. On January 9, 1908, the Tuskegee principal wrote persuasively to Bertram on Fisk's behalf, requesting that the requirement for it to raise new endowment be waived, and six days later Carnegie assented to this request. The construction funds were released, and erection of the building commenced. The rectangular brick building with hipped roof and cupola was designed by the experienced Boston architectural firm of Shepley, Rutan & Coolidge. Of its two floors above grade, the upper was equipped temporarily "to be used for Teachers," and its full basement was set up to serve as a gymnasium for women.[21] Carnegie seldom allowed space in the libraries he donated to be used for such nonlibrary functions, but he appears not to have demurred at the diversion of these spaces. It may, however, have reinforced James Bertram's impression that Fisk had not really wanted a library in the first place. The building, which opened in 1909, was the home of Fisk's library for a relatively short period of twenty-one years until construction of the University's Cravath Library in 1930. It remains standing today.

Livingstone. Booker T. Washington also lent his substantial influence with Carnegie to the cause of Livingstone College, which had been established in Salisbury, North Carolina, in 1879. Livingstone trustee John C. Dancy approached Carnegie in February 1904 requesting $20,000 for a building to house the College library, chapel, and some classrooms, but Carnegie was not interested in multipurpose buildings. Washington later interceded and introduced Livingstone President W. H. Goler to the Scot, who had Bertram write to T. W. Wallace, assistant secretary of the College, on May 24, 1905, offering $12,500 for construction of a library proper.[22] The offer was accepted, and a square two-story brick Classical Revival building was constructed, complete with four fluted Ionic columns supporting a pediment to create a stately portico that sheltered a graceful doorway capped by a delicate fan window. Balancing one-floor wings have been added to the building subsequently, and it has been completely renovated and refurbished (Plate 4d). It is the only one of Carnegie's benefactions to black colleges that remains in use today as a library.

Cheyney. The Cheyney Institute for Colored Youth, precursor to Cheyney State University in Delaware County, Pennsylvania, dates its origin from 1837. It too solicited Carnegie's help in 1905, and its

Principal Hugh M. Brown was informed by Bertram on July 12 of that year that it would receive $10,000 for a library building contingent upon its raising a like amount in new endowment. Although it was difficult, the endowment stipulation was eventually met, and the Institute was able to move into its new library building in 1909.[23] This stone structure featured a baronial hall complete with beamed ceiling and fireplaces at both ends. Added to in 1962, it was finally decommissioned as a library when the Leslie Pinckney Hill Library opened in 1976. It is now the Center for the Department of Business Administration.

Florida A. & M. On July 18, 1905, President Nathan P. Young of Florida A. & M. University in Tallahassee was informed by James Bertram that Carnegie would give the institution $10,000 for a library building if "Ten Thousand Dollars new endowment is raised toward the upkeep and carrying on of the Library in the building." When the President explained in his reply that as a state institution the University was debarred by law from special fund-raising efforts, however, Bertram responded that Carnegie would accept in lieu of new endowment a written guarantee of support from the Chairman of the State Board of Education "as you do not go outside for funds, and are wholly supported by the State and [under the provisions of the second Morrill Act] Federal authorities."

Plans for the new building were drawn up in the University's Department of Mechanical Drawing and Architecture and were then critiqued by the New York City architectural firm of Whitfield & King. When Bertram reviewed the drawings, however, he noted that they showed an office for the University President on the second floor, a feature that he then deleted, stating in his letter to President Young on November 22, 1906, that "the building should be used for Library purposes only." Occupancy, however, would not come soon enough. Just before the new building was completed, on New Years Eve 1905, Duval Hall, which housed the library, burned to the ground, with only about one hundred volumes escaping the flames.[24]

Again the building style opted for at Florida A. & M. University was Classical Revival. A two-story brick veneer structure with a center portico formed by a colonnade of four fluted Ionic pillars and a pediment, with "Carnegie Library" carved into the frieze, was dedicated in February 1908. It was decommissioned as a library forty years later when the present Samuel H. Coleman Library was constructed. Today this Carnegie benefaction, the oldest—and many would say the most majestic—building on the Florida A. & M. campus, houses the University's Black Archives Research Center and Museum.

Johnson C. Smith. Almost as a Christmas present, a letter from James Bertram dated December 23, 1905, informed President D. J. Sanders of Biddle University that Carnegie had approved a gift of $12,500 for the construction and equipping of Biddle's first library building. Biddle was a foundation of the Presbyterian Church in Charlotte, North Carolina, which dated from 1867. Carnegie's requirement that an equal amount be raised in new endowment delayed the project for a number of years. Finally, on May 12, 1910, the Presbyterian Church's Board of Missions for Freedmen, which had the institution in its care, informed the donor that it had fulfilled the matching stipulation, and construction moved ahead.[25]

The delay in construction meant that the Library at Biddle, now Johnson C. Smith University, would be the last of Carnegie's beneficences to black schools to come to fulfillment. A neat and dignified rectangular brick building, with a flat roof and a somewhat smaller center portico, this time with only two Doric columns supporting the pediment, it was finally opened for use in 1912. It is still standing, having served as the institution's library until construction of its subsequent James Biddle Duke Library in the 1970s.

4. Buildings Funded in 1906 and 1907

Wiley. Wiley College was established in Marshall, Texas, in 1873 by the Methodist Episcopal Church. Its president M. W. Dogan requested a library building of Andrew Carnegie in January 1905, but upon reviewing the assets of the College, Bertram replied that

> with a plant consisting of only one building costing Forty-two Thousand Dollars, and no endowment, Mr. Carnegie does not think it would be advisable to sink money in the erection of a special library building.

After retotting its resources and revising its proposal to include library service to the inhabitants of the small local community, Wiley returned a year later with a new request. It also sought the intercession of its parent authority, the Church's Freedmen's Aid and Southern Education Society. This time Carnegie responded with an offer to provide $15,000 for a building and furniture, if $15,000 of new money could be raised for the College endowment fund.

Again Booker T. Washington entered the scene, writing to Carnegie on April 9, 1906. He began by informing Carnegie that Washington's own executive secretary, Emmet J. Scott, who had gained Carnegie's notice and admiration during the latter's visit to Tuskegee three years earlier, was an alumnus of Wiley College, implying that

Scott exemplified the qualities of all good Wiley graduates. He then pleaded that raising the matching endowment would be an especially onerous hardship for Wiley and inquired if a guarantee of library support from the board of trustees would suffice as a substitute for it.

Carnegie believed strongly in helping those who helped themselves, and this matching requirement had by then become an important aspect of his college library grant program. Nonetheless, in this case he relented, but Bertram's next letter to Washington importuned him to

> please see that this matter is arranged so that it is not published in every newspaper from Maine to Texas so that every other college in the country wanting something from Mr. Carnegie unconditionally will not be able to point to Wiley as a precedent.

In his letter of appreciation five days later, Washington promised to be "very careful to see that nothing is said about it in the public press."[26]

A decade later Wiley's Carnegie Library was described in a comprehensive publication of the U. S. Department of the Interior on black colleges as being "of neat design, two stories high, and one of the best libraries in colored schools."[27] It was indeed a stately Colonial-style structure with a recessed portico supported by two columns. It continued to serve both the Wiley staff and students, as well as the Marshall community for some threescore years until the Thomas Winston Cole, Sr., Library was opened in 1967, and it is still in use today for College administrative purposes.

Knoxville. Chartered in 1863 in Tennessee, Knoxville College was a creature of the Board of Freedmen's Missions of the United Presbyterian Church. Its President R. W. McGranahan's representations to Carnegie early in 1907 elicited an offer of $10,000 for a building, if a matching amount of new money were added to the institutional endowment. The president reported that the College contemplated constructing a building rather like Talladega's, but with an assembly hall for lectures on the second floor.[28] This building also remained in use until the 1960s, when it was razed to make room for the College's present Alumni Library, which was then constructed on the same site.

Howard. The last of the black colleges to be offered a library building by Andrew Carnegie was Howard University, chartered in the nation's capital in 1867. Its President Wilbur P. Thirkield first lay his need before the philanthropist in a letter written on January 17, 1907. Howard's inadequate library with its tiny reading room

Plate 4. The Adoption of Classical Revival Architecture for the Columbian Exposition in 1892 Resulted in a Resurgence in Its Popularity for Most Public Buildings, Including Libraries, for Many Years Thereafter.

a) Columbia University (NY), 1897. McKim Mead & White, Architects.

b) Emory University (GA), 1898. S. M. Patton, Architect.

c) Grinnell College (IA), 1905. Hallett & Rawson, Architects.

d) Livingstone College (NC), 1906. Architect not known.

twenty feet by twenty-five feet was then crowded into the southeast corner of the third floor of the Main Building. His bid for a grant was not immediately successful, but on December 2 of that year Carnegie offered $50,000 for a building and equipment, with the standard proviso that the University raise a like amount in new endowment. In a second letter to President Thirkield written the following day, Bertram also suggested that the University might wish to consult the aforementioned New York City architectural firm of Whitfield & King for help in planning its new building. In a postscript Bertram added the following useful bit of intelligence: "Mr. [Henry D.] Whitfield is Mr. Carnegie's brother-in-law." The University did retain Whitfield & King, and, able to satisfy the strict endowment requirement through the substitution of a ten-year support pledge of $5,000 per annum, ground was broken on April 17, 1909.[29]

Dedication of Howard University's new Carnegie Library on April 25, 1910, must have been one of the more elaborate academic library dedications in history.[30] Speakers included Librarian of Congress Dr. Herbert Putnam, donor Andrew Carnegie, and President Howard Taft, in that order. Carnegie's speech may help to explain his extraordinary motivation to make libraries available to society. After noting that books contained all recorded knowledge, and that through libraries knowledge is completely democratized, he summarized his own general motivation to provide them as follows:

> Books are the most perfect instruments of philanthropy that exist. I will tell you why. They do not do anything for nothing. . . . If you are going to get any benefit out of these books, you must work for it. . . . I wish to help those who help themselves.[31]

Beyond this, and doubtless revealing the faith that bred his own further particular motivation to provide libraries to black schools especially, he went on to encourage the students in attendance to use the library to

> keep on, attend your lessons, get education, remember that each one of you bears part of the honor of the race wherever he goes, and the day is not far distant when you will take your place in this country with any other race, and you will progress and the white race will progress; you will come to like each other, and you will live on good terms with each other, and the race problem will be no more forever.

The Library building that Carnegie funded for Howard University was one hundred feet by thirty-five feet in size with a four-tier steel structural stack with glass floors extending to its rear. Neo-

Classical in style, its antae and four columns supported the center pediment that marked the main entrance. On the entry level large reading rooms were situated to the right and left of a central circulation area, which was open to the roof. Off the second-floor gallery were special reading rooms, seminar rooms, a board room, and other administrative spaces. In the basement there was a newspaper room and an assembly hall for lectures. The building is still standing and has been used for various other purposes since the opening of Howard's Founders Library in 1939.

With the opening of the Library at Johnson C. Smith in 1912, eighteen black colleges in the United States had freestanding library buildings, of which Carnegie had funded all but four. Moreover Carnegie had made his offers to all of these institutions except Tuskegee during the very brief span from 1904 to 1907, his library benefactions to them totaling $240,490. In the latter years of the period he had also exacted from the recipient institutions some kind of commitment that the libraries would be supported with an appropriate level of operating funds. Of the fourteen buildings that he funded, eleven are still standing, ten are still serving their institutions in some capacity fully ninety years later, and even today one is still functioning as a library. Surely this was a legacy of signal importance to academic libraries in the United States, and of special significance among black institutions.

And what of Booker T. Washington? Was Andrew Carnegie ever disposed to deny him anything he asked? Perhaps not. Yet, when Washington requested $18,000 for an addition to the Tuskegee Library in November 1913, Carnegie responded as follows: "My dear Friend: Don't you think Tuskegee has had its share from your humble servant. . . ? Think about it."[32] This was not a letter drafted by the curmudgeonly James Bertram but by the Laird of Skibo Castle himself. The Tuskegee Principal withdrew his request.

B. Carnegie Buildings on Other College Campuses.

All told, Andrew Carnegie funded the construction of fully ninety-three library buildings at four-year colleges and universities in the United States. All but five of these projects were initiated during the eleven-year period from 1900 through 1910, although their construction was not finally completed until 1921. Their total cost was $4,176,548, an enormous sum even now but vastly greater in its time.[33] These construction grants ranged in size from the $6,000 given to tiny Benedict College to as much as $227,446 to Wellesley. George Peabody College received $180,000, and $150,000 each was granted to Brown University, Oberlin College, Pennsylvania State University, and Syracuse University. With the exception, however, of these six and four others, all of Carnegie's grants for academic library buildings were five-figure amounts, with the large majority of them falling in the lower half of that category. The median amount granted to the ninety-nine institutions was $27,000.

Carnegie's ninety-three academic library buildings were quite well distributed throughout thirty of the then forty-six states of the nation, and both private and state-supported institutions were well represented among the recipients. More institutions in the state of Ohio received grants than those in any other state; there were eight. Meanwhile Iowa, Kansas, North Carolina, and Pennsylvania each received six, and five each were given to Alabama, Georgia, Maine, and Tennessee.

Just as was the case with the fourteen black colleges discussed above, by far the dominant architectural style among the rest of the Carnegie buildings was Renaissance. Almost all had centered entries. Most required the scaling of at least eight or ten steps to the door as at Grinnell (1905, Plate 4c), Mercer (1908), Otterbein (1908), and Winthrop (1906). Many had rotundas, as did Converse (1904), Furman (1907), Judson (1909), Maine (1906), Miami (1910), Pomona (1908), and Washington and Lee (1908). In fact, Mount Holyoke and Swarthmore, both of which were Gothic and both of which were completed in 1906, were among the very few Carnegie buildings that were not patterned upon the popular Renaissance models.

C. Other Building Donors of the Period

Well before the twentieth century began, of course, American philanthropists had begun to provide funds for the construction of library buildings, both public and academic. A number of them have already been mentioned in the earlier pages of this volume. By the turn of the century, however, this practice was becoming increasingly fashionable, and although Carnegie was the only multiple donor in its first decade, the total given by others for libraries added up to a very considerable amount, no doubt approaching $3 million. Table 3 enumerates many if not all of the institutions that benefited from this generosity.[34]

Then as now the preferences of donors sometimes influenced the shape and style of library buildings. Clearly, however, the preferences of these individuals favored the Renaissance style also. Indeed among all academic libraries constructed during this period—Carnegie-funded as well as separately funded—those that were not

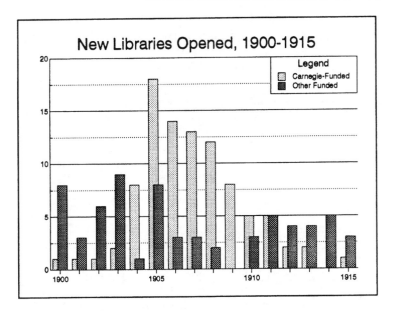

Figure 13. Number of New Academic Library Buildings Constructed in the United States, 1900–1915

basically Renaissance in style can be counted on one's fingers. A half dozen or so buildings in the upper Atlantic states evinced a resurgence there of interest in Gothic, primarily at Bowdoin (1902), Bryn Mawr (1906), Clark (1903), and Vassar (1905), in addition to Swarthmore and Mount Holyoke, which were mentioned earlier. Elsewhere, at least in the early years of the decade, the Romanesque pattern still showed some signs of life, as at Southern Illinois (1904), Tulane (1903), and West Virginia (1902)[35].

D. Publicly-Funded Buildings

So extensive, in fact, was the largesse of Carnegie and his companion philanthropists during this period that the number of publicly funded library buildings constructed tailed down to fewer than one per annum. Although no fewer than twenty-six state-supported institutions opened new library buildings during this eleven-year span, Carnegie funded fully eighteen of them as well, and other donors built two more. Thus fewer than a fourth of the total came to be paid for from the public purse. These included the University of Wisconsin (1900), West Virginia University (1902), Southern Illinois

TABLE 3
Institutions Receiving Buildings from Donors Other than Carnegie, 1900–1910.

NAME OF INSTITUTION	YR.BUILT	NAME OF DONOR	AMOUNT GIVEN
Albion	1902	Lettie Gassette	$ 10,000
Allegheny	1901	W. E. Reis	
Bates	1902	[Coram Library]	
Baylor	1903	F. L. Carroll	75,000
Bowdoin	1902	T. H. Hubbard	300,000
Bryn Mawr	1906	[Multiple Donors]	258,000
Butler	1903	E. C. Thompson	40,000
Cincinnati	1900	A. Van Wormer	60,000
Clark	1904	J. G. Clark	150,000
Duke	1903	J. B. Duke	70,000
Franklin	1903	[Shirk Library]	
Georgia	1905	G. Peabody	50,000
Hampton	1903	Mrs. C. P. Huntington	100,000
Hanover	1905	Mrs. E. S. Hendricks	35,000
Hiram	1900	[Teachout-Price Lib.]	
Hollins	1908	[Cocke Library]	
Lafayette	1900	A. S. Van Wickle	30,000
Lake Forest	1900	A. S. Reid	30,000
Louisiana State	1903	J. Hill	33,000
Middlebury	1900	E. Starr	50,000
Milwaukee-Downer	1905	Mrs. H. A. J. Upham	10,000
Rutgers	1903	R. Voorhees	59,000
Saint Olaf	1902	H. Steensland	
Stanford	1900	T. W. Stanford	320,000
Tulane	1907	Mrs. F. W. Tilton	50,000
Vassar	1905	Mrs. F. F. Thompson	500,000
Washington/Jefferson	1905	W. R. Thompson	60,000
Wooster	1900	H. C. Frick	35,000

University (1903), Peru State University (1906), Indiana University (1907), and Indiana State University (1910).

In conclusion, it should be observed that, insofar as academic library buildings were concerned, the first decade of the twentieth century was no more innovative than the concluding decade of the nineteenth had been. Little if anything that was truly new was brought into library function, and no experimentation of conse-

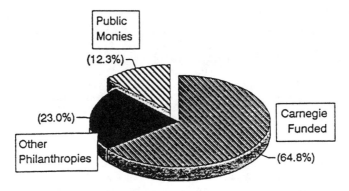

Figure 14. Funding Sources of Academic Libraries Constructed, 1900–1910

quence was attempted. The total number of buildings built was more than four times greater, however, thanks primarily to Andrew Carnegie and secondarily to the large number of other donors. But here too there was a much higher level of uniformity in architectural style in the latter period than there had been formerly. Most of the library buildings built during these years are still recognizable as libraries today.

Notes

1. This story is perhaps most widely known through George S. Bobinski's *Carnegie Libraries: Their History and Impact on American Public Library Development* (Chicago: American Library Association, 1969). But see also Abigail A. Van Slyck, "Free to All: Carnegie Libraries and the Transformation of American Culture, 1886–1917." Ph.D. dissertation, University of California, 1989.

2. For a fuller account of this matter, see the excellent work by Abigail A. Van Slyck, " 'The Utmost Amount of Effectiv (*sic*) Accommodation': Andrew Carnegie and the Reform of the American Library" *Journal of the Society of Architectural Historians* 1 (December 1991): 359–383.

3. Much of the text in this section has been published as David Kaser, "Andrew Carnegie and the Black College Libraries," pp. 119–133, in *For the Good of the Order: Essays in Honor of Edward G. Holley* (Greenwich, Conn.: JAI Press, 1994). I am grateful to the JAI Press for permission to use this material herein. I am also especially indebted in preparing this section to Jessie C. Smith's *Black Academic Libraries and Research Collections; An Historical Survey* (Westport, Conn.: Greenwood Press, 1977), passim.

4. B. N. Puryear, *Hampton Institute* (Hampton, Va.: Prestige Press, 1962), p. 57; "The Huntington Memorial Library of Hampton Institute," *Library Journal* 28 (May 1903): 241–243.

5. Bobinski, p. 14.

6. Florence Anderson, *Carnegie Corporation Library Program 1911–1961* (N.Y.: Carnegie Corporation of New York, 1963), pp. 74, 75.

7. Carnegie's correspondence with colleges and universities is preserved alphabetically by institution in the Carnegie Corporation's "Libraries" files on 89 microfiches, oddly designated as reels 37–39. They have been deposited in the Rare Book & Manuscript Library at Columbia University. They will be cited here simply as Carnegie Corporation "Libraries" files.

8. Theodore Wesley Koch, *A Book of Carnegie Libraries* (N.Y.: H. W. Wilson, 1917), pp. 116–119.

9. Carnegie Corporation "Libraries" files.

10. Booker T. Washington, *Papers*, ed. by Louis R. Harlan and Raymond W. Smock (Urbana: University of Illinois Press, 1977), VII, 119.

11. Andrew Carnegie, *Autobiography* (Boston: Houghton Mifflin, 1920), pp. 276–277.

12. Ibid., Bertram to Merrill, December 23, 1902.

13. Maxine D. Jones and Joe M. Richardson, *Talladega College: The First Century* (Tuscaloosa: University of Alabama Press, 1990), p. 69.

14. January 18, 1904, Carnegie Corporation "Library" files.

15. Ibid., April 24, 1905.

16. Frederick A. McGinnis, *A History and an Interpretation of Wilberforce University* (Wilberforce, Ohio: Brown Publishing Company, 1941), p. 74.

17. Letters dated December 3, 1903; February 21, 1904; March 10, 1904; November 16, 1904; January 27, 1906; February 20, 1906; October 31, 1906; January 11, 1907; Carnegie Corporation "Libraries" files.

18. Ibid.

19. Letters dated February 6, 1904; March 18, 1904; April 28, 1904; June 11, 1904; October 29, 1904; January 29, 1906; ibid.

20. *Library Journal* 31 (November 1906): 789.

21. Letters dated March 15, 1905; March 27, 1905; April 4, 1905; April 5, 1905; January 9, 1908; January 15, 1908; May 4, 1908; Carnegie Corporation "Library" files.

22. Letters dated February 25, 1904; May 24, 1905; ibid. But for a contrarian view of Washington's involvement, see the Boston *Guardian*, March 18, 1905.

23. Letters dated July 5, 1905; November 14, 1908; October 10, 1909; Carnegie Corporation "Libraries" files.

24. Letters dated July 18, 1905; September 18, 1905; January 15, 1906; November 22, 1906; ibid. See also Leedell W. Neyland and John W. Riley, *The History of Florida Agricultural and Mechanical University* (Gainesville: University of Florida Press, 1963), pp. 57–59.

25. Letters dated December 23, 1905; May 12, 1910; Carnegie Corporation "Libraries" files.

26. Letters dated January 10, 1905; February 3, 1905; March 26, 1906; April 9, 1906; May 7, 1906; May 12, 1906; ibid.

27. *Negro Education: A Study of the Private and Higher Schools for Colored People in the United States* (Washington, D.C.: Department of the Interior, Bureau of Education, "*Bulletin*, 1916, No. 38," 1917), I, 583.

28. Letters dated January 22, 1907; March 15, 1907; March 10, 1908; Carnegie Corporation "Libraries" file.

29. *Library Journal* 34 (May 1909): 234.

30. *Public Libraries* 15 (1910): 213.

31. *Library Journal* 35 (June 1910): 264–265.

32. Letter dated November 19, 1913; Carnegie Corporation "Libraries" file.

33. Anderson, pp. 69–87. Note, however, that this list contains several preparatory schools, one building outside the United States, and a building that was never used as a library. Also this list in each case gives the year not that the building was completed for use but rather the year in which the grant was made. Often several years passed before the building was completed.

34. These data have been drawn from the following sources: *Library Journal* 25: 193, 344, 345; 26: 416, 418; 28: 122, 241; 29: 36, 98, 177–78, 182, 249; 30: 434, 497; *Public Libraries* 4: 214; 5: 220; K. J. Fennimore, *The Albion College Sesquicentennial History 1835–1985* (Albion, Mich.: Albion College, 1985), p. 364; R. Rouse, "A History of the Baylor University Library, 1845–1919." Ph.D. dissertation, University of Michigan 1962, p. 177; L. C. Hatch, *The History of Bowdoin College* (Portland, Maine: Loring, Short & Marmon, 1927), p. 431; Ohio Library Commission, *Sketches of Ohio Libraries* (Columbus: F. J. Heer, 1902), p. 295; and M. M. Wilkerson, *Thomas Duckett Boyd* (Baton Rouge: Louisiana State University Press, 1935), p. 202.

35. This handsome building was designed by Stanford White, who was shot and killed by a jealous husband, one Harry Thaw, some four years later. It is ironic that in 1912 the family of White's killer funded the construction of a "Thaw Memorial Library" at Jamestown College in North Dakota, a building that is still standing at the time of this writing.

Chapter Six

Enter the Behemoths, 1910–1945

The third major period of American academic library design—that of fixed-function buildings with multitier structural stacks—began in 1910, and it too lasted thirty-five years. Here also began the period of large library buildings. The term "large", of course, is relative. Presumably the University of South Carolina viewed its first academic library as very large when comparing it with what little had gone before, and every decade or so since then another library has been built that was larger than anything that had preceded it. Indeed several large academic library buildings had been constructed in the years immediately preceding and following the opening of the twentieth century. Columbia's million-dollar Low Library has already been mentioned. In 1910 Wellesley opened a new $250,000 library, and Brown a new $300,000 library, both designed by the Boston firm of Shepley, Rutan & Coolidge. Vassar had opened a new $500,000 library in 1905. Stanford had constructed a new $600,000 library that was virtually completed by the end of 1905, but before it could be occupied it was so totally destroyed by the San Francisco earthquake in April 1906 that it had to be abandoned.

Circumstances in American higher education were such by 1910 that even buildings of these sizes would be dwarfed by several of the new libraries that would be built in the years immediately ahead. It is a commonplace to observe that throughout American history, the sizes of academic library buildings have depended upon an interactive mix comprising three factors: the size of the book collection, the size of the enrollment, and the predominant teaching style used in the institution. By the turn of the century all three of these factors were aligned in a conjunction supportive of seemingly ever-larger library buildings.

In chapter 4 it was observed that even as early as 1875 to 1890 the "seminar" style of instruction, which for the first time required students to consult a multiplicity of primary as well as secondary sources, had begun to pervade American higher education. This came increasingly to be the fashion of instruction especially in institutions that opted, or were driven, to emphasize graduate study, and resulted understandably in the need for unrelenting acceleration in the growth in their library book collections. Parenthetically it resulted also, for the first time in American English-language usage, in some differentiation between the meanings of the words "college" and "university," although even today that difference remains imprecise.

By the beginning of the new century the transition to this seminar method in American universities, as well as in some colleges, was well advanced. In his inaugural address on February 14, 1896, Chancellor George E. MacLean of the University of Nebraska noted this change somewhat effusively as follows:

> Within the decade seminars have spread through all departments of our universities. These seminars are the growing tips of knowledge. The professor in the midst of his volunteer band of fellow-investigators [i.e., those taking elective courses] trains them to be independent workers and teachers of others. He shares with them the first joy of the discovery of truth which stimulates patient and endless research. . . .[1]

No doubt Chancellor MacLean was pleased that his own University had dedicated a new library building, complete with seminar rooms, only two months prior to his inauguration.

Table 4 shows the experiences of a few selected university libraries as regards both enrollment and book collection sizes during the thirty-year period from 1890 to 1920. These figures, which are not atypical, show an average growth rate in enrollment in these institutions of more than 370 percent during the three decades, while the size of their aggregate collections increased more than fivefold. Parenthetically it is interesting to see here that, although the Civil War had ended more than a half century earlier, its impoverishing impact on southern institutions was still evident as late as 1920.

Between 1900 and 1910 these redoubled growth pressures spawned some creative thinking about how twentieth-century library services ought best to be organized, configured, and housed in the new buildings that they would require. All universities planning new library buildings struggled especially with the issues surrounding the needs of seminar-style instruction. Many professors believed that true seminar instruction could not be given except in rooms where all books relevant to the subject of the seminar were sequestered and available only to the students in the seminar, which

TABLE 4
Enrollment and Library Collection Growth in Selected Universities,
1890–1920.

Institution	Library Collection Size		Enrollment	
	1890	1920	1890	1920
Brown	68,000	270,000	285	1,310
Columbia	115,700	747,448	1,671	8,510
Cornell	108,138	630,637	1,329	5,765
Harvard	380,000	2,028,100	2,126	4,650
Michigan	74,599	432,392	2,158	8,652
North Carolina	34,000	93,914	200	1,437
Pennsylvania	90,000	503,572	1,594	6,862
Virginia	45,000	120,000	483	1,638
Yale	200,000	1,250,000	1,477	3,152

was the standard practice in the German universities. Most librarians, on the other hand, felt that such an arrangement would bring chaos into library administration.

No new departures regarding this matter emerged until the second decade of the century. When they did come, however, these departures fell basically into two categories, one of which was so radical that it found few adherents, while the other became so popular that it largely stereotyped university library building design for more than three decades thereafter.

A. Radical Departures

The first category comprised only two institutions: the University of Chicago and Johns Hopkins University. Although the considerations that they brought to bear upon their problems were very similar, their two resolutions of them were very different. Both were young institutions, Johns Hopkins having been founded in 1876 and Chicago in 1891. As a result, neither was freighted down with a baggage of tradition to constrain its thinking; in fact, neither had ever had a university library building before. Moreover, both had been strongly committed from the time of their establishment to seminar-style instruction at the graduate level.

In pondering their requirements for library space, both of these institutions began from the position that the needs of the professoriate were dominant and should be accommodated regardless of any cost to administrative efficiency. These considerations resulted in new buildings at both universities that were greatly different from anything that had gone before, not only in their sizes but also in the internal configuration of their materials and services.

Chicago. The William Rainey Harper Library at the University of Chicago was completed in 1912, but the concept for the building had been settled upon a full decade earlier. At the ALA Conference at Niagara Falls in 1902, University of Chicago Librarian Ernest DeWitt Burton presented a scheme that his university had already adopted. It concluded that the principal literary sources should be divided up by subject and distributed to individual seminar rooms rather than centralized as subject subsets within a single monolithic collection. It furthermore called for these separate departmental libraries to be located not in a central library building, but rather in the teaching departments themselves. Such libraries were planned for the departments of philosophy, history, the social sciences, classics, modern languages, Oriental languages, divinity, law, chemistry, geology, physics, biological sciences, mathematics, and astronomy. Each would have a card catalog of the books it contained. A new central library building meanwhile would comprise a large general study room with a large reference collection, stacks for the remaining general collections as well as infrequently used books, technical services, administrative space, and a union card catalog.

As a concession to the unity of all knowledge, however, the 1902 scheme required that the several departmental libraries be "so closely connected with the general library as to make communication as easy as possible." Since the university was then in the process of planning a complete new campus, it would be possible to effect reasonably convenient access to a centrally located library building across an elaborate system of bridges from the upper floors of the new surrounding classroom structures. The entire new campus was planned with this in mind, again by Shepley, Rutan & Coolidge of Boston.[2]

This arrangement resulted in the new William Rainey Harper Memorial Library's principal service level—complete with main reading room, public catalog, and delivery desk—being situated somewhat anomalously on its third floor, where the bridges from classroom buildings were destined to arrive. The library's second floor housed its administrative activities, while the entire central stack, which was eventually to attain a capacity of more than a million volumes, was on the ground floor. Electric book lifts and pneumatic tubes provided communication between the stack floor and the delivery desk two floors above. The scheme, somewhat optimistically, envisioned that this configuration of library spaces would provide "for the growth of the General Library and the libraries of the Humanities groups . . . for from 75 to 110 years."[3] Actually it served for fifty-eight years until the Regenstein Library was opened at the University of Chicago in 1970.

When completed in 1912, the Harper Library at Chicago was of monumental style and proportions, but rather than adopting the currently popular Renaissance exterior, it chose "English Gothic architecture of the collegiate type."[4] Its two six-story balancing stone towers, each supporting battlemented corner turrets rising 135 feet above the ground, contained other services and study rooms as well as offices. The main reading room, with almost 300 seats, featured a high timbered groin vault and was lighted with seven large arched windows with stone tracery facing both the north and south.

This building cost more than a million dollars to construct, of which John D. Rockefeller provided $600,000. Although the Harper building did contribute over time to a growing taste for "college Gothic" exteriors on academic buildings of many kinds, its interior arrangement of functions appears not to have influenced the layout of any subsequent libraries. Indeed an informed European observer wrote of it twenty years later that its hopes for fusion of departmental and central libraries "remained only on paper."[5]

Johns Hopkins. After wrestling with the same problems addressed at Chicago, Johns Hopkins University arrived at almost, but not quite, as radical a resolution. From the time of his appointment as librarian here in 1908, M. Llewellyn Raney had been laying plans for merging the traditional needs of library service with the new ones presented by seminar-style instruction. His solution was, in effect, to attempt to develop a library "apartment house" where each discipline could find in proximate locations its own books, journals, study space, seminar rooms, and faculty offices, but so configured with those of other disciplines that the overall integrity of the operation and ease of access for all patrons was preserved.

The resulting Daniel Coit Gilman Hall Library, which was opened in 1916, was 204 feet across and 160 feet deep. As may be seen in Figure 15, it was a four-floor hollow square structure with its entry on the foreside of an open court, stacks to the right and left sides of the court, and a large 6,000-square-foot reading room along its rear, available across an interior bridge from the vestibule. Beyond the stacks to the right and left were faculty offices, seminars,

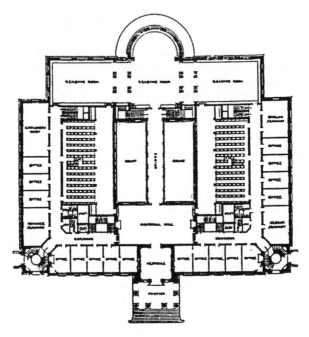

Figure 15. Entry Level of the John Hopkins University Library, 1916

and other class rooms. No books were shelved permanently in seminar rooms, but they were only a few steps away from these distributed seminar rooms and offices to which, if need be, books could be removed temporarily.[6] This Georgian Revival building with centered clock tower backed onto a declining slope so that, although public entry was at the third floor, even the lower floors had access to natural light rearward. Designed by Douglas H. Thomas, Jr., Gilman Hall served as the university library building until the construction of the Eisenhower Library in 1964. As was true of the Harper Library at Chicago, however, it was seldom copied. Its fate was summarized a generation later as follows: "The plan caused great stir at the time; it was thought that the ideal library for students had been made; but it has later found no imitation."[7] This judgment, however, is perhaps a bit harsh, because it is true only when taken as a whole. Some of the components in its design did come to be wrapped into the concepts of several of the nation's other university libraries during the ensuing quarter of a century.

B. More Conventional Solutions

The rest of the new university libraries of this period started with the premise that although sound library administrative principles would be observed, everything possible would be done within them to accommodate the needs of seminars. This resolution nonetheless resulted in some significant alterations in building layout.

California. Chronologically the first new academic library building to be opened with the spatial demands of the twentieth century clearly in mind was at the University of California at Berkeley. Although this building, which was originally planned for 1.25 million volumes, was not completed until 1917, its first phase, paid for with a gift in excess of $744,300 from Charles Franklin Doe of San Francisco, was opened for use in the early summer of 1911. Designed by University of California Professor John Galen Howard in the manner of the French Empire, this structure when completed was 224 feet by 262 feet in size, stood four stories in height, and contained a 100-foot-square nine-level core stack in its center.

Architect Howard no doubt had Charles Follen McKim's 1896 Boston Public Library building in mind as he conceptualized the Doe Library.[8] Entry to the Doe building was gained through a large foyer in the center of the north face of the building. Capacious galleried reading rooms were situated to the right and left of the foyer, and a divided monumental stair directly ahead rose to a sumptuous piano nobile above. This upper floor comprised an ample skylighted delivery hall, large catalog area, an administrative suite, and a massive main reading room with a vaulted ceiling looming upward in its center fully forty-five feet to three skylights (Plate 5e). This huge room contained almost four hundred seats at forty regularly arrayed eighteen-foot tables, which received an abundance of natural light not only from the skylights but also from ten high windows ranged along the room's north wall and enormous arched windows at its east and west ends (Plate 5e). Additional reading rooms, core stack space, seminar rooms, and staff work areas were then added in the second phase of construction completed some six years later.[9]

The Doe Library at Berkeley has been added to and modified several times in its fourscore years of existence, but it remains largely as it was originally planned. Although its design had weaknesses, it also proved to be admirably functional in meeting the academic needs of its era, and as a result it was for a long time very influential in the planning of other large academic libraries. In fact, for the next thirty-five years almost all of the newly built university library buildings were substantially influenced by it in a number of ways. These included entry in the center of a lower floor and a corridor thence below a main reading room to a stair that rose to a principal service floor above, with catalog, delivery desk, and entry to a multitier stack to the rear.

Found to be especially felicitous in the Berkeley building was the vertical spatial relationship between its stack levels and its building

Plate 5. Interior Views of Selected Academic Libraries, 1856–1912.

a) Main Library Hall, College of Charleston (SC), 1856. (College Archives).

b) Rotunda, Lehigh University (PA), 1876.

c) Reading Room, Cornell University, 1890. (University Archives).

d) Main Library Hall, Union College, 1903. (College Archives).

e) Main Reading Room, University of California (CA), 1911.

f) Main Reading Room, University of Texas (TX), 1912.

floors, a feature that was described simply by one contemporary observer as follows: "The regular story heights of the building are 15 ft., a multiple of 7 ft. 6 in., so that every second stack floor is at the same elevation as a floor of the building."[10] This feature in particular came to be copied in subsequent buildings. More will be said later in this study about the multitier stack and this important relationship.

Texas. In the following year the University of Texas opened a new library building that, although considerably smaller than those at Chicago, Johns Hopkins, and California, nonetheless hewed quite faithfully to the internal configuration of services that had been so effectively pioneered by the Doe building. For the Austin institution New York architect Cass Gilbert designed a "modified Spanish Renaissance" T-shaped building with the main section 126 feet by 49 feet and a rearward extension 80 feet by 63 feet.

Entrance to lower-level corridors was gained in the middle front and at the two ends of the main portion. Thence one ascended a flight of stairs to the principal service floor where a two hundred-seat reading room with a high-timbered ceiling ranged across the entire front of the building, and where the delivery desk, public catalog, office, and entrance to the fourth level of a seven-level stack were located (Plate 5f). Except above the reading room and stack, a third floor provided space for several seminar rooms and administrative activities. This building proved to be quite serviceable. Cass Gilbert went on to design other libraries later, although most of them were public rather than academic libraries.[11]

Harvard. In 1913 Harvard University razed Gore Hall, its first library building, in order to erect a new library on the site. The new building would be a memorial to recent Harvard graduate Harry Elkins Widener, who had died in the sinking of the *Titanic* a year earlier. Widener's mother selected well-known architect Horace Trumbauer of Philadelphia to design the building, an assignment that required delicate negotiation of a number of issues between the donor and the university.[12] The building was opened for use late in the summer of 1915.

Harvard's book collections then, as now, comprised the largest university holdings in the hemisphere, and Trumbauer was challenged to design a building large enough to accommodate them. He did this by developing a hollow rectangle, some 200 feet broad and 250 feet deep, surrounded on three sides by a nine-tier bookstack with a shelf capacity of well over 2 million volumes. As at Berkeley and at Texas, one entered here below the principal service floor, proceeded beneath the main reading room to a monumental stair leading upward to the piano nobile with its reference room, reading room, periodical room, public catalog, delivery room, and access to the bookstack.

Although considerably larger than Gilman Hall at Johns Hopkins, there is a faint resemblance to it in Trumbauer's handling of Harvard's central court. Rather than penetrating it with a bridge to a rear reading room as was done in Gilman, Trumbauer appropriately located the Widener Memorial Room and its attendant collections in this prime focal space. Unable, also for the same reason, to place the delivery desk here as was done at Berkeley, it was unusually situated to the far left end of the floor beyond the public catalog. Scattered throughout the building were some eighty-four faculty study rooms ranging in size from 120 to 180 square feet each, a large number of seminar rooms, ample administrative space, and several special reading and service rooms.[13]

Trumbauer's exterior for the building, red brick trimmed in limestone, was less successful than the interior. Its great bulk had to be crowded onto a site that was probably too small for it in the first place, and its massing did little to diminish that perception. One knowledgeable commentator later implied that Harvard had perhaps oriented the Widener building in the wrong direction, a criticism that has been repeated. In his judgment the building

> presented its small rear entrance to Massachusetts Avenue and pushed its colossal façade with giant columns and enormous and fatiguing steps into the small quadrangle at the north, where it dwarfed its more distinguished neighbors.[14]

Despite its intimidating appearance, almost as a sphinx couchant preparing to leap into the Yard, Widener still serves effectively some eighty years later as the centerpiece of Harvard University's impressive library plant facilities.

Stanford. Following the collapse of Stanford's most recent library building in the earthquake of 1906, planning began immediately on the University's third library building in less than a decade, but circumstances delayed its occupancy until 1919. Consistent with H. H. Richardson's original architectural concept for the entire campus, San Francisco architects Bakewell & Brown designed a Romanesque structure 180 feet wide and 235 feet deep, faced on the front with sandstone and roofed with red tile.

Entering a large vestibule from an arcade across its front, one encountered a grand stairway ahead leading up to the delivery hall on the principal service floor. Different from most of the buildings of this genre, however, that featured the delivery desk ahead, all main-floor services here were rotated 90° clockwise. Thus the public catalog was ahead, the delivery desk to the right, the periodical room above the building's entry, and the main reading room was to the left.

Seven stack levels with an estimated shelf capacity of 750,000 volumes occupied the building's right wing with access gained to its fourth level from behind the delivery desk on the main floor. A third floor rising above only the central portion of the forepart of the building contained five seminar rooms with still a different resolution to their need for many books on site. Located adjacent to them was a single large shelf-and-study room where all seminar collections and their users were brought together to facilitate their administration. Document and reserved book rooms were situated at the entry level, and staff work areas were behind the public catalog on the main floor.[15] Although substantially enlarged, this building still houses the main collections of the University.

Michigan. In 1917 the University of Michigan demolished all but the five-tier stack of its 1883 library building in order to erect a much larger replacement on the site. Its new four-floor, 200-foot-by-177-foot structure, called by some "American factory" in style but basically Renaissance, was designed by the pragmatic Albert Kahn of Detroit and was opened for use early in 1920.

This building contained many features now made familiar by the buildings at Berkeley, Texas, and Stanford. The entry hall, which was centered in the building's north facade, proceeded below the main reading room and between a reserved book room on the right and technical services workroom on the left, to a divided stairway leading up to the central hall on the floor above. Here the delivery desk was located on the south side of the hall, the periodical room on the west, the main reading room with 375 seats and a barrel-vault ceiling on the north, and public catalog and administrative suite on the east. Behind the delivery desk opened a cruciform eight-tier structural stack. (See Figure 16).

Michigan handled its need for seminar instruction in a manner somewhat similar to Stanford, but instead of having a single aggregation of seminar collections, it had four. Each of these so-called Graduate Study Rooms was devoted to a cluster of disciplines and was situated adjacent to several seminar class rooms. At the time of construction, Librarian William Warner Bishop reported that

> There are seats for one thousand readers in the new structure, divided between reading and study rooms, seminars, and stacks. It will house one million volumes without extension, and nearly a million more with the extensions planned for.[16]

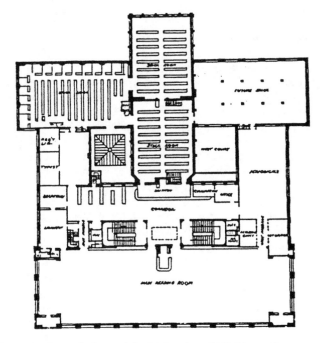

Figure 16. Second Floor of the University of Michigan Library, 1920

This building has been expanded but remains the main library for the University of Michigan.

C. A Stereotyped Pattern, 1920–1945

Previous to the 1920s most academic library buildings were rectangular. When the American Library Association made its first survey of library practice in 1925, it found that, of the buildings built since 1871, "two-thirds of the whole number (79 among 120) [were] reported as rectangular, and all but a very few of the remainder [were] described as T shape."[17] Following 1920, however, that began to change. Now the solution to layout problems pioneered at the University of California and at Michigan became a stereotyped pattern that was used in most of the university libraries, large and small, as well as in some of the colleges constructed during the next quarter of a century. This configuration called for one to enter in the center of the building's front, pass beneath a monumental main reading room, and ascend a grand staircase to the floor above where were situated a delivery hall, catalog and reference rooms, and entrance to a multilevel stack. The stack could either extend rearward from the main portion of the building forming it into a T, or the main portion of the building could wrap around three sides of the stack as in a U, E, or as in the upper half of an H, or it could wrap all the way around the stack as in a squared O. (See Figure 17). Seminar rooms, periodical and reserve activities, technical services, and other facilities could be distributed indifferently throughout the balance of the building.

Among institutions that used this concept virtually without modification were, chronologically by date of opening, the University of Montana (1923), the Universities of Kansas (Plate 6c) and of Minnesota (1924), the University of Arizona (1925), the Universities of Washington and Illinois (1926), UCLA and the University of North Carolina (1929), the University of Oklahoma (1930, Plate 6d), the University of Rochester (1931), Atlanta and Northwestern Universities (1932), Columbia University (1934), the Universities of Arkansas and Utah (1935), Temple University (1936), Brooklyn College

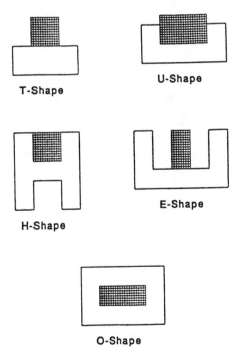

Figure 17. Common Stack Locations in Academic Libraries, 1910–1945

(1937), Howard University (1938), and Vanderbilt University (1941). Even such smaller institutions as Bluffton College (1930), Drake University (1938), and Westminster College in Pennsylvania (1938), managed to configure their traffic patterns similar to their larger counterparts. (See Figure 18).

This is not to say that all of these buildings looked alike. Their numbers of floor levels varied among the larger libraries from three to five, although most had four. Their numbers of stack levels varied from four to twelve. Most of these buildings were of Renaissance design, but Illinois and Howard were Georgian, UCLA was Romanesque, and Kansas, Washington, Oklahoma, Temple, and Northwestern were college Gothic. North Carolina and UCLA featured rotundas, and Rochester had a stack tower.

Several other libraries of the period varied the stereotype only slightly. Dartmouth (1928), for example, Oregon (1937), and Drew (1939) departed from the basic pattern only to the degree that they situated their delivery desks on the entry level rather than on the floor above. The University of Southern California (1932) placed its main reading room in a side wing rather than above the principal entry. Emory University (1926) located the main reading room of its library atop its three-level stack to the rear of the building, rather in the fashion of the New York Public Library. Likewise at Holy Cross (1928) the main reading room was placed above the stack. More details on some of these buildings are shown in Table 5. Al-

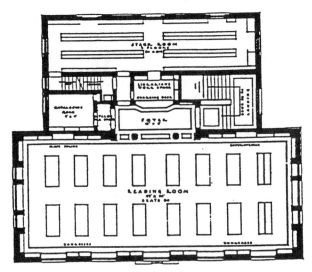

Figure 18. Bluffton College Library, 1930

TABLE 5
Some Large Libraries Constructed, 1920–1945.[18]

Institution	Date	Architect	Cost	Bk. Cap.	Shape
Arizona	1925	Lyman & Place	$ 475,000	225,000	E
Columbia	1934	James Gamble Rogers	$4,000,000	1,609,000	O
Dartmouth	1928	Jens Larson	$1,200,000	450,000	H
Emory	1926	Edward L. Tilton	$ 400,000	300,000	U
Holy Cross	1928	Maginnis & Walsh	$ 750,000		T
Illinois	1926	Charles A. Platt	$1,750,000		U
Kansas	1924	George L. Chandler	$ 313,000		T
Minnesota	1924	C. H. Johnston	$1,253,000	800,000	U
Montana	1923	McIver & Cohagen		180,000	U
Nebraska	1943		$1,000,000	800,000	U
N. Carolina	1929	Atwood & Nash	$ 625,000	450,000	T
Northwestern	1932	James Gamble Rogers	$1,200,000	600,000	T
Oklahoma	1930	Layton Hicks Forsyth		300,000	T
Oregon	1937	Lawrence Holford Allyn	$ 485,000	400,000	T
Rochester	1931	Gordon & Kaelber	$1,500,000	706,000	T
So.California	1932	Cram & Ferguson	$1,100,000	300,000	H
Vanderbilt	1941	Henry Hibbs	$ 823,000	500,000	H
Yale	1931	James Gamble Rogers		2,100,000	O

though enlarged, the great majority of these buildings is still in use, many still serving as their parent institutions' central library buildings.

D. Booms and Busts in Library Construction

A great many new academic library buildings were constructed between 1920 and 1949. All told they numbered at least 289, with no fewer than eighty-four new ones coming on line in the 1920s, 122 in the 1930s, and eighty-three in the 1940s. Counted thus in ten-year spans, they appear to reflect a fairly robust and steady-state industry. When they are viewed year by year, however, it becomes obvious that the appearance of new buildings varied greatly from one time to another, with four years (1920, 1922, 1934, and 1944) seeing only one new building each, and one year (1945) encountering no new openings at all.

Plate 6. A Stereotyped Pattern for Academic Libraries from 1911 to 1946 Featured a Large Reading Room on the Second-floor Front and Multi-tier Stacks to the Rear.

a) University of California (CA), 1911. John Galen Howard, Architect.

b) University of Texas (TX), 1912. Cass Gilbert, Architect.

c) University of Kansas (KS), 1924. George L. Chandler, Architect.

d) University of Oklahoma (OK), 1930. Layton Hicks & Forsyth, Architects.

The graph in Figure 19 shows the numbers of new buildings opened between 1916 and 1950, demonstrating how sensitive the academic library construction industry was during this period to circumstances and events in American society at large. World War I precipitated a substantial decline between 1918 and 1922, the Great Depression brought construction to a very low ebb between 1932 and 1935, and World War II caused a similar decline between 1943 and 1947. Indeed, for the first time since 1880, no new libraries at all were opened in 1945. During other years, however, the number of new openings sometimes reached between twenty and twenty-five.

E. A Single Innovation

The principal innovation of this entire quarter of a century grew from recognition that stack towers could seemingly be pushed ever higher. At the Library of Congress (1897) stacks had been installed that were nine tiers high, but those stacks were made of cast iron, and nine tiers probably approached the upper limit of their technology. In the subsequent quarter century, however, stack manufacturers increasingly moved to steel construction, reopening the possibility that stack towers could be built even taller. The break came at the beginning of the 1930s.

Already mentioned above was the opening of the new library at the University of Rochester in 1931. Although at the time of opening this building contained a stack of twelve levels, it was designed to accept a vertical extension at a future time that would bring it to nineteen levels. Columbia University's Butler Library, opened in 1934, was also originally designed by architect James Gamble Rogers to have nineteen stack tiers, although only fifteen were installed at the time of original construction.

Meanwhile the first truly high-rise stack tower to be completed was the Sterling Memorial Library at Yale University, opened in 1931. This tower sits beyond the delivery desk at the end of a monumental entry hall with nave, colonnades, aisles, and groin vault typifying, except for its huge scale, American collegiate libraries of fourscore years earlier. The sixteen-tier tower 90 feet by 135 feet rises to a height of 150 feet. Also designed by James Gamble Rogers, this entire massive building is wrapped in a pure Gothic exterior.[19]

Other stack towers soon followed. In 1936 the University of Texas opened a very narrow stack tower, only 60 feet by 60 feet, designed by the French-American architect Paul Cret, that could loom upward twenty-seven tiers to the rear of the university's 1911 library.

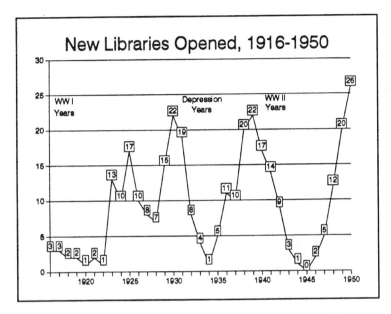

Figure 19. Fluctuations in the Number of New Academic Library Buildings Opened, 1916–1950

And in 1941, Stanford University erected a seventeen-tier stack tower to house its Hoover Institution collections. By the time of World War II, however, the era of the multitier structural stack was drawing to a close, and no more of these magnitudes were destined to be constructed for some three decades thereafter.

Notes

1. University of Nebraska *Journal* February 15, 1896.
2. *Library Journal* 28 (February 1903): 70–71.
3. Ibid.
4. *Public Libraries* 17 (1912): 270.
5. Wilhelm Munthe, "Modern American Library Buildings," *Library Association Record* 3d ser II (1932): 286–287.
6. M. Llewellyn Raney, "Gilman Hall—The New Library of the Johns Hopkins University," *Library Journal* 38 (November 1913): 607–612.
7. Munthe, "Modern American Library Buildings," 287.
8. Meanwhile McKim clearly had the Bibliothèque Ste. Geneviève in Paris in mind when he designed the Boston Public Library.
9. Kenneth G. Peterson, "The History of the University of California

Library at Berkeley, 1900–1945." Ph.D. dissertation, University of California, Berkeley, 1968, pp. 177–97.

10. W. L. Huber, "The Doe Memorial Library, University of California," *Engineering Record* 62 (August 10, 1910): 241.

11. Nathaniel L. Goodrich, "University of Texas Library," *Library Journal* 37 (June 1912): 325–326.

12. The story of these negotiations is well told in W. Bentinck-Smith, *Building a Great Library: The Coolidge Years at Harvard* (Cambridge, Mass.: Harvard University Press, 1976), pp. 54–79.

13. William C. Lane, "The New Harvard Library," *Library Journal* 38 (May 1913): 267–270.

14. John Burchard and Albert Bush-Brown, *The Architecture of America: A Social and Cultural History* (Boston, Mass.: Little, Brown and Co., 1961), p. 289.

15. Leland Stanford, Jr., University Library, *New Building of the Stanford University Library* (Stanford, Calif.: Stanford University, 1919); George T. Clark, "The New Library Building at Leland Stanford Junior University," *Library Journal* 44 (November 1919): 716-717.

16. William Warner Bishop, "New Library Building of the University of Michigan," *Library Journal* 44 (October 1919): 637. See also Edna Ruth Hanley, *College and University Library Buildings* (Chicago, Ill.: American Library Association, 1939), pp. 31–33.

17. *A Survey of Libraries in the United States* (Chicago: American Library Association, 1927), v. 4, p. 190.

18. Principal sources for this table are Hanley, *op. cit.*, *passim*, and *Library Journal* 49:1029–1032; 50:748–749; 52:291–296; 1061–1063, 1162–1164; 54:191–194; 55:55–58, 254–255; 56:343–346, 529–533; 57:894–900; 58:189–196; and 62:940–945.

19. Andrew Keogh, "The Sterling Memorial Library," *Library Journal* 56 (June 15, 1931): 529–533.

Chapter Seven

Changes in Design, Structure, and Style

A. The Era of the Structural Stack[1]

Many significant innovations have enhanced American academic library service during the twentieth century. The Library of Congress Classification Scheme, the Anglo-American Code, microfilm, the Online Computer Library Center (OCLC), and the advent of library research have all left indelible improvements in the quality of library service to university students and scholars. Perhaps no other innovation has been of greater benefit to them, however, than the adoption, immediately after the Second World War, of so-called modular construction methods that enabled library buildings to abandon the traditional multitier structural stack as their chief means of housing their book stocks. Before discussing modular construction, however, some attention must be given to what went before it. Many allusions have already been made herein to the "multitier structural stack," but little explanation of it has yet been given. It will be discussed here.[2]

The multitier structural stack had itself been a significant invention when it was pioneered in the 1840s by the celebrated French architect Henri LaBrouste for storing books in the Bibliothèque Ste. Geneviève and later in the Bibliothèque Nationale in Paris. Readers there were not allowed to consult books on open library shelves but rather had desired volumes fetched to them by library employees to be studied under their scrutiny in large public reading halls. Appropriate to the Bibliothèque Ste. Geneviève, LaBrouste's purpose in developing this kind of installation was not to facilitate public access to library material but rather to compress the largest number of books into the smallest possible cubage. The multitier structural stack served this limited purpose admirably and remained the most economical compact book storage device anywhere on earth for more than a hundred years thereafter.

As American academic libraries began to grow in the later nineteenth century, LaBrouste's invention was imported into the United States and put to work here, first in a new wing on Gore Hall at Harvard in 1877 and soon after in other university libraries as well. By the end of the nineteenth century, virtually all newly constructed academic libraries in this country were using this method of warehousing their books. Just as in Paris, however, library patrons were not allowed access to these stack areas; instead all but a few favored professors had to call for specific books as needed and have them delivered for their use in reading rooms.

This seemingly cumbersome form of access to library books was adequate for those times because book use was then relatively unimportant for success in American universities. As was stated earlier, students had only limited need to consult sources, so they were little discommoded by not being allowed to visit library bookshelves, except of course for "Reference" shelves, which were always open to the public. As the seminar style of college pedagogy percolated throughout American higher education between about 1880 and 1910, however, it bred a much higher incidence of library use. Widespread book and journal use, not just the memorization of lecture notes, became essential for success in college courses.

For the first time, college students began justifiably petitioning for direct access to their library bookshelves, where they could consult a range of books and journals, tasting, sampling, winnowing, and selecting best references for their problem at hand. They now needed seating among the bookshelves, and they sought carrels adjacent to the broad spectrum of literature relevent to their special concern of the occasion. It simply would no longer do for them to select citations from the listings in the card catalog, leave call slips for them at delivery desks, and then carry the volumes off for study in reading rooms when they arrived.

For all of its virtues, LaBrouste's multitier structural stack did not lend itself to this kind of increase in public traffic. Although such stacks came early to have a few perimeter carrels for professors, they were designed solely for purposes of maximum book density and, like a prison constructed entirely of steel, they presented a very inhumane and unwelcoming environment for human habitation. Moreover they were totally inflexible. As is shown in Figure 20, such stacks required the erection of an immovable grid of vertical steel uprights, which soon came to be spaced every 36 inches in one direction (i.e., the length of bookshelves) and every 54 inches in the other direction (i.e., the on-center dimension between stack ranges). These steel posts did more, however, than simply hold up the shelves. They extended the full distance from the floor to the ceiling and constituted the structural members that also held up similar configurations of posts and shelves on the tiers above.

These tiers of stacks did not even have to be attached to the walls, although they were usually tied to them about every six to eight feet. Structurally independent of them, they were simply erected in place on the floor slab after it, the walls, and roof were completed. Even the walking surfaces for the several upper stack tiers were non-structural but rather removable plates laid in channels affixed to the stack posts. Originally these plates were made of metal and were grated to allow the circulation of air and the transmission of light vertically through the multitier stack. Of the academic libraries responding to a survey regarding buildings constructed between 1901 and 1920, however, ten reported using glass panels in their stack-deck floors (to allow light to filter from floor to floor), five used marble (to provide light reflectance), and one used concrete.[3] If a single post were removed from this very constricting grid, everything above it—floors, shelves, books, book trucks, and any chance passersby—all the way to the roof of the building would tumble into the void.

Not only were the lateral dimensions of such stack installations very constricting but so also were their vertical dimensions. Although varying heights were experimented with early, it was soon recognized that stack attendants of average stature could reach

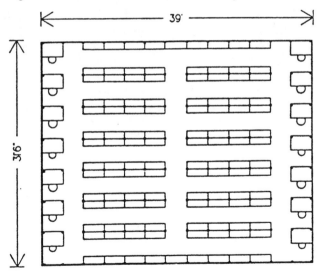

Figure 20. Typical Stack Deck in a Small Academic Library, Showing Vertical Posts

bookshelves up only to about 70 to 80 inches above the floor. This recognition led to the adoption almost universally of tier-to-tier heights in multistory structural stacks of 7 feet 6 inches. By 1925 fully three-fourths of the academic libraries in the nation had adopted this dimension.[4] In their earliest installations, stack attendants carried lamps to light their tasks; with the advent of electricity, however, bulbs were hung below this low ceiling, creating a hazard for tall attendants. With the later advent of modern air treatment moreover, ducts were also suspended from these very low ceilings, exacerbating still further the head room hazard for tall people. Thus their in-the-clear ceiling heights often dropped as low as 6 feet 6 inches, and sometimes lower still.

This 7-foot-6-inch tier-to-tier dimension in the multilevel stack soon began leaving its impress upon the rest of the building as well. Since floor levels elsewhere in these buildings obviously needed to meet those of the stack tiers, their floor-to-floor dimension became fixed—first at the University of California, but soon elsewhere as well—at fifteen feet so that the elevation of every other stack tier would match that of a floor level. Until about the time of World War II, fifteen feet proved to be a felicitous floor-to-floor dimension for library reading rooms and administrative spaces because it accommodated high windows that could serve both for admitting natural light and for evacuating heat buildup. (See Figure 21).

These multitier structural stacks imposed constraints of still other kinds upon library functions. Since it was assumed from the beginning that the library's entire general book stock would be housed in the multitier stack, this area alone in the building was engineered to support the great weight of loaded bookshelves, now normally calculated as live load to be 150 pounds per square foot. That assumption allowed floors in the rest of the building, which comprised mostly large reading halls and administrative offices, to be engineered at the much lower (and cheaper) standard of only 65 to 75 pounds per square foot, which was wholly adequate to support the weight of people and normal room furnishings. Thus, while the tight immovable grid prevented the installation of comfortable reader accommodations within the stack area, so did the limited strength of the floors in the rest of the building prevent the erection of bookshelves outside of the stack area.[5] The sole exception to this constraint was that shelves could be attached to the perimeter walls of reading and reference rooms where their weight was supported by the building's wall structure. The resulting buildings were "fixed-function" structures, destined forever to be used only in accord with the intent of their original planners. Readers and books

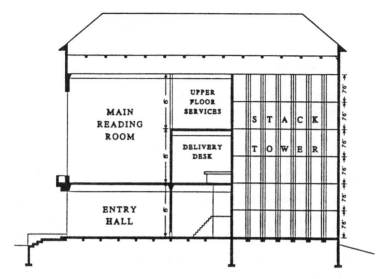

Figure 21. Typical Fixed-Function Library Building with Load-Bearing Walls and Structural Stack Tower (University of Arizona, 1925)

appeared fated never to enjoy the intellectual benefits of intermixture as long as these buildings remained in use.

In the years leading up to the Second World War, increasing numbers of colleges and universities in the United States began to open their stacks to patrons, first to faculty members, later to some graduate students, and eventually to selected undergraduates as well. Nonetheless little could be done to convert their multitier structural stacks into gracious, comfortable places for browsing and study. Their limiting dimensions remained unalterable, and their harsh and hard-surface steel and concrete finishes defied efforts to humanize them. Nonetheless physical access to the books on the shelves became a privilege much cherished by those readers who were allowed it.

B. Advent of the Modular Building

New construction materials and technology in the late 1930s ultimately provided an alternative to the multitier structural stack, but its actual application in libraries was delayed until after the Second World War. Stack manufacturer Angus Snead Macdonald was the first person to recognize that the strength of several stack posts could be aggregated into one larger steel column that could then be located much farther from other similar columns and still support the weight of any and all library activities, including bookshelves, that might be located on the floors above.[6] This arrangement would then allow large open areas that could serve either for reader stations *or* for bookshelves. Almost total flexibility would inhere in the use of such space. Only these large columns and the concrete floor slabs themselves would be fixed permanently in place; all else, at least in theory, could be moved about to meet changing functional needs. Macdonald also designed improved library lighting, and he conceptualized a hollow steel structural column that he visualized using for air circulation, but this was not as readily accepted by librarians as the basic modular concept, primarily because of fear that the resulting flue might prove to be hazardous in case of fire.

Through the closing years of the 1930s and the early 1940s, Macdonald, who had been trained as an architect, was able to gain the attention of some key librarians to the advantages of his modular scheme. An early and effective adherent from within the library profession was Ralph Ellsworth, then director of libraries at the University of Colorado, who worked closely with Macdonald to assure that the concept was developed along practicable lines that would work in a real-world library environment. Because virtually all nondefense construction, including libraries, was halted by World War II, the concept of a modular library structure was a long time in gestation, but the delay allowed for it to be thoroughly critiqued before any effort was made to apply it.

That critique took place under the rubric of an ad hoc group that called itself the Cooperative Committee on Library Building Plans. Responding affirmatively to an invitation tendered by President Harold W. Dodds of Princeton, library representatives from fifteen universities that planned to construct new libraries after the war convened themselves at Princeton in December 1944 to discuss common problems. The meeting was successful, and another session was scheduled for October 1945 at Orange, Virginia, where Angus Snead Macdonald had, at his own expense, constructed for demonstration purposes a full-scale, two-story mock-up of a modularly planned library unit, fully furnished and equipped. Although this model was criticized, primarily for its low ceilings, it helped the librarians in attendance for the first time to see just what such a library could look like and how it could work, and it paved the way for its increasing acceptance. In its six meetings over a four-year period this Cooperative Committee, together with some eighteen of the nation's leading architects, reviewed exhaustively a comprehensive range of library building issues. Nothing received more attention from Committee members, however, than the relative merits of the new modular concept for library buildings.

Other innovations also appeared on its agenda. Fluorescent lighting was new, and its relative advantages and disadvantages for library purposes were evaluated in its sessions. Air conditioning, which was first used in an academic library at Southern Methodist University in 1940 and then at Tulane and Vanderbilt in 1941, was also the subject of much attention. Discussion was devoted too to appropriate building space for audiovisual materials and services; microform production, storage, and use; proper floor covering; acoustics; and desirable distribution of library functional areas throughout the building. Time was also spent discussing some innovations that have not survived into today's world, such as rapid selectors and smoking rooms.

These meetings between leading librarians and architects, held over several years, were very salutary. Both the librarians and the architects in attendance learned to understand better and to respect more highly the concerns and thoughts of the others. The dialogue between the two professional groups led to a high level of consensus among them as to the issues that had to be addressed and resolved regarding library buildings in the years following the war when civilian construction could once again begin. A large backlog of buildings would need to be replaced, and these sessions assured that they would be planned in relative harmony. Indeed a survey made in 1949 revealed that of the 146 institutions that reported having constructed new library buildings in the previous twenty years, sixty-three were already filled to capacity and needed replacement.[7]

Among the architects who attended one or more of the sessions of the Cooperative Committee on Library Building Plans were Henry R. Shepley, whose firm was the most experienced library designer in the nation and would soon plan the Lamont undergraduate library at Harvard (1949); Alfred Githens, who was to plan the University of Georgia library building in 1953; Walter H. Kilham, Jr., whose firm would soon design, among others, the new libraries at Princeton (1948), Louisville (1955), and Colgate (1959); Ralph Walker, who would design a new MIT library in 1950; and John F. Staub, whose firm would design the Fondren Library at Rice (1949), probably the only library building anywhere on earth to have its reading room walls covered with cowhide. All of these buildings would contain at least some of the elements of the modular concept.

Previous to this time only a very few academic librarians had served as library building consultants. Theodore Koch at Northwestern, A. F. Kuhlman at Vanderbilt, Louis R. Wilson at North Carolina, and Edna Ruth (Hanley) Byers at Agnes Scott were notable exceptions. The work of the Cooperative Committee was instrumental in changing this, however, and resulted in a substantive increase in their numbers in the years following World War II. Among librarians in attendance at the deliberations of the Cooperative Committee were Duke's B. E. Powell, MIT's Vernon Tate, Rutgers's Donald F. Cameron, Ralph Parker from Missouri, Colorado's (and later Iowa's) Ralph Ellsworth, Harvard's Keyes Metcalf, Indiana's Robert Miller, and North Carolina's Charles Rush. All of these librarians also served other institutions in subsequent years as library building consultants, bringing to the academic community at large the benefit of these extensive colloquia carried out under the ægis of the Cooperative Committee on Library Building Plans. The Committee duplicated full minutes of its sessions and made them available to all who requested them, and in addition it sought and received a grant from the Rockefeller Foundation to cover the costs of editing them into an invaluable volume entitled *Planning the University Library Building* that was published in 1949 by the Princeton University Press. It remains a useful volume for reference by building planners even today.[8]

In laying out in 1945 the performance requirements for the new library it would build as soon as possible after the cessation of hostilities, the Massachusetts Institute of Technology included the following statement:

> (1) The structural design shall be such as to permit full flexibility, not only for minor changes such as might occur in the humanities reading room, but for much more consequential changes in the whole plan of library administration.[9]

In other words, it would be a modular rather than a traditional fixed-function building. This document was published in the journal *College & Research Libraries* early in 1946, influencing other librarians to adopt similar goals.

The first library building to begin to incorporate these innovations, including the modular plan, was completed at Hardin-Simmons College in 1947. Others followed quickly thereafter, at Princeton in 1948; at Bradley, Washington State, and North Dakota State in 1950; and at the University of Iowa in 1951.[10] In 1948 the architect for the building at Washington State, John W. Maloney, published a paper in the *Architectural Record* making the new design concept more widely known throughout the architectural profession.[11] In this new, so-called modular construction, the stack posts were no longer needed to hold up the floors above. Floors came instead to be supported on the building's own structural system, and a new kind of stack posts, now freestanding, were needed only to support the bookshelves themselves. For the first time book shelves could be located anywhere in a library building, or indeed could be removed from anywhere in a building, without jeopardizing the building's structural integrity.

From the standpoint of library function, the great virtue of this new modular style of construction was that books and reader spaces could now be intermixed. All patrons could, for the first time in almost a century, go direct to library shelves now arrayed in spacious, open areas, outfitted also with varied reading and study accommodations adjacent to the books and journals. Macdonald's interest went even into the appropriate size of the module. As early as 1943, and with the advice of mechanical engineers, he concluded that a square bay 22½ feet on centers would be optimal as regards steel construction costs. Moreover, this bay size would fit perfectly the sizes of standard library equipment and furniture. Assuming that columns would need to be 16 inches square, this bay size would permit the erection of six 3-foot sections of shelving between columns in one direction and the location of five ranges of shelving 4½ feet apart in the other direction. Furthermore, if the library staff ever found it necessary in the future to reorient its bookshelves in the opposite direction, they would still fit perfectly. This felicitous dimension became almost frozen into academic library building planning until the 1990s when the Americans with Disabilities Act practically mandated that ranges be situated no less than 5 feet on centers.[12]

All of this was such a vast improvement over what had gone before that wherever possible American colleges and universities in the subsequent four decades scrapped their old fixed-function library buildings with structural stacks in favor of these new "modular" structures. Nonetheless many fixed-function libraries remain in use today, especially in large universities where the cost of their replacement would be prohibitive. Such libraries as those at California (1911), Harvard (1915), Michigan (1920), Illinois (1926), and Columbia (1934), still operate in fixed-function buildings with multi-tier stacks. Other institutions, such as Cornell (1960), Pennsylvania (1962), Brown (1965), and Indiana (1969) managed to replace them with modular structures.

An obvious impediment to the replacement of the older fixed-function library buildings was that, for the most part, they were just as impervious to alteration for other academic purposes as they were to modification for other library uses. It proved especially difficult to identify possible alternative applications for their book-stack areas. Moreover, in most cases these fixed function buildings even proved overcostly to enlarge. With the availability in recent times of good artificial lighting and modern air treatment, high ceilings are no longer necessary anywhere in the library. Thus to match in a new addition today the fifteen-foot floor-to-floor dimensions of these older buildings can result in the unnecessary construction of as much as 10 or 15 percent of superfluous cubage. This consideration has often rendered them uneconomical to enlarge.

Where multitier structural stacks have been retained, well-nigh heroic efforts have sometimes been made to "humanize" them for complete library use. Their steel finishes have been painted, carpet has sometimes been put underfoot, lighting has been improved, and better air treatment has been installed, all of course at considerable cost, but they remain what they were originally designed to be: rigid, inflexible nineteenth-century book storage mechanisms. They still have vertical steel posts from floor to ceiling every three feet in one direction and every four feet six inches in the other. They still have ceiling heights so low as to be a hazard even to people of average stature. And they still do not provide the kind of hospitable environment wherein scholars and students can find pleasant reading accommodations for study and learning surrounded by shelves laden with books.

For all of their residual problems today, however, multitier structural stacks served very effectively for almost a century the purpose for which they were originally devised—namely compact book storage. They still serve quite well where closed stacks are needed, as say in housing rare book collections. It was not indeed until fourscore years after their introduction in Paris that methods for more densely compacting library books were attempted and eventually brought to a practicable level of effectiveness. It is perhaps ironic that these newer methods of book compaction are beset today with the same problem that plagued LaBrouste's invention, namely that they also work best when a library's books are to be removed from proximity with its readers.

Today, however, modular construction techniques permit welcoming, open-access buildings where scholars can set themselves up and work amid the entirety of the library's literature relevant to their topics of the moment, week, month, or year without having to utilize the services of a staff intermediary. (See Figure 22). In this environment they experience quicker access to requisite materials, increased efficiency and confidence in their work, improved benefits of serendipity through browsing, and greater satisfaction with their literature searches. Angus Snead Macdonald's concept of multiuse space in library buildings has proved to be a boon of great consequence to modern readers and researchers.

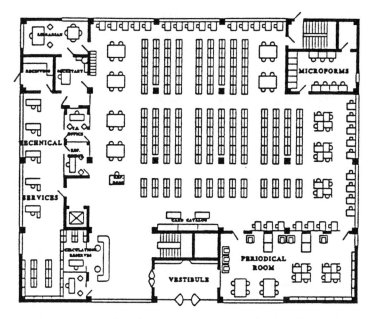

Figure 22. J. Russell Bailey's Modular Plan for the Meredith College
Library Building, 1969

C. The Need For Building Expertise

As post-war college enrollments soared into the 1950s, higher education faced a growing need for new and enlarged modular library buildings. The pool of library building experience and understanding, however, remained largely constant. Following the demise in 1952 of the Cooperative Committee on Library Building Plans, retirement began to take its toll from among the individuals who had gained building understanding through its deliberations, and concern grew in the library community about how to replenish the dwindling supply of knowledgeable consultants.

This need for building expertise was further exacerbated in the 1960s by the entry of the federal government into the funding of academic library construction. With the passage of the Higher Education Facilities Act late in 1963, huge amounts of federal grant and loan money were for the first time made available for academic building construction, including libraries. Under the HEFA, up to one-third of the construction cost of academic buildings could be funded from federal coffers, and during the course of the program (1964–1972), some $2.669 billion was granted or lent to 5,550 institutions. Although federal statistics were not kept in a way that allows the determination of the exact amount that was thus made available specifically to library projects, more than 15 percent of the funded projects contained library space, including the construction or expansion of 605 separate academic library buildings.[13] It has been calculated that during the five-year period beginning January 1, 1967, alone, almost $1 billion was spent on academic library buildings in the United States and Canada,[14] much of it federal money.

Understandably, this sudden infusion of so much new money into the library construction market resulted in a great surge of activity. Figures 23 and 24 show that during the same five-year period from 1967 to 1972, fully 257 new academic library buildings fitting the parameters of the present study were completed and opened to the public. This represented an increase of 210 percent over the number of new buildings that had been opened in the previous five years and 240 percent above the number that would be opened in the next five years. Here, it was hoped by educators, was indeed a new Mæcenas who would top the library giving record even of Andrew Carnegie himself. The federal government, however, disappeared from the funding scene even more quickly than Carnegie had done.

In order to enlarge the pool of qualified library building consultants, many felt that the library schools should teach courses on building planning, and a few such courses were initiated. Upon reflection, however, it appeared that this could not solve the problem. Few institutions, after all, were destined to erect new libraries more often than once in two or three decades, and it seemed inappropriate for library school students to invest up to one-twelfth of their professional educations taking a course that they would likely be called upon to apply only once or twice in their entire careers. Librarians working in the field, moreover, had similarly infrequent opportunities (again perhaps once in twenty or thirty years) to gain building planning understanding from personal experience at the work site. And in the last analysis, taking a course or working on only one or two (or perhaps even three, four, or five) building projects was probably not enough to make a person a building expert.

There was, to be sure, some literature that could be consulted even in the 1950s. The aforementioned *Planning the University Library Building* (Princeton University Press, 1949) was an invaluable source. Herman Fussler's collection of papers entitled *Library Buildings for Library Service* (American Library Association, 1947) also contained helpful advice. James Thayer Gerould and Edna Ruth Hanley had both produced books[15] in the pre-war period that were still useful. The *Library Journal* and, especially since its establishment in 1939, *College & Research Libraries* occasionally published articles devoted to building planning. But a wider array of sources of information was badly needed.

Additional writings became available during the 1960s, some of them early enough to help the library profession meet the tidal wave of federally funded projects. This is not the proper place for a bibliography of library building literature, but two authors, both participants in the Cooperative Committee on Library Building Plans, made signal contributions to the evolution of the post-war library building and deserve special mention. In 1965 Keyes Metcalf's "big book" was published,[16] making available much of the building expertise that he had developed during his extensive career as an academic library building consultant. It immediately became a vade mecum to grace the desks of all academic librarians involved in library building planning. Ralph Ellsworth also drew upon his own equally extensive building experience to produce several smaller planning manuals, replete with helpful and cautionary advice to novices.[17] As time passed, the body of relevent literature grew quite large and became increasingly valuable to building planners.

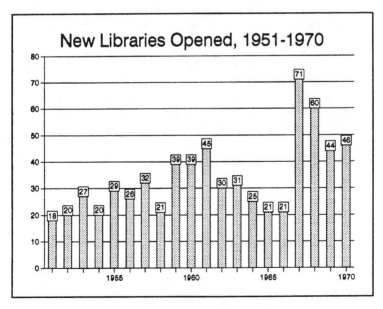

Figure 23. New Academic Library Buildings Opened in the United States, 1951–1970

Another fountainhead of continuing education for librarians, as well as for architects and others who had concern for library buildings, was the series of Library Buildings and Equipment Institutes that was sponsored by divisions of the American Library Association following the discontinuation of the Cooperative Committee on Library Building Plans. Through the 1950s these institutes were held, usually once or twice a year for two days, under the oversight of what was then called the Association of College and Reference Libraries (ACRL). Proposed plans for new buildings were critiqued at these institutes, and informational papers were presented. The institutes or workshops, which sometimes attracted as many as five hundred attendees, were later continued under the auspices of the Library Administration and Management Association, where they understandably addressed the needs not only of academic libraries but of other types of libraries as well. Proceedings of the institutes were published and made available also to others who were unable to attend. Under somewhat varying formats these institutes continue today, their very tenacity itself bespeaking clearly their great utility to the profession.

In an effort to enlarge the pool of experts, the Educational Facilities Laboratories, Inc., a creature of the Ford Foundation, sponsored in the summer of 1964 an institute at the University of Colorado for the training of academic library building consultants. Instructors in the program were Ralph Ellsworth, Keyes Metcalf, and William Jesse, director of libraries at the University of Tennessee as well as a very sound and widely experienced building consultant. Twenty-five librarians were selected to attend, all of whom had already accrued some consulting experience, along with sixteeen architects, all of whom had designed academic library buildings. The syllabus covered a wide range of building-related issues, including the role of the consultant, writing building programs, campus planning procedures, basic dimensions and specifications, growth calculations, evaluation of architectural drawings, and other similar matters. The group also visited a half dozen recently constructed college and university libraries.[18]

This institute solved the problem of trained consultants for the next quarter of a century, as most of the attendees went on to consult on future library construction projects. Whereas some of them worked on only six or eight, others—Stanford's David C. Weber, Ellsworth Mason of Hofstra and Colorado, North Carolina's Jerrold Orne, and David Kaser of Cornell and Indiana, for example—worked on very large numbers of libraries in subsequent years. Several other individuals came to develop substantial expertise on academic library buildings through other routes. Jay Lucker at MIT,

Robert Walsh of the Virginia State Library, and Nancy McAdams at the University of Texas were not products of the Boulder Seminar, but all three made major contributions as building consultants. It has been estimated that all told, the librarians who attended this institute at the University of Colorado consulted on no fewer than seven hundred library construction projects during the next three decades, including new buildings, renovations, and expansions. Nonetheless, by the end of the period covered by this study, even this new pool of experienced people had begun to dwindle, and again there was no obvious mechanism in view with which to replace them.

D. Innovations and Improvements

All of the ferment in the academic library building field during the 1950s and 1960s resulted in a climate favorable for the introduction of a number of important innovations and improvements. Among them were the use of carpet, small group study rooms, accommodations for computers, and seating styles and configurations based upon research into student preferences. These will be discussed here seriatim.

Carpet. Perhaps no new practice in the latter half of the twentieth century contributed more to the desired study ambience of the library than the introduction of carpet as the principal floor covering. Except for an occasional rug to accent a special area, carpet had not been used in academic libraries prior to the 1960s. Many other materials had been used for this purpose, including wood, ceramic tile, lineoleum, slate, concrete, terrazzo, marble, brick, asphalt tile, rubber tile, and cork tile. Each had its respective advantages and disadvantages in such areas as the costs of purchase, installation, and maintenance; in terms of such safety features as slip resistance and flammability; as well as in acoustical properties, light reflectance, design, and resiliency. Until about the time of the second World War, the floor covering that was most favored in library reading rooms, when all of these considerations were taken into account, had been cork tile. Yet cork tile could burn, it was costly to install and maintain, it was easily indented, and its color range was largely limited to three shades of brown. Thus already by 1950 it was being replaced for the purpose by vinyl asbestos tile, which could offer many of the benefits of cork without some of its disadvantages.

Although carpet had been used as a floor covering since Assyrian times, its high cost had always made it impractical to consider for commercial purposes. Beginning about 1950, improved technology in its manufacture tended to reduce its purchase cost considerably, although except for marble, good quality carpet remained the most expensive of all floor coverings to purchase. It was soon recognized, however, that in terms of its "life cycle" costs, including its much lower maintenance cost, carpet was more economical to use in the United States than almost any other satisfactory product. With this recognition, it came quickly to be used extensively in academic libraries.[19]

Perhaps the first four-year college library to carpet almost its entire floor area was Lafayette College in 1963.[20] It was used there on all floors and stairways "except the receiving room, closed stacks, rest rooms, staff galley, janitorial quarters, and the area behind the circulation desk."[21] Earlham College also made widespread use of carpet in its new building in the same year, as did Brown University in 1964; Amherst, Asheville-Biltmore, Bowdoin, and Butler in 1965; as well as Baltimore, Boston University, and Saint John's in 1966. The topic was addressed at the ALA Library Equipment Institute in 1964, where it was suggested that the total cost of carpet was only about half that of other floor-covering materials, understandably giving carpet a new burst of popularity. Almost immediately following the publication in 1968 of a study by ALA's Library Technology Project that demonstrated its clear superiority in cost as well as other desirable qualities,[22] its use became well-nigh universal in American institutions.[23]

Everyone liked carpet. Librarians, who had long chafed at their reputation for having to hush patrons, could now forgo the activity entirely in view of its cherished acoustical properties. Custodial personnel welcomed its vastly lower maintenance cost. Students immediately began using it as an alternate seating accommodation, which they had never done with the earlier hard-surface floors. It was reported, moreover, that students even deported themselves better when there was carpet underfoot. Interior designers found it much easier to work with, and acoustics engineers were glad to be able now to rely on the floor as an area's principal sound-attenuating surface instead of the traditional acoustical ceiling tile. This last benefit, however, was short-lived, because the ceiling was quickly taken over by illumination engineers for mounting larger fluorescent light panels than had been used previously.

Small Group Study Rooms. So-called seminar rooms had become a design feature in American academic library buildings when the German seminar became the dominant pattern for college instruction here in the 1880s and 1890s. In Germany, however, seminar materials had been the property of the individual professor who directed the seminar to place wherever he wished and to organize as he saw fit, so he uniformly shelved them together permanently in the room where he taught his seminar and made them available only to members of his seminar. The German seminar model was thus not a perfect fit for institutions in the United States where study and research materials needed for seminars were almost always the property of the university library to be arranged by and under the curatorship of the librarian. As was related earlier herein, American institutions experimented with various ways of accommodating this important difference, but the practice of keeping seminar materials permanently shelved in rooms available only to members of specific seminars never became widespread.

This meant that the term "seminar rooms" in American usage came, somewhat anomalously, to mean simply small classrooms located in the library, containing no books at all, but used for seminar-type instruction or indeed any other kind of instruction that the Registrar chose to schedule there. Most library buildings built into the 1960s had one or more of these rooms. They usually had from eight to twenty chairs arrayed around a large table and had a chalkboard located at one end. Except when the room was in use for a scheduled class it was open to anyone to use as study space. As would be expected, however, almost the only times that more than one student was found studying in them they were friends. Sometimes seminar rooms even came almost to be the private turfs of fraternities, football squads, or other cliques. Nonetheless they did serve a useful purpose as locales for group study.

Beginning in the 1960s, group assignments, as distinct from traditional individual assignments, began to become popular in American pedagogical style. As long as such assignments were infrequent, seminar rooms were able to accommodate these study groups, but the rooms were almost always overlarge for the sizes of assignment groups, which usually tended to comprise only three or four persons. As group assignments became increasingly popular in college courses, the library profession began to realize that library buildings could serve better if they provided more small "group study rooms" and fewer large "seminar rooms," so they began to appear in that new format. The University of Notre Dame and the University of Northern Iowa (both 1964) were among the first libraries to incorporate large numbers of small group study rooms designed to accommodate only four students each, but others followed soon thereafter. Hofstra, the University of Pittsburgh, and Austin Peay State University incorporated them into their new buildings in 1967, and Northwestern University and Washington College provided them in 1970.

Small group study rooms only 10 feet by 10 feet, it was determined, could accommodate a four-foot-by-six-foot table, four chairs, and a chalkboard. That was only 25 square feet per reader, the same amount of floor area needed to seat a reader in a large open shelf and study facility. With this recognition that they were so economical in their use of floor space, small group studies came into almost universal use, giving the library a new and extended utility in its service to the academic program of its parent institution. An attendant benefit to the scholarly ambience of the building, of course, was that such small group study rooms allowed patron conversations to move from open study areas into special spaces that were designed acoustically to handle them.

Electronic Technology. The early 1960s were also the years when computer technology first began to make itself felt in college and university library building planning. A second surge of activity resulting from concern for this issue came a quarter century later and will be discussed in the final chapter of this study. In its earliest manifestations, however, its advent elicited both extravagant claims from some and bitter scorn from others. To many, it was quite clear very early that its eventual impact would indeed be substantial, although just how, when, and even why were questions that were either ignored ostrichlike, or debated vociferously within the library community specifically and within the academic community generally. Most of the early attempts to "computerize" library activities or operations collapsed, some of them producing failures on the grand scale, yet in most cases lessons were learned from them that improved the chances for success on the next experiment.

Until the early 1960s there was little viable dialogue between rank-and-file computer advocates and rank-and-file librarians. "Tell us what you want to have done," proffered the former group, "and we will do it for you." "No," responded the latter group. "You tell us what your computers can do, and we will tell you if we need it." Although there had been some "back-channel" colloquies on the topic earlier, the first fairly broadscale public dialogue between librarians and information systems people came in May 1963 when a Conference on "Libraries and Automation" was held at Airlie House in Virginia. One hundred persons, divided equally between librarians and others, were invited by the sponsors—the National Science Foundation, the Council on Library Resources, and the Library of Congress—to a relatively unstructured three-day assembly to discuss, argue, and debate, but most of all to learn from one another. The results were unequivocally successful. Mutual respect was bred at the meeting, and thenceforward there was productive dialogue rather than diatribe between the two factions.[24]

More rapid progress was made thereafter in automating libraries, but for a long time it remained unclear just how, if at all, these changes should be factored into new building planning. New buildings, after all, could be expected to serve for as much as a half century or more, and surely these new technologies would in some way impact upon their spatial requirements in so long a time. This particular issue was addressed at another conclave four years later sponsored by the aforementioned Educational Facilities Laboratories, Inc. (EFL). Here a select group of librarians, information technologists, and architects was assembled to explore "the wisdom of continuing to build libraries along traditional lines, and plumb available knowledge for cues on how to prepare buildings for the new era."[25] The resulting document was a twenty-one page pamphlet entitled "The Impact of Technology on the Library Building." After suggesting some functional requirements that future library buildings would likely have to meet, the report concluded that, at least for the next twenty years,

> library planners can proceed . . . with confidence that technological developments . . . will not alter radically the way libraries are used. In planning library buildings today, we should start with the library as the institution we now know it to be. Any departures in the future should be made from this firm base.[26]

The publication of this pamphlet, with the cachet of the respected EFL, reduced anxiety among building planners that they might be constructing libraries that would soon be outmoded. Many new buildings thereafter included concessions, small or large, to the future impact of technology. The new libraries at NYU, the University of California at San Diego, and Fisk, for example, all of which opened in 1970, invested heavily in such innovations as under-the-floor cable trays, oversized risers to handle future cables throughout the building, and computer rooms. Most, however, settled for more modest adjustments such as perimeter bus ducts surrounding each floor and greater flexibility in the use of floor area. EFL's prediction proved to be quite accurate. Relatively small changes accommodated rather well the needs of computerization in libraries for the next twenty years, although by 1990 many libraries had found it necessary to resort to such unsightly expedients as exposed wire molds and power poles to bring telecommunication and power to unanticipated locations.

Seating Configurations. The 1960s also brought another phenomenon to bear upon library building planning for the first time. That phenomenon was research. Until that time there had been a great deal of experience and lore to guide building planners, but knowledge born of empirical research was in very short supply. A major portion of this new research concerned student preferences in library study accommodations and seating configurations, and most of it was initiated not by librarians but rather by psychologists and sociologists. Perhaps the principal producer of this research was Robert Sommer, best known for his book *Personal Space: The Behavioral Basis for Design* (Englewood Cliffs, N.J.: Prentice-Hall, 1969), although his investigations into the subject in libraries and his publication of journal articles on it had begun a decade earlier.

Since there had really been only two ways of accommodating student study needs in the earlier fixed-function libraries—namely at large multiple-station tables in monumental reading rooms or at perimeter carrels in multitier stacks—no one had bothered to ask students what they would prefer. The same arrangements were simply continued into the early modular buildings. Thus it came as somewhat of a surprise to building planners to learn, when researchers did begin to ask, that students really wanted a wider variety of options, including not large tables but smaller ones, with a much higher percentage of individual study stations (perhaps as much as 50 percent of the seating), not arrayed in large "institution-size" reading rooms but in smaller "human-size" spaces, and accompanied by an ample sprinkling of lounge seating, all configured in various patterns and mixes, rather than regimented row on row as in the past.

An influential report in 1965 was researched not in four-year colleges and universities but in community and junior colleges.[27] Nonetheless its findings were easy to extrapolate to senior institutions, and they were quickly wrapped into the interior design of subsequent academic libraries of all kinds. It marked the demise of big reading rooms comprising large multi-place study tables in favor of "semi-social" and informal settings and the increased provision of individual study tables. It also contributed to the advent of carpeted floors and small group study rooms, which was mentioned earlier. It was a significant event when, only three years later, a new library building at Marywood College could boast that it had "no main study areas or reading rooms,"[28] although nostalgia and the designer's affection for grand reading rooms with lofty ceilings lingers on in some circles even to this day.

Notes

1. Much of the material in the first two sections of this chapter appeared originally in the author's "Rise and Demise of the Multi-Tier Structural

Stack," pp. 33–41 in *Trends in International Librarianship*, ed. by N. Qure-shi and Z. Khurshid (Karachi: Royal Book Company, 1991) and is reprinted here with the kind permission of the publisher.

2. For a thorough account, see Charles H. Baumann's excellent *Influence of Angus Snead Macdonald and the Snead Bookstack on Library Architecture* (Metuchen, N.J.: Scarecrow, 1972). The present author has drawn heavily from this excellent book. See also the informative volume produced by Snead & Co., *Library Planning, Bookstacks and Shelving* (Jersey City, N.J.: Snead & Co., 1915).

3. *Survey of Libraries in the United States* (Chicago: American Library Association, 1927), v. 4, p. 196.

4. Ibid., v. 4, p. 194.

5. *Planning the University Library Building* (Princeton, N.J.: Princeton University Press, 1949), pp. 60–61.

6. Angus Snead Macdonald, "A Library of the Future," *Overbiblioteker Wilhelm Munthe pa Femtiårsdagen 20. Oktober 1933* (Oslo: Grøndahl, 1933), pp. 168–184.

7. Robert H. Muller, "College and University Library Buildings, 1929–1949," *College & Research Libraries* 12 (January 1951): 261–265. Of the 146 libraries reported as having been constructed during the period, the average book storage capacity was 184,000 volumes, and the average number of study seats was 420.

8. Ralph E. Ellsworth, *Ellsworth on Ellsworth* (Metuchen, N.J.: Scarecrow, 1980), pp. 56–58.

9. This document, which was drafted by MIT Library Director John E. Burchard, was later published as "Buildings and Architecture," *College & Research Libraries* 7 (January 1946): 78–79.

10. Ellsworth, pp. 40–50.

11. John W. Maloney, "Modular Library Under Construction," *Architectural Record* 104 (July 1948): 102–109.

12. Ralph E. Ellsworth, *Planning the College and University Library Building*, 2d ed. (Boulder, Colo.: Pruett Press, 1968), p. 113.

13. Edward B. Stanford, "Federal Aid for Academic Library Construction," *Library Journal* 99 (January 15, 1974): 113.

14. Jerrold Orne, "The Renaissance of Academic Library Building 1967–1971," *Library Journal* 96 (December 1, 1971): 3947–3967.

15. James Thayer Gerould, *The College Library Building: Its Planning and Equipment* (N.Y.: Scribner's Sons, 1932); and Hanley, *College and University Library Buildings* (Chicago: American Library Association, 1939).

16. *Planning Academic and Research Library Buildings* (N.Y.: McGraw-Hill, 1965). This volume was later revised and brought up to date by Philip C. Leighton and David C. Weber and issued as a second edition (Chicago: American Library Association, 1986).

17. See, for example, Ellsworth, *Planning . . .*

18. "Institute for College Library Building Consultants," *College & Research Libraries* 25 (September 1964): 424–425.

19. The earliest public exposure to the concept of carpeting college and university libraries came at the ALA Library Equipment Institute in June

1964; see Joe B. Garrett, "The Carpeted Library," *The Library Environment: Aspects of Interior Planning* (Chicago: American Library Association, 1965), pp. 57–59.

20. However, the Undergraduate Library at the University of South Carolina and several community colleges—Foothill College in California, for example—preceded the four-year institutions in this innovative move.

21. Clyde L. Haselden, "Lafayette in Sequence," *Library Journal* 88 (December 1, 1963): 4577–4579.

22. Bernard Berkeley, *Floors: Selection and Maintenance*, LTP Publications No. 13 (Chicago: American Library Association, 1968).

23. The only area in academic libraries that institutions were slow to carpet was the lobby floor, just inside from the vestibule. It was argued that the traffic here was so great that carpet would wear out too soon. As a result, hard surfaces—especially terrazzo, slate, or even marble—continued for many years to be used in this location. It is an irony that, precisely because it is so congested an area, exacerbated by necessary talking at proximate reference and circulation counters, this practice served to pollute the acoustical environment of the building at its most fragile point.

24. "The Airlie Conference," *College & Research Libraries* 24 (July 1963): 337–338.

25. "The Impact of Technology on the Library Building" (N.Y.: Educational Facilities Laboratories, [1967]), p. 7.

26. Ibid., p. 19.

27. *A Study on Studying: A Report from the Community College Planning Center on Student Study Facilities* (Stanford, Calif.: Stanford University School of Education, [1965].

28. "Octagon for Marywood," *Library Journal* 93 (December 1968): 4513.

Chapter Eight

The Contemporary Modular Building[1]

The fourth period in American academic library building design—
that of modular integration of book and reader spaces—began with
the conclusion of the Second World War, and at the time of this
writing it still continues. It has, however, gone through several modifications and adaptations.

A. The Classic Module

Modular planning was used increasingly in the years immediately
following its introduction at Hardin-Simmons (1947). Within a decade this simple design concept had totally superseded the fixed-
function character that had dominated American academic library
building planning during the first half of the twentieth century. In
a modular building the floor is divided into equal rectangles, each
of which is usually defined by structural columns at its corners, as
well as by uniformity in ceiling heights, air and light treatment, and
floor-loading capacities, thus allowing its use to be economically
modified as needs change. The compelling virtues of the new style
were that (1) it was readily adaptable to post-World War II library
service concepts requiring that readers have direct physical access to
books on open shelves, (2) it lent itself readily to the profession's
contemporary concern for improving the "time-and-motion" effi-
ciencies of libraries and their users, and (3) it was remarkably flexible.

Readers were no longer restricted to massive reading rooms with
floor structures unable to support the weight of the books they
wished to consult. Librarians could now fulfill their social contracts
in modest structures rather than in palatial halls. Library interiors
could now, as they could not previously, be rearranged easily and
cheaply. Those flexible interiors moreover could be wrapped in al-

most any kind of exterior skin that the site called for, as long as it was basically rectangular to reflect the modular rectangularity of its bays. Princeton's Firestone Library (1949) took a Gothic Revival appearance, as did the libraries at Virginia Polytechnic (1955), Saint Thomas College in Minnesota (1959), the University of the South (1964), and Scarritt College (1966). A few were Georgian. The great majority of the libraries built in the latter half of the 1940s and the 1950s, however, were of the so-called "Modern" or "International" style, shorn of such concessions to history or traditional motifs, and reflective of the Bauhaus movement of which they were a part. Most were flat-roofed with uniform fenestration, austere and unimposing, with entry at grade level rather than on elevated podiums. It is small wonder that modular academic library buildings were so quickly adopted by the librarians who were to work in them and by the architects who designed them. All of this resulted from the consensus among architects and librarians that had been forged in the Cooperative Committee on Library Building Plans between 1944 and 1948.

In fact, the consolidation of the modular concept's strengths and the further resolution of most of its principal weaknesses occurred so rapidly that by 1960 its use in academic library buildings had probably arrived as close to perfection as it was fated to come. Because of its unadorned severity and stark simplicity, its uncompromising adherence to Louis Sullivan's dictum that "form must follow function," and the almost brutal economy of its structural style, classicists found the very tenets of their professional and aesthetic creeds embodied within the design of the early modular buildings. Among buildings built in this early tradition were the libraries of Louisiana State (1958), Colgate (1958), Brigham Young (1958), and St. Louis (1959) universities. In each, the facade displayed the very skeleton itself of the building, adumbrating not only the uniform interior floor levels laterally but also the column lines vertically.

Some, however, came early to feel that the new modular building lacked visual interest. Its reliance on uniformly rectangular components was boring and cried out for relief. It was ugly, they said, and looked "like a box," although a box was indeed exactly what library functional requirements warranted, with its rectangularity dictated by the real library "module"—the book itself—of which the building must economically accommodate hundreds of thousands or even millions. Nevertheless, it soon became clear that the "box" was going to have to be dressed up to look less like a box (Plate 7).

It did not take long for this change in architectural preference to become apparent. Ellsworth was especially critical of the movement then gaining momentum to depart from the simple, flexible, modular structure. Writing in the *Journal* of the American Institute of Architects in 1965, he placed the onus for the retrogression on the backs of

> some of the big-name architects in the East [who] are going back to pre-World War II traditions and are designing libraries that are not capable of meeting the needs of a modern university library, even though they may be superlatively beautiful. This new trend will surely cause the same kind of trouble we had with the pre-war buildings. . . . The[se architects] tend to think of the beauty of the shell rather than the beauty of the operation.[2]

In the last analysis, however, it had to be admitted that although architects were designing these retrospective libraries, they would never be built if client institutions were not also accepting them.

This movement to disguise the box certainly did not originate among librarians. Contemporary discussion, the literature, and the recollections of librarians who participated in the scene, all indicate that the library profession was very aware of how well off it was with the box and desired to remain with it. It is easy to hypothesize that donors may have been among the first to want more than a box. They, after all, were in some cases to have their names memorialized by these buildings and might have been disposed to favor something grander than a mere box. Or it may have been university presidents and trustees who wanted something more elaborate than a box. The early record is largely silent on the matter. Soon, however, some campus administrators began calling for their new library buildings to serve not only as libraries, but also as symbols, statements, signatures, or embodiments, of institutional style, real or imagined.

As soon as these dual expectations began to arise, the overall utilitarian quality of academic library building design in the United States began to decline. Library buildings were no longer allowed to serve one simple, straightforward function that would determine their form. Now library buildings were expected to serve two functions, one bibliothecal and the other symbolic, and just as no slave can serve two masters, no form can serve two functions without one of them suffering.

Although architects had expressed just as much pride in the boxes they designed in the 1950s as their owners had, they were generally quick to abandon the box in favor of more esoteric forms, wherever their clients would agree. Thereafter, many architects were found in the vanguard of the movement away from simplicity. Also, whether as cause or effect, the consensus generated in the Cooperative Committee on Library Building Plans more than a decade earlier began slowly to unravel.

Plate 7. Early Modular Academic Library Buildings in the 1950s Tended to Take on a Boxlike Appearance That Many Felt Was Dull.

a) University of Iowa (IA), 1951. Keffer & Jones, Architects.

b) LaSalle University (PA), 1952. Architect not known.

c) University of Louisville (KY), 1955. O'Connor & Kilham, Architects.

d) Saint Louis University (MO), 1956. Leo A. Daly, Architect.

As memories of the productive dialogues between architects and librarians in the Cooperative Committee receded with the passage of time, and as architectural ennui with the new modular boxlike libraries increased, the two groups found themselves once again drifting into two camps regarding how libraries should be designed. Librarians continued to favor the simple Bauhaus quality of the function-driven rectangular loft spaces that characterized the library buildings of the late 1940s and 1950s. Having been chafed for years by the rigid constraints of the fixed-function spaces and load-bearing walls of the earlier period, they cherished the reassurance of the new kinds of spaces that could be cheaply and easily modified as needed to meet the exigencies of change. Architects, on the other hand, came increasingly to propose new postmodern theories of design that, in the eyes of librarians, threatened to subordinate function to alien considerations and limited the flexibility of library spaces.

For example, Robert B. O'Connor, who designed the libraries at the University of Louisville (1955, Plate 7c) and Colgate University (1959), animadverted eloquently upon his frustrations in trying to provide "flexibility" in library design:

> In attempting to cope with this immense and rapid change, we have almost insensibly placed our main reliance on "flexibility". For the first time in architectural history we are deliberately designing for something that does not now exist and which in the premises we cannot really know [sic]. Whereas "form has followed function" since time immemorial, we are now faced with the perplexing problem of giving form to unknown functions. The result is the strange disembodied quality of so much of modern architecture and the tendency to make up for this organic vacuity by dragging in the latest architectural tricks from the illustrated magazines irrespective of logic or propriety.[3]

Librarians found such statements inscrutable at best and arrogant at worst. It is a feckless exercise, they responded, to rage in the face of uncertainty. When expecting uncertainty, one should plan for uncertainty. Surely that principle should militate in support of libraries that comprise simple, rectangular, loft spaces that could now be built with modular techniques. To O'Connor's credit, however, it must be said that, this commentary to the contrary notwithstanding, his library buildings at Louisville and Colgate hewed faithfully to the principles of flexibility and simplicity, although both were criticized by some for their dullness and their boxlike appearance. It is ironic that architect H. S. Newman's 1982 addition to O'Connor's building at Colgate was criticized not for its "dullness and box-like" character but rather for its unnecessary inflexibility and complexity (Plate 9f).

As time passed, others came increasingly to question the sacrosanctity of "function" as the sole or even the dominant determinant of form. In commenting upon his design of the Bobst Library at New York University in 1970, Philip Johnson opined that ". . . we've gone too far the other way in reaction to McKim, to Low Library. You need something more than utility to make you think of the library. The utilitarian aspects of the library will adapt themselves."[4] This, librarians countered, was exactly what they did not want to happen; they had grown weary through decades of adapting the "utilitarian aspects" of their libraries to the immutable constraints of bricks and mortar. Since it was now possible, with modern structural techniques, to build flexible utilitarian spaces, they felt it would be a retrogression—if not a transgression—to fail to do so.

During the conceptualization of his widely acclaimed "Field Theory" of architectural design, architect Walter Netsch designed several academic library buildings, including those at the University of Illinois at Chicago (1964), Wells College (1968), Northwestern University (1970), the University of Chicago (1970), and Texas Christian University (1982). Field Theory has been described as

a way of laying out spaces and/or space-enclosing architectural masses by making them grow diagonally as diagonally oriented squares or more complicated star-shaped clusters, specifically avoiding the buildup of large rectangular volumes or boxes with outthrusts—the almost universal way of building architectural shapes.[5]

Or stated differently, Netsch sought in his buildings "to get away from the boredom of the square box."[6] To a library profession that knew from experience that it could do its work best in "a square box," such statements were a tocsin of impending danger. Subsequent experience with library buildings based upon the Field Theory of design demonstrated that their apprehension was well-founded.[7]

Even well-intentioned efforts sometimes went astray when they departed too far from the traditional wisdom. Writing of his design of the library at Clark University (1968, Plate 8d), once hailed as "the mod reply to modular construction,"[8] John M. Johansen evinced strong concern for library function. This building, he said, "represents an attempt to find the essential nature of 'library'. It is simply doing a job; it is performing. . . . The will at work here is the will of the program, rather than the will of the fine-arts-minded architect."[9] The resulting design did indeed reflect admirably that intention, but most librarians felt that the effort was flawed ironically by its too rigid contemporary adherence to the program, resulting in failure also to provide requisite flexibility in the future use of the space. Discrete functional areas at canted angles, each with its own specialized lighting treatment, and a monolithic stack tower surrounded by open wells, have impeded the building's ability to adapt economically to changes in its functional requirements.

B. . . . and the Romantic Module

Some art historians might say that beginning about 1960 the period of classicism in academic library building design gave way rapidly to a strong romantic movement. Others might say that it was the beginning of decadence in the art form—that by 1960 it had risen to its zenith and that thereafter efforts to change it could only harm it. Certainly the trappings of romanticism pervaded much of the work that came to be done in subsequent decades. Contorted shapes, unusual textures, artistic license, emphasis upon effect, revulsion against constraint and discipline, return to tradition (or what was perceived as traditional) or to nature (or what was perceived as natural)—all began showing up with increasing frequency in new library buildings. As a result, the simple modular planning so consistent with classic theories of design, and so much appreciated by librarians, became unfashionable. These romantic elements were also partially responsible for the rapid increase in building costs during the period. Boxes were, and are, simply cheaper to build than more complex containers.

It is ironic that this period of romanticism set in at almost the very moment that the classical modular form was attaining its highest point, so much so that both styles can be seen in a single watershed building. The library at Washington University in St. Louis, designed by architects Murphy & Mackey in the late 1950s and opened in 1962, has been described by many informed observers as the modular building brought to its highest level of success. It is a square structure, indeed almost a cube, with its grade-level entry in the middle of the third of its five stories, providing the most efficient access to all of its interior spaces, square bays sized to library modular equipment, low ceilings, uniform air and light treatment throughout, and distribution of activities based solely upon the functions themselves. These qualities led Ralph Ellsworth to call it simply "the best"[10] (Plate 8a). Few commentators have departed markedly from that assessment.

Yet the beginning of decline is also evident in Washington University's fine modular library. Two features were incorporated into the design primarily to keep it from looking too much like a box; both cost extra money to construct, and one of them impaired function (although only slightly). One of these features was a wide deck that circumscribed the building at the second level above grade. The other was a tree court notched into one corner of the building. The deck was claimed to be necessary to shade a collar of glass used at grade level to make the building appear to "float" on the campus, thereby appearing to diminish its bulk. The tree court was rationalized as a device to bring natural light to the main stair, reserve area, and special collections suite.[11] Both of these purposes were accomplished handsomely. But a deck twenty-seven feet wide completely around the building (including the north side) was certainly not needed just to screen out the sun, and since the interior of the building was amply and ambiently lit artificially, natural light was not needed from a tree court. The court used up space needed for library activities, especially at grade level, thereby obtruding upon function. Both were extremely pleasant features, however, and they did relieve the perceived monotony of an otherwise box-shaped building.

Not all academic library architecture broke so immediately during the early 1960s for the more euphoric and emotional style of the romantic movement. Some buildings designed during this period even won AIA/ALA awards, a program initiated in 1962, for their classical commitment to functionalism. Among such early award winners were the undergraduate library at the University of South Carolina, completed in 1960, and the libraries at Lafayette College (1963), the University of Miami (1964), and LeMoyne College in Memphis (1964). Although each of these buildings had some functional problems (as virtually any library will), none resulted from a lack of modularity. All of these buildings were square or rectangular, and all evinced restraint in design. As the years passed, however, these qualities became increasingly rare in newly minted academic library buildings, especially among those selected for AIA/ALA awards. In fact, for the next thirty years the deliberations of the AIA/ALA award juries, comprising some librarians but usually with architects in the majority, have been fraught with disagreement about the degree to which library buildings should be judged for their form or for their functionality.[12]

C. Problem Areas

What were some of the problems that increasingly insinuated themselves into American library building design during the subsequent years? Few were new problems; most instead were old problems that now tended to get out of hand. Most were already obvious to Keyes Metcalf in the early 1960s when he drafted his comprehensive volume, *Planning Academic and Research Library Buildings.* Among those that he enumerated in that book were (1) irregular shapes, (2) interior or exterior courts, (3) monumentality, and (4) too much or too little glass.[13] These four potential areas of weakness will be discussed here with a view to their prominence in buildings constructed in the next two decades.

Irregular Shapes. Other things being equal, simple squares or rectangles that can be entered near the center of the long side, especially at the building's middle level, lend themselves best to economical library use and operation. They also create minimal exterior wall area requiring expensive cosmetic treatment. Of course, other things are seldom if ever equal, and legitimate factors, often relating to irreconcilable site considerations, frequently impinge upon a building's design. Some have argued, however, that in too many cases this economy of construction and operation has been forgone for no apparent reason save to attain a desired aesthetic effect or, more frequently, to keep the box from looking like a box.

Some of these irregularly shaped new buildings were round, although, as has already been recognized in this volume, that was certainly not a new shape for libraries. Semicircular libraries were built as early as Roman times, and the first of several completely circular libraries was built in the late seventeenth century. Since books and off-the-shelf library furniture are rectangular, however, round buildings (or indeed buildings of any other non-rectangular form) are profligate in their use of floor space. Radial shelving layouts, for example, require a certain minimum distance (perhaps three feet) between ranges at their hub ends simply to allow persons to pass through. The farther the ranges radiate from the center, however, the wider the distance between the ranges becomes, creating large areas of unusable floor space, which reduce the efficiency and drive up the cost of the building. Building contractors, moreover, can construct buildings with 90 angles cheaper than they can contend with curvilinear or other nonright-angular structures.

These considerations prompted a six-decade hiatus in the construction of round libraries following the openings of the new libraries at Columbia in 1897 and at NYU in 1899. The only exception was Frank Lloyd Wright's round library building, which was opened at Florida Southern College in 1942.[14] Wright's building was largely an aberration, however, and, perhaps due to the onset of World War II, gained little contemporary notice. Paul Turner was essentially correct when he observed of the entire Florida Southern campus that "its nonrectilinear geometries and complex building shapes, largely out of step with the increasingly accepted International Style, seems to have had little effect on campus architects,"[15] until considerably later.

Despite their proven inefficiency, round libraries began again in the 1960s to be built with unabashed frequency. The University of Corpus Christi built one in 1963, as did Chabot College in 1966, Saint Peter's College and Heidelberg College in 1967 (Plate 8c), and Saint Michael's College in 1968. Some of these, such as Saint Michael's, later covered up their curvilinear facades with new rectangular facings, but their impact upon the original interiors proved to be more difficult to disguise. Meanwhile in pursuit of his Field Theory, Walter Netsch, after experimenting unsuccessfully with radial stacks at Wells College in 1968, proceeded to design three round stack towers for Northwestern University two years later.[16] Other institutions built libraries that were only partially curved, such as Nevada Southern University and Worcester Polytechnic Institute, both in 1967. It is ironic that at the same time that some architects were attempting to disguise rectangular boxes, others were trying to disguise these rotund "hat boxes" by modifying their roundness. Thus Marywood College opened a gear-shaped library in 1967, and Worcester State College built a ratchet-shaped building in 1970.

Some other institutions, while eschewing rectangles, at least opted for rectilinear forms. Oral Roberts University built a hexagon in 1966, and Drexel University (1959) and Marymount College (1967) built octagons. Widener College (1969), Wright State (1974), and Sangamon State University (1976) settled for triangles, and the University of Texas built a parallelogram in 1978. Western Illinois University opened a library shaped like a pinwheel in 1978, with each level rotated forty-five degrees from the floors immediately above and below. The shape of Netsch's library building at the University of Chicago (1970), while retaining a semblance of rectangularity, nonetheless defied simple description, and Pereira's library at the University of California at San Diego (1970, Plate 9b) took the shape of a mushroom cloud. Still others failed to assume any discernible shape, such as the aforementioned Wells College Library, which, in Ralph Ellsworth's words, "oozes down the hillside" toward Cayuga Lake.[17]

Interior and Exterior Courts. There was a time, before modern lighting and air treatment became available, when interior and exterior courts were necessary in order to make central spaces in large buildings usable. Atria and light wells are thus among the world's oldest architectural refinements, and they have been used effectively since long before the Christian era. High vaulted ceilings and clerestory lighting were essential standard features of the seventeenth- and eighteenth-century alcoved book halls used as libraries following their introduction by Sir Christopher Wren at Trinity College, Cambridge, in the 1690s.

By the end of World War II, however, good ambient artificial light and efficient ventilating and air-conditioning systems were available at low cost, so that open wells, courts, and high ceilings were seldom if ever thereafter required for any functional purpose. With the need for them gone, their great inefficiency soon became apparent. It was immediately recognized that four kinds of problems, none susceptible to easy resolution, resulted from the use of wells. The first was that they increased construction cost by swelling the bulk of the building, thereby increasing the amount of its exterior skin that needed to be finished off. The second was that they increased maintenance costs by creating large blocks of unusable interior cubage that had to be heated in the winter and cooled in the summer. Third, they usually blocked more direct and efficient circulation of patrons and staff, or they were in locations that could have served better for assignable library purposes. And fourth (and doubtless most annoying to patrons), they permitted the transmission of noise vertically from floor to floor, impairing the library's essential acoustical ambience. Also, floor areas below atria and in high-ceilinged rooms were difficult to light, and they reduced flexibility in the future use of a building. Obviously, exterior courts experienced only some of these problems, but they were nonetheless deserving of concern.

For these reasons, few atria were used in the early (i.e., pre-1960) modular library buildings, although occasional mezzanines and high ceilings made appearances, largely as vestiges of the fixed-function buildings that preceded them. Law school libraries especially continued to favor mezzanines, but some also turned up in general academic libraries. The Lamont Library at Harvard (1949) and the libraries at MIT (1950), Georgia Institute of Technology (1955), Grinnell College and St. Louis University Library (1959), and Colorado College (1962) can be counted among the early modular buildings that utilized mezzanines. High ceilings tended in this early period to be limited to entryways, as at Southern Illinois University (1954) and Clemson University (1966).

Despite their functional deficiencies, however, atria and wells, both open and interior, became widely used during the next two decades. In fact, for a time following the opening in 1967 of Atlanta's Regency Hyatt Hotel, resplendent with a cavernous atrium, libraries seemingly all came with holes in the middle. Not only did wells increase in numbers, but they also increased in size. The library atria at Rice University (1949) and Butler University (1963) were relatively modest in scale, as was the one at Providence College (1968), while those at the Countway Medical Library (1966), the undergraduate library at Stanford University (1967), the University of Utah (1968), and the undergraduate library at the University of Washington (1972) yawned ever larger.

The trend to bigger interior wells had to end somewhere, and it appears to have done so with the opening in 1970 of New York University's Bobst Library, which boasted a gaping 10,000-square-foot maw that loomed upward fully twelve stories from its entrance on Washington Square. This building, which was designed by Philip Johnson, contained two ironies. The first was that for almost a century the nation's largest interior library well had been that of the Peabody Library in Baltimore (1878), which because of *its* great size (only two thousand square feet and six levels high) had signaled the conclusion of the earlier book-hall style of library architecture. The second irony is that on the outside the NYU Library looks like an unmitigated box.

By this time, however, some of the more deleterious effects of atria in libraries were becoming apparent, and efforts were made to render them less intrusive. In the first place, they were scaled back in size. Some, such as Lehigh University (1984), glassed in their atria and wells from the start to reduce the lateral transmission of sound into upper floors. A fortunate few, such as Stanford University's undergraduate library, were able to obtain funds later to encase their atria in glass in order to diminish the decibel levels on the floors above the entry lobby. Some others, such as Western Illinois University (1978), reduced the acoustic problems of their atria from the start by lining them at all levels with utilities or other functions less likely to be disturbed by reflected sound. Meanwhile some with existing wells attempted to mask the obtrusive sounds transmitted through them by installing bubbling fountains at the lowest level. Called "sound perfume" by some, this device was considered at Delta State University (1968), Illinois Wesleyan University (1968), and elsewhere, and it was tried at Simpson College (1964), Butler University (1963), and Atlanta University (1982) but with little success.

Despite uniformly poor experience with wells and high ceilings in academic libraries, they continued to be built in ever-increasing numbers. The library buildings at Clark University (1968), the University of Chicago (1970), Hamilton College (1972), and Saint Mary's College at Notre Dame (1982) are only a handful of the many libraries built in the United States during recent decades that

Plate 8. Attempts of Many Kinds Were Made in the 1960s and 1970s to Disguise the Boxy Appearance of the Modular Library Building.

a) Washington University (MO), 1962. Murphy & Mackey, Architects.

b) Butler University (IN), 1965. Minoru Yamasaki, Architect.

c) Heidelberg College (OH), 1967. Richards Bauer, Architect.

d) Clark University (MA), 1968. John M. Johansen, Architect.

have been plagued to a greater or lesser degree by one or more of the four problems of wells and atria cited above.

Along with the movement to the use of atria came a concurrent resurgence in the use of skylights for lighting the central wells of buildings. It will be recalled that skylighted areas were common in academic libraries of the late 1800s, as at Lehigh in 1876, for example, Brown in 1878, and the University of Pennsylvania in 1891. In the early 1900s, however, they largely disappeared and remained uncommon for some threescore years thereafter. By the mid-1960s, however, they were back, with Asheville-Biltmore College (1965), Saint Mary's Dominican College (1967), Clark University (1968), Providence College (1968), and Rosary College (1971) among the vanguard. Except for their proneness to leakage, however, and the very wide swings of illumination they provide during daylight hours, they have created fewer functional problems for academic libraries than the atria in which they are so often situated.

Monumentality. Considering the very recent cathedral and palatial heritage of library architecture, it should not surprise that the fixed-function libraries built between 1910 and 1945 continued to use monumental elements. Monumentality in library buildings can take many forms. In general, the term refers to almost any building element that exceeds in size or cost what is necessitated by its function. Thus much of what was discussed earlier in this chapter on irregular shapes and open wells can also be classed as monumentality. Overbroad entries, elevated podiums, sumptuous building materials, grandiose staircases, as well as conspicuously crafted accessories, can, and in library buildings usually do, constitute monumentality.

The modular style, when used in conjunction with modern lighting and air treatment, eliminated all functional need for library ceiling heights to exceed 9½ to 10 feet, thus for the first time uncoupling library design from its princely and priestly origins and allowing the development of utilitarian library structures appropriate to their present-day egalitarian societal role. Yet, as with atria, some vestigial monumentality in ceiling heights continued to survive. Examples may be seen in Marcel Breuer's library at Saint John's University (1966) and H. S. Newman's library expansion at Colgate University (1982) where high ceilings were used for aesthetic rather than functional reasons. High ceilings, as do atria, necessitate larger areas of exterior skin to enclose the building, and they create sonic, illumination, and air treatment problems that are no longer necessary.

Most other kinds of monumentality declined in use following the advent of the module. To be sure, a softer material with better acoustical properties would have been more practical in the vast NYU library lobby than its pretentious, expensive, and resounding marble. Curvaceous stairs can be very fetching and achieve a monumental effect, but they are also conducive to vertigo and seem likely eventually to be eliminated by building codes. Nonetheless they continued to be widely used in libraries during this period, as at the U. S. Air Force Academy (1959), Adelphi College (doubled in appearance by a mirror wall) in 1963, Scarritt College (1968, Plate 10a), Fisk University (1969), Rosary College (1970), Hanover College (1973), Sarah Lawrence College (1974), Ball State University (1976), Trinity University in Texas (1979), among other institutions.

In other efforts to achieve monumentality, some library buildings designed in subsequent years forsook the total flexibility of the module, so much appreciated by librarians, and returned to some of the fixed-function constraints of the earlier period. The libraries at Clark University (1968) and at Saint Mary's College at Notre Dame (1982), for example, both incorporated very low ceilings where stacks were initially installed and very high ceilings or wells with fixed-task lighting in some other locations, rendering any future effort to revise layout difficult, if possible at all, to accomplish. Perhaps the greatest impairment of future flexibility has been the relinquishing in many buildings of the principle of modular ceiling lighting. A desire to "play," "bathe," and "landscape" with light, rather than use it for library purposes, led to the construction of some buildings, as at Wells College (1968) and the School of Business at Indiana University (1981), that are virtually unalterable because it would be too costly to change the lighting.[18] Other libraries, meanwhile, lost flexibility by varying the floor-loading capacities in the structure, thereby restricting the relocation of bookshelves into certain areas. An example may be seen in the cantilevered extensions of the upper levels of the Sangamon State University building (1976).

Too Much or Too Little Glass. Only one of the problems reported by Metcalf in 1956 eased somewhat in subsequent decades; that was the use of too much or of too little glass. Direct sunlight has never been good for reading purposes, and indirect natural light is available for reading during only half of the hours a library is open. Even during daylight hours, natural illumination levels can be very fickle, varying widely from sunny through cloudy periods. For these reasons librarians have long been uncomfortable with windows on any but the north facades of their buildings. Prior to the availability of modern fluorescent lighting, libraries had to rely heavily on natural light, and the extensive fenestration used in many of the older fixed-function buildings was carried over into the early modular libraries.

Furthermore, as a recently developed building material, glass enjoyed an unusually wide popularity that, although perhaps warranted in some kinds of structures, caused severe problems for libraries. Among libraries from this period that suffered from overuse of glass were those at Grinnell College (1959)—although trees that were subsequently planted along its south side have somewhat ameliorated the problem there in the summer time—Butler University (1963, Plate 8b), Claflin College (1967), and the University of California, San Diego (1970, Plate 9b).

Overuse of glass in the 1950s and early 1960s brought on a modest revulsion against it, resulting in some buildings being built with few if any windows instead. To be faddish, it seemed that a building constructed around 1965 had to be faced either entirely of glass or completely without it. Among "under-windowed" library buildings constructed in this era were those at Oral Roberts University (1966), Rochester Institute of Technology (1967), and Indiana University (1969, Plate 9a). This ambiguous situation prevailed at the time that Metcalf animadverted upon the misuse of glass in libraries.

For the most part, relatively good sense has been used in the employment of glass in library buildings since that time. The introduction of mirror glass for building exteriors in the mid-1970s led for a time to its overuse. The Benedict College Library (1976), for example, was built of mirror glass, and the addition to the Vassar College Library (1976) was originally planned in mirror glass, but it was changed prior to construction because of its energy inefficiency. In most recent library buildings, however, concern for function has resulted both in limited fenestration, based upon the needs of library users rather than upon some counterproductive aesthetic effect, and in the proper use of exterior sunscreens rather than reliance upon drapes or indoor blinds requiring frequent replacement. Windowpanes with ultraviolet filters have also come increasingly to be used in order to reduce paper disintegration in library materials. Nevertheless, because of the large number of poorly fenestrated library buildings already in use, librarians justifiably study with a jaundiced eye all proposals for windows in new library space.

D. Architects

When firms design effective library buildings, of course, they are often invited to try to repeat their successes at other institutions, so it does not surprise that some architectural firms of this modular period were able to ply their skills on several additional library projects. After designing a highly successful building at Cornell University (1961), for example, Warner Burns Toan & Lundy of New York City went on to do equally fine libraries at a number of other institutions, including Brown University (1964), Emory University (1969), Oberlin College (1974), and Sarah Lawrence College (1974). Perhaps the oldest architectural firm in the land, and certainly the firm with the most library experience, Shepley Bulfinch Richardson & Abbott in Boston, provided highly satisfactory libraries to such institutions as Northeastern University (1952), Merrimack College (1967), Vanderbilt University (1969), LaSalle University (1988), Macalester College (1988, Plate 9d), and Augustana College (1990). Hellmuth Obata & Kassabaum of St. Louis were responsible for very functional libraries at Southern Illinois University at Edwardsville (1965), the University of Wisconsin at Parkside (1972), the University of Denver (1972), Western Illinois University (1978), and elsewhere.

Other firms, meanwhile, became well known for their good academic library buildings in particular regions of the country. J. Russell Bailey, an early associate of Angus Snead Macdonald, became dominant in the Southeast by preparing creditable modular libraries for Converse College (1951), Randolph-Macon College (1961), Hampden-Sydney College (1961), Emory & Henry College (1967), Meredith College (1969), and others. In fact, in his lifetime Bailey served as architect or consultant on more than a hundred library buildings.[19] His preeminence in that region of the country was then superseded for a time by that of Lyles Bissett Carlisle & Wolfe, who were responsible for good buildings at Clemson University (1966), South Carolina State College (1968), Winthrop College (1969), Wofford College (1971), the University of South Carolina (1975, Plate 10b), and Benedict College (1976). The Architects Collaborative (TAC) did some fine buildings in New England, including Bates College (1973), Boston College (1984), and Northeastern University (1990). Other areas had their specialist firms as well.

This is not intended to imply that all of the good buildings were designed by repeating firms. In most cases, a firm has to satisfy its first library client in order to be short-listed for others subsequently. Occasionally, moreover, a firm has done competent work on its first commission only to provide to subsequent clients pale duplicates of the design that earned their first success. Many fine libraries erected in the country during this period were designed as maiden library efforts by their architects, who simply never had subsequent opportunities to try their hands at others. The aforementioned building at Washington University may be the nation's outstanding example.

TABLE 6
Ten Largest Libraries Built in the United States, 1964–1984[20]

Institution	Library Gross Sq.Ft.	Year Completed
Univ. of Chicago	584,886	1970
Indiana Univ.	582,185	1969
Univ. of Texas	500,673	1977
New York Univ.	471,144	1970
Univ. of Notre Dame	446,943	1964
Univ. of North Carolina	436,600	1982
Univ. of Massachusetts	405,000	1972
Northwestern Univ.	398,000	1970
Univ. of Minnesota	382,313	1968
SUNY Binghamton	356,370	1975

E. New Directions

Outward . . . , Many very large library buildings were constructed during the years from the middle of the 1960s to the middle of the 1980s. The table above shows the nation's ten largest academic library buildings to be erected during this two-decade span, calculated in terms of their gross square feet of floor area.

As of the time this was written, these sizes had not been exceeded by any other academic library buildings in the United States itself, although the library of the University of Toronto (1973) was approximately twice the size of the building at the University of Chicago. It should be noted moreover that the above figures represent only spaces in newly built (i.e., not enlarged) central structures. The total area allocated to library purposes at Harvard University, for example, is more than triple the amount in the Regenstein Library at the University of Chicago as shown above.

Upward . . . , Among the many restricting realities that faced academic library building planners in these later decades were the rising cost of real estate, dwindling construction space, and reluctance to obtrude buildings unnecessarily upon remaining vistas or green space. As a result, an increasing number of high-rise and below-grade library buildings have been constructed during this period. If these had been the only reasons for their use, high-rise and below-grade buildings might have rested comfortably in their accomplishment, but unfortunately other, nonfunctional, considerations sometimes came into play, limiting their success.

High-rise library buildings were not an invention of the 1960s and 1970s. The New York Mercantile Library and the first John Crerar Library buildings were high-rise structures, and both were built well over seventy years ago, but they were not academic libraries. As has already been noted herein, the stack tower at Yale (1931), the Cravath Library at Fisk (1931), Paul Cret's tower at Texas (1936), and the Hoover Library at Stanford (1940) were academic libraries, so academic librarians in 1960 were not wholly lacking experience with them. Thus when the University of Notre Dame erected its fourteen-story library building (1963), many old heads questioned its wisdom. Rather than its mass being dictated by library functional factors, this building's height was determined by the University's desire for a symbol of its academic excellence that would outshine its reputation for football prowess. The library fulfilled that symbolic purpose admirably, with its mosaic-bedecked facade visible from fully 60 percent of the seats in the adjacent football stadium. Happily, also, the building worked quite well as a library, since the assignable area on each tower floor was large enough to permit the effective deployment of an ample admixture of shelf and reader facilities, a condition not true of the earlier tower buildings at Texas, Fisk, and Stanford.

Notre Dame's use of the first high-rise library in a quarter of a century inspired others to attempt similar schemes, but perhaps none has been so successful, and some have been abysmal failures. Were it not for its unique program requirement to bring departmental libraries under a single roof and yet enable them to retain some semblance of their individual integrities (a dubious political decision rather than a sound library decision), the fourteen-story science library at Brown (1966) would certainly have been disproportionately tall. The ten-story height of the library at Hofstra University (1967) may have exceeded an optimal ratio to its breadth and depth, and the fourteen-story stack tower at Memphis State University (1968) clearly did so. The misbegotten twenty-eight-level library structure at the University of Massachusetts (1972), designed by Edward Durell Stone, has the single virtue that no one has yet attempted to exceed it in height. If history can serve as a guide, however, and if institutions continue to demand that their library buildings serve symbolic functions, then it seems likely that even

Plate 9. In the Last Third of the Century Some Libraries Assumed Modest forms While Others Were Extreme.

a) Indiana University (IN), 1969. Eggers & Higgins, Architects.

b) University of California, San Diego (CA), 1970. William J. Pereira, Architect.

c) Tougaloo College (AL), 1975. Gunnar Birkerts, Architect.

d) Macalester College (MN), 1988. Shepley Bulfinch Richardson & Abbott, Architects.

this towering ziggurat will eventually be surpassed, doubtless with equally dismal results.

. . . and Downward.[21] Burying library buildings, or at least large portions of them, below grade was an innovation of the period being discussed here, and this was generally much more successful than the aforementioned efforts to go up. When this movement commenced in the 1960s the principal reasons for constructing library buildings below grade were (1) to keep their large bulk from overwhelming adjacent structures or areas, and (2) to keep an important site or view unobstructed. The first reason accounted for the location below grade of fully half of the floor area of the Washington University Library in 1962 and of Saint John's University Library in 1966, as well as more than three-fourths of the Johns Hopkins University Library in 1964.

Meanwhile, the second consideration accounted in 1967 for Hendrix College's decision to construct the first library building anywhere to be located completely below grade. Here the only satisfactory site was at the center of the one campus quadrangle, where a conventional building would have blocked all views and circulation. As a resolution to the problem, Philip Johnson conceived a two-level library building that was sunk into the ground, and he used the occasion to relandscape the quadrangle above. In 1968 two other academic libraries—the science library at Vanderbilt University and the undergraduate library at the University of Illinois—were built completely below ground for somewhat similar reasons (Plate 10e). The former was sited below ground to enable it to serve an engirdling ring of laboratory and classroom buildings without visually encroaching upon their quadrangle. The latter was built below grade to attain requisite proximity to the main library without casting a profaning shadow upon the sacrosanctity of the Morrill experimental corn plots, a compelling concern in the state of Illinois.

In the early 1970s a third reason for building below ground became prominent. It was the energy efficiency of such structures, and a number of underground, or partially underground, libraries were built in order to gain this economy. Some were set into hillsides, cropping out to the leeward, or to the sunward, such as the libraries of Scripps Institute of Oceanography (1976) and Saint Meinrad College (1983), which was designed by Evans Woollen. Others continued to be built for reasons other than energy efficiency, although they enjoyed that benefit as well. Among them was the Pusey Library at Harvard, completed in 1976. Here the need to effect a juncture with the Lamont, Widener, and Houghton libraries while at the same time preserving the integrity of the Harvard Yard led to the planning of a five-level below-grade structure, although for cost reasons its height was reduced to three levels before it was built. Likewise for site reasons, architect Gunnar Birkerts expanded the University of Michigan Law Library below grade in 1981 with much more success than a previous expansion in 1955, when a ghastly appendage in glass and aluminum had been grafted upon the side of the graceful Gothic splendor of the Cook law quadrangle.

Considering the level of popular apprehension regarding underground libraries, surprisingly few problems have been encountered with them. No more water came into them than came through skylights, or, for that matter, through so-called flat roofs. Since they require little if any costly exterior facade, they can often be constructed as cheaply as, or cheaper than, conventional above-grade structures. Modern lighting and air treatment can render them as habitable and gracious as any other interior space. Since they have no exterior visible form, there is no temptation to contort them into irregular shapes or masses inimical to sound library function.

One problem common to almost all below-grade libraries built thus far, however, has been their reliance upon exterior wells to bring natural light (and usually vegetation) down into their interiors. Obviously done to mask over the troglodyte character of these spaces, such wells nonetheless create the same library dysfunctions below grade as when they are used above grade. The light wells at the University of Illinois, Harvard, and the Beinecke Library at Yale University (1964), for example, all pierced the service floors and therefore obtruded upon library needs. The one at Vanderbilt was better located to the side rather than in the middle of the library. Only Hendrix College resisted the temptation to utilize a light well, and two full levels of uniformly good, rectangular, totally flexible space were made available for library use. By the middle 1980s, below-grade library space had been totally accepted.

Notes

1. Much of this chapter appeared originally as the author's "Twenty-Five Years of Academic Library Building Planning," *College & Research Libraries* 45 (July 1984): 268–281, and is reprinted here with little change. He is grateful for permission to use it in this way.

2. Ralph E. Ellsworth, "The College and University Library as a Building Type," *AIA Journal* 43 (May 1965): 69–72.

3. Robert B. O'Connor, "Problems of Modern Materials," *Planning a Library Building*, ed. by Hoyt R. Galvin (Chicago: American Library Association, 1955), pp. 30–34.

4. Paul Goldberger, "Form and Procession," *Architectural Forum* 138 (January–February 1973): 45.

5. "Walter A. Netsch," *Interiors* 130 (November 1970): 110–115.

6. "Netsch, Walter A(ndrew Jr.)," *Contemporary Architects*, ed. by Muriel Emanuel (N.Y.: St. Martin's Press, 1980), pp. 585–586.

7. For a measured report, see William G. Jones, "Academic Library Planning: Rationality, Imagination, and Field Theory in the Work of Walter Netsch—A Case Study," *College & Research Libraries* 51 (May 1990): 207–220.

8. Brendan Connolly, S. J., "The Fixed-Function Library," *Wilson Library Bulletin* 44 (April 1970): 858–860.

9. "John M. Johansen Declares Himself," *Architectural Forum* 124 (January–February 1966): 64–67.

10. Ralph Ellsworth, *Planning the College and University Library Building* (Boulder, Colo.: Pruit Press, 1968), p. 123.

11. John P. McDonald, "Campus Contemporary," *Library Journal* 87 (November 1, 1962): 4376–4379.

12. See Roscoe Rouse, Jr., "The Library Buildings Award Program of the American Institute of Architects and the American Library Association," *Advances in Library Administration and Organization* (Greenwich, Conn.: JAI Press, 1989), v. 8, pp. 241–252.

13. Keyes D. Metcalf, *Planning Academic and Research Library Buildings* (New York: McGraw-Hill, 1965), pp. 21–23.

14. See *Architectural Forum* 88 (January 1948): 134–135 and 97 (September 1952): 120–127; as well as William A. Storrer, *Architecture of Frank Lloyd Wright* (Cambridge Mass.: MIT Press, 1978), p. 252. This building was poorly lit, and lamps had to be brought in to supplement the installed illumination. It is said that thereafter when Wright would come to visit the building, all of the lamps would be removed and stored until after his departure.
It is useful to note that this inflexible building was used as a library for less than a quarter of a century before the college's present library building replaced it in 1966. Wright's original building is now used for administrative purposes.

15. Paul V. Turner, *Campus* (Cambridge, Mass.: MIT Press, 1984), p. 257.

16. "The Northwestern University Library," *Architectural Record* 148 (July 1970): 89–96.

17. Ralph Ellsworth, *Academic Library Buildings* (Boulder: Colorado Associated University Press, 1973), p. 42.

18. For a thorough review of this subject, see Ellsworth Mason, "The Development of Library Lighting," *Advances in Library Administration and Organization* 10 (1992): 129–144.

19. Charles H. Baumann, *The Influence of Angus Snead Macdonald and the Snead Bookstack on Library Architecture* (Metuchen, N.J.: Scarecrow Press, 1972), pp. 156–157, 180.

20. Although variant sizes have been ascribed to some of these buildings, the figures given here were taken from the reports of new library buildings published annually in the December issues of *Library Journal*.

21. The most thorough studies of below-grade library buildings have been made by a German scholar. See Rolf Fuhlrott, "Bibliotheken unter der Erde," *ABI-Technik* 5 (1985): Nr. 1, 1–13; and his "Underground Libraries," *College & Research Libraries* 47 (May 1986): 238–262.

Chapter Nine

The Rise of the "Anti-Building"

This study has said little about the costs of academic library building construction because they have varied so extensively over time and region as to make their comparison impossible. It probably suffices to state here, however, that academic library buildings have always been expensive. Institutional histories are replete with chronic, recurring threnodies upon their inability to house their libraries satisfactorily because of the unavailability of adequate funding. They have always represented a large draft upon an institution's capital assets with no possibility of recouping it through a resulting generation of new revenue.

Until about the time of the second World War, colleges and universities had few courses of action available to them when existing library space was filled up except to build more of it. Since mid-century, however, alternatives to costly new construction have increasingly been considered and, in some cases, adopted, so that recent years can perhaps be more accurately viewed as a period of the library "anti-building" than a new period in its evolution. The graph in Figure 24 shows the impact on new library construction, not only of the disappearance following 1972 of federal funds, but also of the increasing reliance by colleges and universities on one or more of these newly available alternatives instead of constructing de novo. It may be seen here that the average number of new libraries built per year from 1980 to 1989 dropped to fewer than eight, the lowest number since the decade of the 1910s.

Principal among the alternatives to new construction that have been most utilized by institutions are the following: (a) the construction of building additions rather than entirely new structures; (b) the compaction of library materials, either on-site or in remote locations; (c) resorting to the provision of "access to information materials" as distinct from their local ownership; and (d) increasing reliance upon non-codex information formats requiring vastly

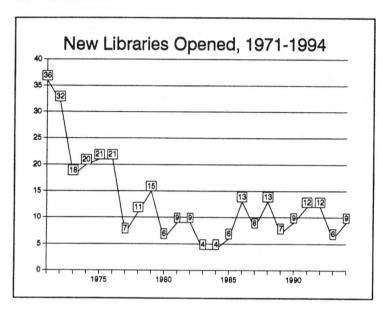

Figure 24. Number of New Libraries Built in the United States, 1971–1994

smaller amounts of floor space. These will be discussed here in this order. Since they are relevent to the present study only in a negative sense, however—that is, they explain why new libraries were *not* built rather than what kind of buildings were built—discussion of them will be brief. Large bodies of literature already exist on each of them.

Building Additions. As has been emphasized here, one of the principal virtues ascribed to the modular design concept was its flexibility, and this quality in postwar library buildings was destined to benefit many colleges and universities, especially in the last quarter of the twentieth century. Since the standard planning period for academic library construction was twenty to twenty-five years, all of the buildings constructed in the 1950s and 1960s found themselves filled to capacity by the 1970s and 1980s. Different, however, from their fixed-function predecessors, these new modular buildings could be easily adapted and added to as needed, and as a result most institutions gladly forwent the cost of constructing new buildings in favor of the cheaper alternative of renovating and enlarging their existing structures.

In general, the earlier (and simpler) modular buildings were easier to enlarge than the later, more complex ones. Latter-day planners of additions often wished for a somewhat larger bay size than the popular twenty-two-foot-six-inch-square of the early modular structures, but it was usually possible for the addition to match that dimension on at least one side of the added bays. Perhaps the most difficult constraint to accommodate was the limited floor-to-floor dimension of the earlier buildings, not because new ceiling heights had to exceed the older 9-foot to 9-foot 6-inch ceiling heights, but rather because more and more paraphernalia (deeper light fixtures and cabletrays, larger ducts, etc.) had to be fitted into the plenum between the ceiling and the slab above. The open wells, curved elements, varied ceiling heights or floor levels, and other such complications that so often marked the designs of the later modular period, however, were usually more difficult to adapt. Nonetheless, as a consequence of their inherent flexibility, and as the accompanying Figure 25 displays, the average number of library additions constructed annually from 1980 to 1994 was 11.3. Except for the single year 1977, this was the first time in the nation's history that the number of library additions built in a particular time span exceeded the average number of new buildings erected, which was 8.6. It was a trend that could be expected to continue.

The Compaction of Library Materials. Even before World War II

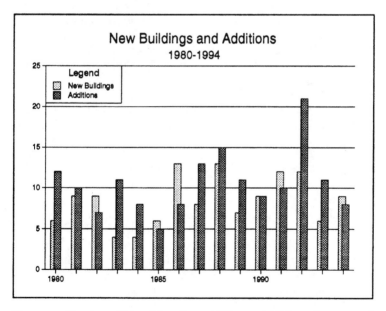

Figure 25. Number of New Libraries and Library Additions Constructed, 1980–1994

some academic libraries were delaying costly new construction by compressing more and more books into the same amount of a building's cubage or floor area. Such shelving devices as arranging books by size, narrowing stack aisles where possible, shelving books two deep, and shelving higher than seven shelves where possible were all tried, although some of these steps were difficult to implement in the conventional structural book stacks of the times. Furthermore, none of them lent themselves easily to the contemporary shift from closed to open shelves.

Compaction of materials became more prevalent following mid-century largely because new mechanisms for book compression, mostly based upon movable shelving, became available at this time. One early device of this kind was the "door-type," where an entire section of double-faced shelves was hinged snugly to one side of a fixed section rearward of it so that it could be pulled outward to reveal both its own rear shelves and the front face of the fixed section behind it. Such an installation was put in use in the Center for Research Libraries in 1951. Another kind of movable-shelf mechanism was the "drawer-type" stack, wherein ranges comprised deep drawers that could be pulled individually into the aisles. The University of Michigan made use of such a system in its storage building, which opened in 1955, and in 1957 D'Youville College installed it for its entire collection, although it was later removed in favor of conventional shelving. In still another variation of this theme, individual shelves could be moved laterally to allow access to other shelves hung directly behind them, although this style of shelving was little used in academic libraries.

The method of compact shelving that came to be most widely used in college and university libraries was the movable range, where adjacent ranges were moved laterally on tracks to open up a desired aisle. Among early installations of this kind in the United States was one at the American University Library, but many others have been used subsequently. They have been especially useful in closed stack areas, such as rare book and archive collections, and for the storage of least-used materials. They have therefore been more frequently installed in large research libraries that have adequate amounts of such materials to warrant their compaction, but some smaller institutions have found them useful, even in some cases in open-shelf areas. Because of their much greater weight when loaded, few existing library buildings have had adequate structural capacities to permit the installation of compact shelves on any but their lowest floor. Thus their greatest use has been in new central and satellite structures and in new wings on existing buildings. Compaction has obviously diminished the pressure for new library buildings.

"Access v. Ownership". Interlibrary Loan has been practiced for many centuries, but in earlier times it was done only on bilateral or ad hoc bases. Broader cooperative programs of interlibrary borrowing among academic libraries became available in this country when the Interlibrary Loan Code was first adopted in 1917. Subsequent revisions of this code, as well as successive revisions of standards for academic libraries, both promulgated by the ALA, have become increasingly emphatic in promoting the notion that libraries must "provide access to," rather than "own," a substantial range of the materials needed by their patrons. For many valid reasons, this has not been an easy goal to attain, but nonetheless it has tended to retard somewhat the unrelenting growth rate of collections of books owned in local libraries. That, in turn, slowed the construction of new central library buildings. Here again is a trend that can be expected to continue and to grow.

Various combinations of these schemes have also been tried since mid-century, including the cooperative development by several institutions of joint storage space for their overflow or least-used materials. These have usually entailed some new construction, but since these buildings are not central libraries, they fall outside the parameters of the present study.

The Use of Non-Codex Information Formats. The microfilming of library books, records, and other documents began in the 1930s, and over time large bodies of library materials came to be held in one or another of the several microformats. Since the storage of microform materials requires less than one fourth as much floor space as their equivalent texts in codex volumes, it may be seen that this technique enabled many libraries to delay considerably their need for additional space. Although many patrons were originally reluctant to use this alternate format, its acceptance increased with the passage of time.

The 1980s, however, brought with them the practical applied use of a new alternative information format that provided vastly greater compressibility than had microforms, namely electronic texts. Electronic texts, moreover, presented a myriad of additional qualities that bid fair eventually to alter very greatly the character and spatial requirements of academic library buildings. Electronic texts could be searched and accessed instantaneously, manipulated with enormous ease, filed effortlessly, and were probably destined someday to become cheaper for institutions to provide to their constituencies than would ever have been possible with texts in codices. In a trice, moreover, they could be transmitted to anywhere or obtained from

Plate 10. Interior Views of Selected Academic Library Buildings, 1965–1982.

a) Main Lobby, Scarritt College (TN), 1966.

b) Current Periodicals Area, University of South Carolina, 1975.

c) Shelf and Study Area, University of Minnesota, 1981.

d) Shelf and Study Area, Vassar College, 1975.

e) Below-Grade Shelf and Study Area, University of Illinois, 1965.

f) Reading Room, Colgate University, 1982.

anywhere on earth, meaning that for the first time in human experience "the library could come to the people instead of the people having to come to the library." Thus its implications for library seating were almost imponderable.

Indeed so extensive was the potential impact of this change that the academic world did not know how best to adjust to it, although through the late 1980s some modest changes were made in new library construction. As in the late 1960s, efforts were redoubled to provide cable infrastructures widely throughout new library construction to accommodate impending changes in the use of spaces, and the importance of flexibility was again emphasized to facilitate it. In long-range extrapolations of new or added spatial requirements, some institutions for the first time ever assumed a deceleration in the growth rates of their codex collections as well as modest reductions in per capita library seating.

Understandably, some academic disciplines were able to posture themselves to adapt to the new bibliothecal concept more rapidly than others, often exacerbating old stresses in campus faculties. Journalists especially contributed to the growing anxiety of future shock by providing glib descriptions of paperless societies possessed of miraculous black boxes that would contain all of the texts in the Library of Congress. For the most part, although not totally, librarians kept on the growing edge of this evolving technology, dragging their parent institutions toward the twenty-first century more rapidly than many of them were wont at first to go. A few foresighted institutions moreover began to place their computer centers into cohabitation with their libraries to facilitate their future cooperation, if not their eventual merger.

The fragile consensus of the late 1980s began to fragment in the early years of the 1990s. Although there tended to be little argument as to the nature of the changing scenario, there were widely varying views regarding its timetable. The line separating libraries from computer centers became increasingly blurred until to many it was indistinguishable. To some, the word *library* became almost a term of opprobrium, as voices—not uncommonly from among college and university trustees, state legislators, and other laypersons—were heard inveighing against the construction of any more outmoded "book warehouses." To change the popular image from one of miles upon miles of bookshelves, some institutions began designating newly constructed library buildings as their "centers for information service," "gateways," or other euphemism instead of "libraries," and indeed perhaps the new terms were more appropriate.

If the electronic image is to be society's new "information format of choice," as now appears likely, the transition may well elicit a fifth kind of library building to replace the modular structure that has now been in use for a half century. On the other hand, it may not. If the modular building is indeed as flexible as has long been touted, it may be able to serve as effectively in the age of electronic images as it has in the time of printed codices. One salutary difference that could influence structures designed to house this "new age" kind of information center might result from its removal from the temple and palace antecedents that have so long influenced the design of conventional libraries. Thus far, at least, campus computer centers have been allowed to assume utilitarian forms without being expected also to fulfill any traditional monumental qualities.

Appendix 1.

Libraries Constructed, 1840–1994

Preliminary Checklist of Buildings Designed to Serve Primarily as New Central Library Buildings for Four-Year Colleges and Universities in the United States

1840	South Carolina, SC		Denison, OH
1841	Harvard, MA		South, U. of the, TN
1846	Yale, CT	1879	Roanoke, VA
1847	Williams, MA	1881	California, CA
1851	North Carolina, NC	1882	Washington & Lee, VA
1853	Amherst, MA	1883	Centre, KY
1856	Charleston, SC		Michigan, MI
	Ohio Wesleyan, OH	1884	Columbia, NY
1862	Centre, KY		Mills, CA
1864	Haverford, PA	1885	Dartmouth, NH
1868	Wesleyan, CT		Hobart & William Smith, NY
1870	Marietta, OH		Oberlin, OH
	Mount Holyoke, MA	1886	Dickinson, PA
1871	Saint Lawrence, NY		Vermont, VT
1872	Hamilton, NY	1887	Grinnell, IA
1873	Princeton, NJ		Kenyon, OH
1876	Lehigh, PA	1888	Drew, NJ
	Rochester, NY	1889	Mississippi, MS
1877	Union, NY		Syracuse, NY
1878	Brown, RI	1890	Colgate, NY
			Indiana, IN

165

Olivet, MI
Pennsylvania, PA
Peru State, NE

1891 Cornell, NY
Wabash, IN

1892 Wittenberg, OH

1893 Baldwin-Wallace, OH
Bard, NY
Ohio State, OH

1894 Colorado College, CO
Doane, NE
Kansas, KS
Northwestern, IL

1895 Nebraska, NE

1896 Carleton, MN
Case Western Reserve, OH

1897 Columbia, NY
Illinois, IL

1898 Claflin, SC
Emory, GA
Franklin & Marshall, PA
Lincoln, PA
Ohio Wesleyan, OH
Saint Augustines, NC
Virginia, VA

1899 New York, NY

1900 Cincinnati, OH
Emporia, KA
Hiram, OH
Lafayette, PA
Lake Forest, IL
Middlebury, VT
Stanford, CA
Wisconsin, WI
Wooster, OH

1901 Allegheny, PA
Saint John's, MD
South, Univ. of, TN
Tuskegee, AL

1902 Albion, MI
Bates, ME
Bowdoin, ME
Saint Lawrence, NY
Saint Olaf, MN
Upper Iowa, IA
West Virginia, WV

1903 Baylor, TX
Butler, IN
Cornell College, IA
Duke, NC
Emporia State, KA
Franklin, IN
Hampton, VA
Louisiana State, LA
Oklahoma, OK
Rutgers, NJ
Southern Illinois, IL

1904 Alabama A & M, AL
Benedict, SC
Clark, MS
Converse, SC
Lebanon Valley, PA
Pennsylvania State, PA
Tufts, MA
Washburn, KS
Yankton, SD

1905 Beloit, WI
Bethany, KS
Bethany, WV
Bucknell, PA
Davidson, NC
Drake, IA
Fargo, ND
Georgia, GA
Georgia State, GA
Grinnell, IA
Hanover, IN
Lawrence, WI
Lincoln Memorial, TN
Milwaukee-Downer, WI
Mississippi U, MS

North Carolina-Greenville, NC
Norwich, VT
Pacific, OR
Parsons, IA
Simpson, IA
Stanford, CA
Syracuse, NY
Talladega, AL
Vassar, NY
Washington Univ., MO
Washington & Jefferson, PA

1906 Alabama A & M, AL
Atlanta, GA
Baker, KS
Berea, KY
Bryn Mawr, PA
Cedarville, OH
Denver, CO
Livingstone, NC
Maine, ME
Marietta, OH
Midland, TX
Mills, CA
Mount Holyoke, MA
Northern Colorado, CO
Peru State, NE
Swarthmore, PA
Winthrop, SC

1907 Earlham, IN
Furman, SC
Georgia Institute of Tech, GA
Hamline, MN
Indiana, IN
Juniata, PA
Knoxville, TN
McPherson, KS
Monmouth, IL
New Hampshire, NH
North Carolina-Chapel Hill, NC
Oregon, OR

Shurtleff, IL
Tulane, LA
Wilberforce, OH
Wiley, TX

1908 DePauw, IN
Florida A & M, FL
Guilford, NC
Hastings, NE
Hollins, VA
Mercer, GA
North Central, IL
North Dakota, ND
North Dakota State, ND
Oberlin, OH
Otterbein, OH
Pomona, CA
Radcliffe, MA
William & Mary, VA

1909 Auburn, AL
Cheyney State, PA
Fisk, TN
Kentucky, KY
Rollins, FL
Smith, MA
Stetson, FL
Wichita State, KS

1910 Baylor, TX
Brown, RI
Howard, DC
Indiana State, IN
Judson, AL
Miami, OH
Northern Iowa, IA
Wellesley, MA

1911 Agnes Scott, GA
Augustana, IL
California, CA
Heidelberg, OH
Loyola, LA
Ohio State, OH
South Dakota, SD
Tennessee, TN

Wells, NY
William Jewell, MO

1912   Chicago, IL
Dropsie U, PA
Hebrew Union, OH
Jamestown, ND
Johnson C. Smith, NC
Kenyon, OH
Texas, TX

1913   Alfred, NY
Centre, KY
Kentucky Wesleyan, KY
Phillips, OK
Purdue, IN
Saint Elizabeth, NJ

1914   Hamilton, NY
Kutztown, PA
Nevada, NV
Trinity, CT
Utah, UT

1915   Capital, OH
Central Methodist, MO
Harvard, MA
Ohio, OH

1916   Akron, OH
Johns Hopkins, MD
Missouri, MO

1917   Amherst, MA
Notre Dame U, IN
Tennessee-Chattanooga, TN

1918   McKendree, IL
Oregon State, OR

1919   George Peabody, TN
Stanford, CA

1920   Michigan, MI

1921   Luther, IA
Oklahoma State, OK

1922   Illinois Wesleyan, IL

1923   Baylor, TX
Birmingham-Southern, AL
Columbia College, SC
Connecticut College, CT
Lane, TN
Montana, MT
Montana State, MT
Montevallo, AL
Nebraska Wesleyan, NE
North Carolina-Greenville,
    VA
Randolph Macon, VA
Williams, MA
Wyoming, WY

1924   Albertson, ID
East Carolina, NC
Elon, NC
Kansas U, KS
Michigan State, MI
Minnesota, MN
Minot State, ND
Occidental, CA
Western Michigan, MI
Wilson, PA

1925   Alabama, AL
Arizona, AZ
Asbury, KY
Bowling Green, OH
Brigham Young, UT
Campbell, NC
Delaware, DE
Florida, FL
Florida State, FL
Hawaii, HI
Iowa State, IA
Millsaps, MS
North Carolina State, NC
Pacific, CA
Texas Christian, TX
Union, TN
Ursinus, PA

1926   Berry, GA
Central Washington, WA

Emory, GA
Fordham, NY
Fort Hays State, KS
Illinois, IL
Louisiana State, LA
Meredith, NC
Missouri Valley, MO
Washington, WA

1927 Ball State, IN
Elmira, NY
Hendrix, AR
Kansas State-Manhattan, KS
Kansas State-Pittsburg, KS
Memphis, TN
South Dakota State, SD
Wesleyan, GA

1928 Colorado State, CO
Dartmouth, NH
Dayton, OH
Holy Cross, MA
Knox, IL
Wesleyan, CT
Western Kentucky, KY

1929 Alma, MI
Boston College, MA
California-Los Angeles, CA
Chadron State, NE
Gettysburg, PA
Illinois College, IL
Kent State, OH
Lehigh, PA
New Hampshire-Keene, NH
New Mexico State, NM
North Carolina, NC
Randolph Macon-Women,
   VA
Southwestern State, OK
Sweet Briar, WV
Whittier, CA

1930 Albright, PA
Arizona State, AZ
Bluffton, OH

Cincinnati, OH
Duke, NC
East Tennessee State, TN
East Texas State, TX
Eastern Michigan, MI
Fisk, TN
Huntingdon, AL
Kalamazoo, MI
Lindenwood, MO
Loyola, IL
Mississippi State-Women,
   MS
Muhlenberg, PA
Oklahoma, OK
Reed, OR
Stephen Austin State, TX
Sul Ross State, TX
Texas A & M, TX
Tulsa, OK
Utah State, UT

1931 Central Michigan, MI
Coe, IA
Geneva, PA
Glenville State, WV
Hebrew Union, OH
Kentucky, KY
Marshall, WV
Maryland, MD
Millikin, IL
Murray State, KY
Ohio, OH
Radford, VA
Ripon, WI
Rochester, NY
Scripps, CA
Trenton State, NJ
West Virginia, WV
Yale, CT

1932 Atlanta, GA
Bethune Cookman, GA
Georgia State-Women, GA
Northwestern, IL

Pennsylvania College-
Women, PA
Southern California, CA
Tennessee, TN Tuskegee,
AL

1933 California State-Chico, CA
Denver, CO
Girard, PA
Shippensburg State, PA

1934 Columbia, NY

1935 Albany State, GA
Arkansas, AR
Massachusetts, MA
Principia, IL
Utah, UT

1936 Agnes Scott, GA
American, DC
Catholic, DC
Linfield, OR
Missouri, MO
Missouri-Kansas City, MO
Northwestern Louisiana, LA
Rosemont, PA
Temple, PA
Texas, TX
Union, NE

1937 Andrews, MI
Benedict, SC
Brooklyn, NY
Denison, OH
Manhattan, NY
Milwaukee-Downer, WI
North Texas State, TX
Oregon, OR
Rhode Island, RI
Xavier, LA

1938 Albion, MI
Bluefield State, WV
Drake, IA
Drew, NJ
Franklin & Marshall, PA

Howard, DC
Lee, TN
Mercyhurst, PA
Morehead State, KY
New Mexico, NM
Saint Bonaventure, NY
Salem, NC
Sam Houston State, TX
Southwestern, TX
Texas Tech, TX
Texas-El Paso, TX
Virginia, VA
Virginia State College, VA
Westminster, PA
Willamette, OR

1939 Alabama State, AL
Babson, MS
Bennett, NC
Central Missouri, MO
Connecticut, CT
Delta State, MS
Drew, NJ
George Washington, DC
James Madison, VA
Longwood, VA
New Rochelle, NY
Northwest Missouri State,
MO
Pepperdine, CA
Slippery Rock State, PA
South Georgia, GA
Southeast Missouri State,
MO
Southwestern Louisiana, LA
Talladega, AL
Virginia Military Institute,
VA
Western State, CO
Wichita State, KS
Winona State, MN

1940 Alabama, AL
Colorado, CO
Eastern Washington, WA

Fort Valley State, GA
Girard, PA
Goshen, IN
Illinois State, IL
North Georgia, GA
Northern Colorado, CO
Pennsylvania State, PA
Rockford, IL
Saint Ambrose, IA
Skidmore, NY
Southeastern Louisiana, LA
Southern Methodist, TX
Tennessee-Chattanooga, TN
Washington College, MD

1941 Allen, SC
Davidson, NC
Hood, MD
Limestone, SC
MacMurray, IL
Mary Washington, VA
Northland, WI
South Carolina, SC
Southern, LA
Tulane, LA
Union, KY
Valdosta State, GA
Vanderbilt, TN
Washington and Lee, VA

1942 Carroll, WI
Florida Southern, FL
Lenoir Rhyne, NC
Manhattanville, NY
Saint Mary's, IN
Saint Olaf, MN
San Jose State, CA
Tennessee Wesleyan, TN
Wilmington, OH

1943 Macalester, MN
Nebraska, NE
U.S. Coast Guard Academy,
CT

1944 Northwest Nazarene, ID

1945

1946 Hardin-Simmons, TX
Walla Walla, WA

1947 Colby, ME
Maine, ME
Our Lady of the Lake, TX
Paine, GA
Tri-State, IN

1948 Alabama A & M, AL
Bemidji State, MN
Central State, OH
Dana, NE
David Lipscomb, TN
Florida A & M, FL
Gannon, PA
Indiana Wesleyan, IN
Kansas Wesleyan, KS
Mount Saint Vincent, NY
Pacific Lutheran, WA
Virginia Union, VA

1949 American International, MA
California Polytechnic, CA
Cameron State, OK
Carson-Newman, TN
Concordia, IL
Culver-Stockton, MO
East Central State, OK
Harding, AR
LaGrange, GA
Lincoln, MO
Philadelphia Col. of Textiles,
PA
Princeton, NJ
Rice, TX
San Francisco, CA
Tennessee Tech, TN
Troy State, AL
Villanova, PA
Washington State, WA
Widener, PA
Wofford, SC

1950 Arkansas-Little Rock, AR
Atlantic Christian, NC
Bethel, MN
Bradley, IL
Bucknell, PA
Eastern Illinois, IL
Elizabethtown, PA
Greensboro, NC
Greenville, IL
Gustavus Adolphus, MN
Langston, OK
Loyola, LA
Massachusetts Inst. of Tech,
 MA
Mississippi, MS
Montana State, MT
Mount Union, OH
North Carolina-Greenville,
 NC
North Dakota State, ND
Ouachita Baptist, AR
Rhodes, TN
Rollins, FL
Science & Arts Univ., OK
South Dakota, SD
Southern Oregon State, OR
Taylor, IN
Texas College, TX

1951 Converse, SC
Detroit, MI
Eastern Oregon, OR
Fairmont State, WV
Georgian Court, NJ
Green Mountain, VT
Houston, TX
Iowa, IA
Kansas State-Pittsburg, KS
Mississippi State, MS
Northeastern State, OK
Northern Michigan, MI
Oregon College, OR
Tri-State, IN
Trinity, TX

West Texas State, TX
Westminster, MO
William Woods, MO

1952 Baylor, TX
Caldwell, NJ
Catawba, NC
Eastern New Mexico, NM
Emporia State, KA
Fort Hays State, KS
Fort Valley State, GA
Hanover, IN
Kansas State-Emporia, KS
Keuka, NY
LaSalle, PA
Lycoming, PA
Northeastern, MA
Notre Dame, CA
Oakwood, AL
Panhandle State, OK
Southwestern, KS
Thiel, PA
Trinity, CT
Valley City State, ND

1953 Bethel, KS
California State-Sacremento,
 CA
California-Riverside, CA
Claremont Graduate School,
 CA
Georgia, GA
Georgia Inst. of Technology,
 GA
Goucher, MD
Howard Payne, TX
Humboldt State, CA
Ithaca, NY
Marquette, WI
Midland, NE
Minnesota-Duluth, MN
New Mexico State, NM
Northern Illinois, IL
Northern State, SD
Oklahoma City, OK

Oklahoma State, OK
Russell Sage, NY
Toledo, OH
Wake Forest, NC
Wayne State, MI
West Virginia Wesleyan, WV
Western Carolina, NC
Wheaton, IL
Wisconsin, WI
Youngstown State, OH

1954   California-Santa Barbara,
        CA
        Centenary, NJ
        Colorado School of Mines,
        CO
        East Carolina, NC
        Georgetown, KY
        Grove City, PA
        Huntington, IN
        Idaho State, ID
        Loma Linda, CA
        Lynchburg, VA
        Newberry, SC
        North Central, IL
        Our Lady of Cincinnati,
        OH
        Puget Sound, WA
        Queens, NY
        Southern Illinois, IL
        Sterling, KS
        Tift, GA
        Transylvania, KY
        Wisconsin-River Falls, WI

1955   Adams State, CO
        Air U, AL
        Antioch, OH
        Augsburg, MN
        Augusta, SD
        Augustana, SD
        Carleton, MN
        Case Western Reserve, OH
        Clarkson, NY
        Gordon, MA

Hollins, VA
Incarnate Word, TX
Iona, NY
John Brown, AR
Louisiana College, LA
Louisville, KY
Millsaps, MS
North Carolina A & T, NC
North Carolina State, NC
Queens, NC
Regis, MA
Richmond, VA
Siena, NY
Southern Arkansas State, AR
Southwest Missouri State,
    MO
Union, TN
Virginia Polytechnic, VA
Waynesburg, PA
Wittenberg, OH

1956   Anderson, SC
        Assumption, MS
        California State-Fresno, CA
        Central Michigan, MI
        Clarke Memorial, MS
        Concordia, MN
        Defiance, OH
        DePauw, IN
        Evansville, IN
        Fairleigh Dickinson, NJ
        Hawaii, HI
        Jersey City State, NJ
        Mars Hill, NC
        Michigan State, MI
        Ottawa, KS
        Pacific, CA
        Paterson State, NJ
        Regis, CO
        Rutgers, NJ
        Saint Xavier, IL
        Seton Hall, NJ
        Stillman, AL
        SUNY-Geneseo, NY

Washburn, KS
Wayne State, NE
West Virginia State, WV

1957   Alfred, NY
Anderson, IN
Blue Mountain, MS
Central, IA
City College, NY
Cornell, IA
Corpus Christi, TX
Decatur Baptist, TX
D'Youville, NY
East Texas Baptist, TX
Freed Hardeman, TN
Furman, SC
General Beadle State, SD
Gonzaga, WA
Grand Canyon, AZ
Holy Names, CA
Idaho, ID
Kilgore, TX
Lamar, TX
Lebanon Valley, PA
Nazareth, NY
Northern State, SD
Northwest Christian, OR
Pine Manor, MA
Portland, OR
Salisbury State, MD
San Jose State, CA
Stephen Austin State, TX
Tabor, KS
Texas Wesleyan, TX
Whitman, WA
Wisconsin-LaCrosse, WI

1958   Alderson-Broaddus, WV
Berry, GA
Canisius, NY
Central State, OK
Concordia Senior, IN
Elmhurst, IL
Hofstra, NY
Maryland, MD

Middle Tennessee State, TN
Mississippi College, MS
North Park, IL
Purdue, IN
Saint Vincent, PA
San Diego, CA
Seton Hill, PA
Texas Southern, TX
Towson State, MD
Wayland Baptist, TX
Western Michigan, MI
Western New Mexico, NM
Wyoming, WY

1959   Albany State, GA
Baldwin-Wallace, OH
Bluefield, VA
Bowie State, MD
Brandeis, MA
Brescia, KY
Briar Cliff, IA
California State-Northridge,
   CA
Colgate, NY
Davis and Elkins, WV
Drexel, PA
Drury, MO
East Texas State, TX
Elizabeth City State, NJ
Grinnell, IA
Gwynned-Mercy, PA
Hunter, NY
Jackson State, MS
Louisiana State, LA
Mankato State, MN
Marin, CA
Minot State, ND
Muskingum, OH
New Hampshire, NH
New School for Social Work,
   NY
Saint Francis, PA
Saint Lawrence, NY
Saint Louis, MO

Saint Thomas, MN
San Diego State, CA
San Francisco State, CA
Savannah State, GA
Susquehanna, PA
Teikyo Marycrest, IA
Union, NY
U.S. Air Force Academy,
    CO
Wabash, IN
Wartburg, IA
Wingate, NC

1960 Alabama State, AL
Appalachian State, NC
Assemblies of God College,
    TX
Baldwin, GA
Bennington, MA
Bethany, WV
Bluefield, VA
Brooklyn, NY
California State-Chico, CA
California State-Long Beach,
    CA
California State-Los
    Angeles, CA
California Western, CA
Carnegie-Mellon, PA
Central State, OH
Chaffey, CA
Church College, HI
Citadel, SC
Colorado College, CO
East Stroudsburg State, PA
Florida State, FL
Hartnell, CA
Huston-Tillotson, TX
Jacksonville, FL
Kentucky State, KY
Loras, IA
Loyola Marymount, CA
Maryland-Baltimore MD
Moorhead State, MN

Mount Saint Agnes, MD
Olivet Nazarene, IL
Rocky Mountain, MT
Saint Anselm's, NH
Saint Catherine's, MN
Saint John's, KS
Saint Procopius, IL
Scranton, PA
Valparaiso, IN
Virginia State, VA
Washington State, WA

1961 Akron, OH
Ashland, OH
Baker, KS
Brigham Young, UT
Central Washington State,
    WA
Chestnut Hill, PA
Concordia Teachers, NE
Cornell, NY
Creighton, NE
Dickinson State, ND
Dillard, LA
Great Falls, MN
Hampden-Sydney, VA
Hartford, CT
Holy Family, WI
Indiana-Pennsylvania, PA
John Carroll, OH
Marietta, OH
McNeese State, LA
Menlo, CA
Miles, AL
Milligan, TN
Mount Saint Joseph, OH
Mount Saint Mary's, MD
North Dakota-Grand Forks,
    ND
Oakland City, IN
Pan American, TX
Porterville, CA
Queens, NC
Randolph-Macon, VA

Rensselaer Polytechnic, NY
Saint Joseph, CT
Simmons, MA
South Florida-Tampa, FL
Southern Mississippi, MS
SUNY-Cortland, NY
Tennessee Temple, TN
Trevecca Nazarene, TN
Tusculum, TN
Union, NY
Vermont, VT
Wagner, NY
Wilson, PA
Wisconsin-Eau Claire, WI
Wisconsin-Milwaukee, WI

1962　Andrews, MI
Auburn, AL
Aurora, IL
Beloit, WI
Bridgewater, VA
California State, PA
California-San Diego, CA
Calvin, MI
Centenary, LA
Eckerd, FL
Fairleigh Dickinson, NJ
George Fox, OR
Illinois Institute of
　Technology, IL
Kenyon, OH
Lambuth, TN
Le Moyne-Owen, TN
Miami, FL
Montana State, MT
Nevada-Reno, NV
Pacific, CA
Pennsylvania, PA
Roanoke, VA
Stonehill, MA
Texas Technical, TX
Tri-State, IN
Washington Univ., MO
Western Maryland, MD

Wichita State, KS
Wisconsin State-Oshkosh,
　WI
Wooster, OH

1963　Adelphi, NY
Adrian, MI
Albright, PA
Beaver, PA
Boise State, ID
Cedar Crest, PA
Delaware, DE
Dominican of San Raphael,
　CA
Earlham, IN
Hastings, NE
Houghton, NY
IUPUI-Fort Wayne, IN
Judson, AL
Juniata, PA
Kearney State, NE
King, TN
Lafayette, PA
Loretto Heights, CO
Montclair State, NJ
Northeast Louisiana, LA
Northwestern State, OK
Oregon State, OR
Parsons, IA
Philander Smith, AR
Rhode Island College, RI
Rowan, NJ
Seattle Pacific, WA
Spring Arbor, MI
Temple, PA
Trinity, DC
Upsala, NJ

1964　Alma, MI
Brown, RI
California-Irvine, CA
Eastern Baptist, PA
Florida Atlantic, FL
Franklin, IN
Illinois Benedictine, IL

Illinois-Chicago, IL
Johns Hopkins, MD
Methodist, NC
Nebraska-Omaha, NE
New Orleans, LA
Northern Iowa, IA
Notre Dame, IN
Ozarks, AR
Regis, CO
Rhode Island Univ., RI
Saint Mary of the Woods, IN
Simpson, IA
Southeastern Louisiana, LA
Stetson, FL
U. S. Military Academy, NY
Wagner, NY
Whittier, CA
William Penn, IA

1965 Amherst, MA
Arkansas State, AR
Asheville-Biltmore, NC
Belmont, TN
Boca Raton, FL
Bowdoin, ME
Butler, IN
Charlotte, NC
Colorado State, CO
Ithaca, NY
Keene State, NH
Lake Forest, IL
Manchester, IN
Mercer, GA
Santa Clara, CA
South, U. of the, TN
Southern Ill.-Edwardsville,
   IL
Tufts, MA
Washington & Jefferson, PA
Weber State, UT
Westminster, UT

1966 Baltimore, MD
Berea, KY
Boston Univ., MA

California Inst. of
   Technology, CA
California State-Fullerton,
   CA
Central Michigan, MI
Chabot, CA
Clemson, SC
Florida Southern, FL
Goshen, IN
Grand View, IA
Knoxville, TN
Limestone, SC
Northwest Nazarene, ID
Ohio Wesleyan, OH
Oral Roberts, OK
Saint John's, MN
Scarritt, TN
Skidmore, NY
SUNY-Albany, NY
Wilkes, PA

1967 Agricultural, Mech. &
   Normal, AR
Alabama A & M, AL
Albertson, ID
Angelo State, TX
Austin Peay State, TN
Bemidji State, MN
Bloomsburg State, PA
Bowling Green State, OH
California College of the
   Arts, CA
California-Santa Cruz, CA
Cedarville, OH
Centre, KY
Chadron State, NE
Chapman, CA
Claflin, SC
Dickinson, PA
Eastern Michigan, MI
Emory & Henry, VA
Ferris State, MI
Florida, FL
Fontbonne, MO

Fort Lewis, CO
George Mason, VA
Graceland, IA
Heidelberg, OH
Hendrix, AR
Hofstra, NY
Indiana Wesleyan, IN
Johnson C. Smith, NC
Kalamazoo, MI
Lewis & Clark, ID
Louisiana State-Unica, LA
Mary Baldwin, VA
Marymount Col. CA
Marywood, PA
Merrimack, MA
Millersville State, PA
Milton, WI
Montevallo, AL
Moravian, PA
National Col. of Education, IL
New England, NH
North Carolina Wesleyan, NC
Pacific Lutheran, WA
Pacific, OR
Pennsylvania Col. of Textiles, PA
Pfeiffer, NC
Pittsburgh, PA
Quincy, IL
Radcliffe, MA
Rochester Inst. of Technology, NY
Rockford, IL
Rockhurst, MO
Saint Francis, IL
Saint Mary's, CA
Saint Mary's Dominican, LA
Saint Teresa's, MN
Shaw, NC
South Dakota, SD
Southern Oregon State, OR
Southwest State, MN

SUNY-Geneseo, NY
Tulsa, OK
Vermont Technical Institute, VT
West Florida, FL
Wiley, TX
William Paterson, NJ
Windham, VT
Winston-Salem State, NC
Worcester Polytechnic, MA
Xavier, OH

1968 Arkansas, AR
Arkansas College, AR
Augusta, GA
Barry, FL
California Polytechnic, CA
Clark, MA
Clinch Valley, VA
Dakota State, SD
Delta State, MS
Eastern Montana, MT
Elon, NC
Emporia, KS
Eureka, IL
Fairfield, CT
Florida Technological, FL
Hawaii, HI
Illinois Wesleyan, IL
Iowa Wesleyan, IA
Ithaca, NY
Jersey City State, NJ
Kutztown, PA
Louisiana State-Alexandria, LA
Lycoming, PA
Mankato State, MN
Marylhurst, OR
Missouri-Rolla, MO
Missouri-St. Louis, MO
Montana State-Billings, MT
Newark State, NJ
North Adams State, MA
Northeastern State, OK

Northern Michigan, MI
Ohio Northern, OH
Pembroke State, NC
Portland State, OR
Providence, RI
Saint Benedict's, KS
Saint Elizabeth's, NJ
Saint Mary's, TX
Saint Michael's, VT
Sam Houston State, TX
Shippensburg State, PA
South Alabama, AL
Southwest Texas State, TX
Spalding, KY
SUNY-Fulton, NY
SUNY-Oswego, NY
Tampa, FL
Tennessee A & I, TN
Tennessee-Martin, TN
Thomas More, KY
Tulane, LA
Urbana, OH
Utah, UT
Virgin Islands, VI
Wells, NY
Wesleyan, GA
West Georgia, GA
Westmont, CA
Wisconsin State-Superior,
   WI

1969   Alabama-Huntsville, AL
Alaska, AK
Carlow, PA
Christian Brothers, TN
Dana, NE
Elmira, NY
Emory, GA
Farmington State, ME
Findlay, OH
General Beadle State, SD
Goddard, VT
Grand Valley State, MI
Indiana, IN

Kansas State-Ft. Hays, KS
Lees-McRae, NC
Long Island, NY
Luther, IA
McKendree, IL
Meredith, NC
Mississippi State for Women,
   MS
Missouri-Kansas City, MO
Mount Angel, OR
Mount Saint Mary's, CA
Mundelein, IL
Nebraska Wesleyan, NE
North Carolina-
   Wilmington, NC
Notre Dame, NY
Ohio, OH
Redlands, CA
Ricker, ME
Roger Williams, RI
Sacred Heart, CT
South Carolina State, SC
Southwestern State, OK
Sul Ross State, TX
SUNY-Fredonia, NY
Towson State, MD
Troy State, AL
U.S. International, CA
Unity, ME
Virginia Wesleyan, VA
Western Montana, MT
Winthrop, SC
Wisconsin State-Platteville,
   WI

1970   Abilene Christian, TX
Alcorn A & M, MS
Bethany, KS
Blackburn, IL
Bryn Mawr, PA
Capital, OH
Chicago, IL
Doane, NE
Faulkner, AL

Fisk, TN
Franklin Pierce, NH
Georgetown, DC
Green Mountain, VT
Hampshire, MA
Hartford, CT
Hawaii Loa, HI
Kent State, OH
Lock Haven State, PA
Louisiana State-Shreveport, LA
Marian, IN
McPherson, KS
Monmouth, IL
New Mexico Inst. of Mining, NM
New York, NY
Northland, WI
Northrop Inst. of Technology, CA
Northwestern, IL
Rust, MS
Saint Francis, ME
Saint Peters, NJ
Salem, WV
South Dakota Mines, SD
Southern Utah State, UT
SUNY-Alfred, NY
Texas Lutheran, TX
Thomas, ME
Ursinus, PA
Valdosta State, GA
Virginia Commonwealth, VA
Washington College, MD
Wesley, DE
West Liberty, WV
Western Connecticut State, CT
Widener, PA
Worcester State, MA
Yankton, SD

1971 Baptist, SC

Bethune Cookman, FL
Boise State, ID
Bridgewater State, CT
Cal. State-Hayward, CA
Cal. State-San Bernardino, CA
Connecticut-Waterbury, CT
Covenant, TN
Dayton, OH
Eastern Connecticut State, CT
Eastern Mennonite, VA
Evergreen State, WA
Francis Marion, SC
Hillsdale, MI
Jamestown, ND
Lake Superior State, MI
Malone, OH
Nazareth, MI
North Carolina-Charlotte, NC
North Texas State, TX
Notre Dame, OH
Ohio Dominican, OH
Oklahoma City, OK
Otterbein, OH
Rosary, IL
Sacred Heart, KS
Salem State, MA
San Diego State, CA
Slippery Rock State, PA
Southern A&M-Shreveport, LA
Springfield, MA
Susquehanna, PA
Tougaloo, AL
Voorhees, SC
Western, OH
Western Kentucky, KY
Wofford, SC

1972 Alabama-Birmingham, AL
Bryant, RI
Central Connecticut State, CT

Charleston, SC
Concordia, MN
Denver, CO
Elmhurst, IL
Gannon, PA
Gustavus Adolphus, MN
Hamilton, NY
Hamline, MN
Indiana State, IN
IUPUI, IN
Lincoln, PA
Lyndon State, VT
Massachusetts, MA
Miami, OH
Mississippi Valley State, MS
Norfolk State, VA
North Georgia, GA
Occidental, CA
Plymouth State, NH
Saint Cloud State, MN
Saint Thomas, TX
Southeastern Mass., MA
Southern Indiana, IN
Stephen F. Austin State, TX
SUNY-Binghamton, NY
SUNY-Cobleskill, NY
Syracuse, NY
U.S. Naval Academy, MD
Wisconsin-Parkside, WI

1973   Adams State, CO
Bates, ME
Chicago State, IL
Erskine, SC
George Washington, DC
Hanover, IN
Indiana-New Albany, IN
Jacksonville State, AL
Keuka, NY
Loyola-Notre Dame, MD
Northwestern Louisiana, LA
Oakwood, AL
Saint Augustines, NC
Stockton State, CA

SUNY-Oneonta, NY
Toledo, OH
Union, NJ
U.S. Coast Guard Academy, CT

1974   Belhaven, MS
Bridgewater, CT
Columbus, GA
Davidson, NC
Lowell State, MA
Massachusetts-Boston, MA
Minnesota-Morris, MN
Montana, MT
Morgan State, MD
Oberlin, OH
Ohio-Chillicothe, OH
Our Lady of the Elms, MA
Presbyterian, SC
Rose-Hulman, IN
Sarah Lawrence, NY
Southern Arkansas, AR
SUNY-Cortland, NY
Tennessee-Chattanooga, TN
West Texas State, TX
Wright State, OH

1975   California State-Sacramento, CA
Central, FL
Central Washington, WA
Fitchburg State, MA
Florida International, FL
Fort Valley State, GA
Frostburg State, MD
Georgia Southern, GA
Hardin-Simmons, TX
Illinois State, IL
Lawrence, WI
Long Island-Brooklyn, NY
Northern Kentucky, KY
Notre Dame, CA
Pittsburgh-Greensburg, PA
Purdue-Westville, IN
Saint John Fisher, NY

Shorter, GA
South Carolina, SC
Williams, MA
Youngston State, OH

1976 Allegheny, PA
Arizona, AZ
Ball State, IN
Benedict, SC
Birmingham Southern, AL
Central Wesleyan, SC
Cheney State, PA
Colorado-Denver, CO
Connecticut, CT
Coppin State, MD
Hobart & William Smith,
  NY
Lamar, TX
Maine, ME
Old Dominion, VA
Olivet Nazarene, IL
Rensselaer Polytechnic, NY
Sangamon State, IL
Savannah State, GA
Temple, PA
Texas-San Antonio, TX
Wilberforce, OH

1977 Bowie State, MD
Idaho State, ID
Illinois College, IL
Northern Illinois, IL
South Dakota State, SD
SUNY-Plattsburgh, NY
Texas, TX

1978 California State, PA
Clarkson, NY
Coastal Carolina, SC
Connecticut Univ., CT
Indianapolis, IN
Lander, SC
Lassen, CA
Miles, AL
Millikin, IL

Northeastern Illinois, IL
Western Illinois, IL

1979 American, DC
Atlantic Christian, NC
Cincinnati, OH
East Texas Baptist, TX
Friends Bible, KS
Louisville, KY
Morris, SC
Northern Colorado, CO
Northwest Bible, ND
Pan American, TX
Ramapo, NJ
SUNY-Buffalo, NY
Trinity, TX
Washburn, KS
Washington & Lee, VA

1980 Albion, MI
Christopher Newport, VA
Hebrew Union, OH
Indiana-Gary, IN
John Brown, AR
North Florida, FL

1981 Babson, MA
California Poly-San Luis,
  CA
Gallaudet, DC
Gettysburg, PA
Michigan-Dearborn, MI
Pennsylvania State-Media,
  PA
Sheridan, WY
Southwest Missouri State,
  MO
Wisconsin-Stout, WI

1982 Atlanta, GA
Hawaii-Hilo, HA
John Wesley, NC
Le Moyne, NY
North Carolina, NC
Northern Montana, MT
Saint Mary's, IN

Suffolk, MA
SUNY-Old Westbury, NY

1983 Bethel, IN
Saint Meinrad, IN
Saint Thomas, FL
Western New England, MA

1984 Boston College, MA
Drexel, PA
Pace, NY
Southern A & M-Baton
Rouge, LA

1985 California Lutheran, CA
CBN, VA
Rollins, FL
Southeastern Louisiana, LA
SUNY-Utica, NY
Texas-El Paso, TX

1986 Aguadilla Regional, PR
Austin, TX
Bethel, KS
Gwynned-Mercy, PA
Lee, TN
South Florida-Sarasota, FL
Southeastern Louisiana, LA
Taylor, IN
Texas Woman's, TX
Trinity, VT
Westbrook State, ME
Willamette, OR
Wisconsin-Stevens Point,
WI

1987 Cedarville, OH
Clarke, IA
Daniel Webster, NH
Huntington, IN
Saginaw Valley State, MI
Saint Benedict's, MN
Saint Mary, NE
Texas A & M-Galveston, TX

1988 Academy of the New
Church, PA

Allentown, PA
Arizona State, AZ
Assumption, MA
Fayetteville State, NC
Florida Internat'l-N.Miami,
FL
La Salle, PA
Macalester, MN
Prairie View A & M, TX
Queens, NY
Shawnee State, OH
Texas Wesleyan, Tx
Wright State, OH

1989 Indiana-South Bend, IN
Mary Washington, VA
Medgar Evers, NY
Mercer, GA
Muhlenberg, PA
Park, MO
Tennessee Technical, TN

1990 Alaska-Juneau, AK
Atlantic, College of the, ME
Augustana, IL
Elizabethtown, PA
Galveston, TX
Mills, CA
Northeastern, MA
Reformed Bible, MI
Southwest Texas State, TX

1991 Atlanta Christian, GA
California-San Francisco,
CA
David Lipscomb, TN
Edgewood, WI
Greenville, IL
Hampton, VA
Longwood, VA
Millersville State, PA
Miramar, CA
Paine, GA
Roger Williams, RI
Salve Regina, RI

1992 Arkansas-Little Rock, AR
Baylor, TX
De Paul, IL
Drury, MO
Hood, MD
Minot State, ND
New Jersey Inst. of Tech., NJ
New Mexico Inst. of Mining, NM
New Mexico State, NM
North Idaho, ID
Scranton, PA
Shenandoah, WV

1993 Albany State, GA

Defiance, OH
Gonzaga, WA
IUPUI, IN
Memphis, TN
Xavier, LA

1994 California State-Bakersfield, CA
Dekalb, GA
Hendrix, AR
Loyola, IL
Memphis, TN
Pennsylvania State-Erie, PA
Seattle Pacific, WA
Seton Hall, NJ
Southwestern Adventist, TX

Sources

ARCHIVES

The archives of many institutions were consulted in developing the information used in this study. Those at the following institutions were especially helpful:

Amherst College
Auburn University
Baldwin-Wallace College
Bard College
Brown University
Carleton College
Centre College
Colgate University
College of Charleston
Colorado College
Columbia University
Denison College
Dickinson College
Drew University
Emory University
Florida A. & M. University
Franklin & Marshall College
Goucher College
Grinnell College
Haverford College
Indiana University
Iowa State University
Kansas State University
Lehigh University
Marietta College
Mills College

New Brunswick Theological Sem.
Northern Iowa University
Oakwood College
Oberlin College
Ohio Wesleyan University
Olivet College
Peru State College
Princeton Theological Sem.
Roanoke College
Saint Lawrence University
Saint Louis University
Stephens College
Syracuse University
Union College (NY)
University of Illinois
University of Kansas
University of Michigan
University of Mississippi
University of Nebraska
University of Rochester
University of Vermont
Valparaiso University
Wabash College
Washington & Lee University
Wittenberg University

In addition to these institutional archives per se, two other archives located within institutional archives were also helpful. The first were the American Library Association archives, which are located in, and administered by, the University of Illinois Archives. The second were the archives of the Carnegie Corporation of New York, which are located in, and administered by, the Rare Book & Manuscript Library at Columbia University. The latter comprise the major portion of the sources for the discussion in Chapter 5 of Andrew Carnegie's provision of library buildings to American colleges and universities.

The author is grateful to all of these institutions for their assistance.

Dissertations, Theses, and Unpublished Papers

Abbott, John C. "Raymond Cazallis Davis and the University of Michigan Library 1877–1905." Ph.D. dissertation, University of Michigan, 1957.

Allan, J. M. "The Library of Hamilton College, Clinton, NY, from January 1793 to January 1963." Fellowship thesis, Library Association [of the United Kingdom . . .], 1968.

Ambrose, Lodilla. "A Study of College Libraries." Master's thesis, Northwestern University, 1892.

Andrews, Thelma. "Trends in College Library Buildings." Master's thesis, University of Chicago, 1945.

Boll, John J. "Library Architecture: A Comparison of Theory and Buildings, with Emphasis on New England College Libraries." Ph.D. dissertation, University of Illinois, 1961.

Kaufman, Peter S. "American Academic Library Architecture, 1876–1890: An Introduction and Survey," unpublished paper submitted November 12, 1976, in *Architecture* 648, Cornell University.

Lee, Sang Chul. "Planning and Design of Academic Library Buildings." DLS dissertation, Columbia University, 1985.

Linderman, Winifred B. "History of the Columbia University Library, 1876–1926." DLS dissertation, Columbia University, 1959.

Lowell, Mildred H. "Indiana University Libraries, 1829–1942." Ph.D. dissertation, University of Chicago, 1957.

Malo, Paul. "The Herring-Cole Library," unpublished paper dated January 22, 1968, in the Special Collections of the Owen D. Young Library, St. Lawrence University.

Peterson, Kenneth G. "The History of the University of California Library at Berkeley, 1900–1945." Ph.D. dissertation, University of California, Berkeley, 1968.

Ratcliffe, Thomas E. "Development of the Buildings, Policy and Collection of the University of Illinois Library in Urbana, 1897–1940." Master's thesis, University of Illinois, 1949.

Reynolds, Helen M. "University Library Buildings in the United States." Master's thesis, University of Illinois, 1946.

Rouse, Roscoe, Jr. "A History of the Baylor University Library, 1845–1919." Ph.D. dissertation, University of Michigan, 1962.

Stanley, Ellen L. "The Earlham College Library: A History of Its Relation to the College, 1847–1947." Master's thesis, University of Illinois, 1947.

Van Slyck, Abigail A. "Free to All: Carnegie Libraries and the Transformation of American Culture, 1886–1917." Ph.D. dissertation, University of California, Berkeley, 1989.

Books

American Almanac and Repository of Useful Knowledge for the Year 1840. Boston, Mass.: David H. Williams, 1840.

Anderson, Florence. *Carnegie Corporation Library Program 1911–1961.* N.Y.: Carnegie Corporation of New York, 1963.

Baumann, Charles H. *The Influence of Angus Snead Macdonald and the Snead Bookstack on Library Architecture.* Metuchen, N.J.: Scarecrow Press, 1972.

Bazillion, Richard J. and Connie Braun. *Academic Libraries as High-Tech Gateways; A Guide to Design and Space Decisions.* Chicago: American Library Association, 1995.

Beach, Arthur G. *A Pioneer College: The History of Marietta.* Marietta, Ohio: 1935.

Bentinck-Smith, William. *Building a Great Library: The Coolidge Years at Harvard.* Cambridge, Mass.: Harvard University Press, 1976.

Berkeley, Bernard. *Floors: Selection and Maintenance,* "LTP Publications No. 13." Chicago: American Library Association, 1968.

Bobinski, George S. *Carnegie Libraries: Their History and Impact on American Public Library Development.* Chicago: American Library Association, 1969.

Bond, Horace Mann. *Education for Freedom: A History of Lincoln University.* Jefferson City: Mo. Lincoln University, 1976.

Bryan, John Morrill. *Architectural History of the South Carolina College, 1801–1855.* Columbia, S.C.: University of South Carolina Press, 1976.

Bullock, Henry M. *A History of Emory University.* Nashville, Tenn.: Parthenon Press, 1936.

Burchard, John, and Bush-Brown, Albert. *The Architecture of America: A Social and Cultural History.* Boston, Mass.: Little, Brown and Co., 1961.

Cabaniss, Allen. *The University of Mississippi; Its First Hundred Years,* 2d ed. Hattiesburg, Miss.: University and College Press of Mississippi, 1971.

Carnegie, Andrew. *Autobiography.* Boston, Mass.: Houghton Mifflin, 1920.

Chessman, G. Wallace. *Denison: The Story of an Ohio College.* Granville, Ohio: Denison University, 1957.

Clemons, Harry. *The University of Virginia Library, 1825–1950.* Charlottesville, Va.: University of Virginia Library, 1954.

Corbin, Edward T. *A Manual of the Reformed Church in America.* N.Y.: Board of Publication of the Reformed Church, 1902.

de Laborde, Leon. *Etude sur la Construction des Bibliothèques.* Paris: A. Franck, 1845.

Diehl, Carl. *Americans and German Scholarship*. New Haven, Conn.: Yale University Press, 1978.

Easterby, J. H. *A History of the College of Charleston*. N.Y.: Scribner, 1935.

Ellsworth, Ralph E. *Academic Library Buildings*. Boulder, Colo.: Colorado Associated University Press, 1973.

————. *Ellsworth on Ellsworth*. Metuchen, N.J.: Scarecrow Press, 1980.

————. *The Economics of Book Storage*. Washington, D.C.: Association of Research Libraries, 1969.

————. *Planning the College and University Library Building*. 2d ed. Boulder, Colo.: Pruit Press, 1968.

Fairbanks, George R. *History of the University of the South*. Jacksonville, Fla.: H. & W. B. Drew, 1905.

Fennimore, K. J. *The Albion College Sesquicentennial History 1835–1985*. Albion, Mich.: Albion College, 1985.

Fitch, James M. *American Building*. Boston, Mass.: Houghton Mifflin, 1948.

Fussler, Herman H., ed. *Library Buildings for Library Service*. Chicago: American Library Association, 1947.

Galpin, W. Freeman. *Syracuse University: The Pioneer Days*. Syracuse, N.Y.: Syracuse University Press, 1952.

Gerould, James T. *The College Library Building: Its Planning and Equipment*. N.Y.: Charles Scribner's Sons, 1932.

Griffin, Clifford S. *The University of Kansas: A History*. Lawrence, Kan.: University Press of Kansas, 1974.

Halliburton, Cecil D. *History of St. Augustine's College*. [Raleigh, N.C.]: St. Augustine's College, 1937.

Hamlin, Arthur T. *The University Library in the United States*. Philadelphia, Pa.: University of Pennsylvania Press, 1981.

Hanley, Edna R. *College and University Library Buildings*. Chicago: American Library Association, 1939.

Harding, Thomas S. *College Society Libraries*. Brooklyn, N.Y.: Pageant Press, 1971.

Harvard University Library, 1638–1938. Cambridge, Mass.: Harvard University Library, 1969.

Hatch, L. C. *The History of Bowdoin College*. Portland, Maine: Loring, Short & Marmon, 1927.

Hollis, Daniel W. *South Carolina College*. Columbia, S.C.: University of South Carolina Press, 1951.

Hubbart, Henry C. *Ohio Wesleyan's First Hundred Years*. Delaware, Ohio: Ohio Wesleyan University, 1943.

Impact of Technology on the Library Building. N.Y.: Educational Facilities Laboratories [1967].

Jones, Maxine D., and Richardson, Joe M. *Talladega College: The First Century*. Tuscaloosa, Ala.: University of Alabama Press, 1990.

Jones, Rufus M. *Haverford College: A History and Interpretation*. N.Y.: Macmillan, 1933.

Jordy, William, and Monkhouse, Christopher. *Buildings on Paper; Rhode Island Architectural Drawings, 1825–1945. Catalogue of an Exhibit*. Providence, R.I.: Rhode Island School of Design, 1982.

Kaser, David. *Books and Libraries in Camp and Battle.* Westport, Conn.: Greenwood Press, 1984.

Koch, Theodore W. *A Book of Carnegie Libraries.* N.Y.: H. W. Wilson Co., 1917.

Kondayan, Betty R. *Historical Sketch of the Library of Washington and Lee University.* Lexington, Va.: Washington and Lee University, 1980.

Langill, Ellen. *Carroll College: The First Century; 1846–1946.* Waukesha, Wis.: Carroll College Press, 1980.

Larson, Magali S. *The Rise of Professionalism.* Berkeley, Calif.: University of California Press, 1979.

Leland Stanford, Jr. University Library, *New Building of the Stanford University Library.* Stanford, Calif.: Stanford University, 1919.

Lloyd, James B. *The University of Mississippi; The Formative Years.* University, Miss.: University of Mississippi, 1979.

Malmstrom, R. E. *Lawrence Hall at Williams College.* Williamstown, Mass.: Williams College Museum of Art, n.d..

McGinnis, Frederick A. *A History and an Interpretation of Wilberforce University.* Wilberforce, Ohio: Brown Publishing Company, 1941.

Mendel, Mesick, Cohen, firm. *The Nott Memorial: A Historic Structure Report.* Albany, N.Y.: Prepared for the Trustees and Alumni Council of Union College, 1973.

Metcalf, Keyes D. *Planning Academic and Research Library Buildings.* New York: McGraw-Hill, 1965.

———. *Planning Academic and Research Library Buildings.* 2d ed. by Philip C. Leighton and David C. Weber. Chicago: American Library Association, 1986.

Mumford, Lewis. *The South in Architecture.* N.Y.: Harcourt Brace, 1941.

Negro Education: A Study of the Private and Higher Schools for Colored People in the United States. Washington, D.C.: Department of the Interior, Bureau of Education, *"Bulletin,"* 1916, No. 38," 1917.

Neyland, Leedell W., and Riley, John W. *The History of Florida Agricultural and Mechanical University.* Gainesville, Fla.: University of Florida Press, 1963.

Nollen, John S. *Grinnell College.* Iowa City, Iowa: State Historical Society of Iowa, 1953.

Ochsner, Jeffrey K. *H. H. Richardson: Complete Architectural Works.* Cambridge, Mass.: Massachusetts Institute of Technology, 1983.

Oehlerts, Donald E. *Books and Blueprints; Building America's Public Libraries.* N.Y.: Greenwood Press, 1991.

O'Gorman, James F. *The Architecture of Frank Furness.* Philadelphia, Pa.: Museum of Art, 1973.

Ohio Library Commission. *Sketches of Ohio Libraries.* Columbus, Ohio: F. J. Heer, 1902.

Parsons, Kermit C. *The Cornell Campus: A History of Its Planning and Development.* Ithaca, N.Y.: Cornell University Press, 1968.

Pilkington, Walter. *Hamilton College, 1812–1962.* Clinton, N.Y.: Hamilton College, 1962.

Planning the University Library Building. Princeton, N.J.: Princeton University Press, 1949.

Puryear, B. N. *Hampton Institute.* Hampton, Va.: Prestige Press, 1962.

Rhees, William J. *Manual of Public Libraries, Institutions, and Societies in the United States and British Provinces of North America.* Philadelphia, P.A.: J. B. Lippincott, 1859.

Rudolph, Frederick. *The American College and University; A History.* N.Y.: Vintage, 1968.

Sellers, Charles C. *Dickinson College: A History.* Middletown, Conn.: Wesleyan University Press, 1973.

Sharp, Katherine L. *Illinois Libraries, Part III; College, Institutional and Special Libraries.* Urbana, Ill.: University of Illinois, 1907.

Shiflett, Orvin L. *Origins of American Academic Librarianship.* Norwood, N.J.: Ablex, 1981.

Small Library Buildings. Boston, Mass.: A.L.A. Publishing Board, 1908.

Smith, Jessie C. *Black Academic Libraries and Research Collections; An Historical Survey.* Westport, Conn.: Greenwood Press, 1977.

Smythe, George F. *Kenyon College; Its First Century.* New Haven, Conn.: Yale University Press, 1924.

Snead & Co. *Library Planning, Bookstacks and Shelving.* Jersey City, N.J.: Snead & Co., 1915.

Sommer, Robert. *Personal Space: The Behavioral Basis for Design.* Englewood Cliffs, N.J.: Prentice-Hall, 1969.

Soule, Charles C. *How to Plan a Library Building for Library Work.* Boston, Mass.: Boston Book Company.

Storrer, William A. *Architecture of Frank Lloyd Wright.* Cambridge Mass.: MIT Press, 1978.

Study on Studying: A Report from the Community College Planning Center on Student Study Facilities. Stanford, Calif.: Stanford University School of Education, [1965].

Survey of Libraries in the United States. Chicago: American Library Association, 1927.

Tewksbury, D. G. *The Founding of American Colleges and Universities before the Civil War.* Hamden, Conn.: Archon, 1965.

Turner, Paul V. *Campus.* Cambridge, Mass.: MIT Press, 1984.

Washington, Booker T. *Papers,* ed. by Louis R. Harlan and Raymond W. Smock. Urbana: Ill. University of Illinois Press, 1977.

Wilkerson, M. M. *Thomas Duckett Boyd.* Baton Rouge, La.: Louisiana State University Press, 1935.

Williams, Howard D. *History of Colgate University 1819–1969.* N.Y.: Van Nostrand, 1969.

Wilson, Louis R. *Library of the First State University.* Chapel Hill, N.C.: University of North Carolina Library, 1960.

Articles

"Academic Library Building. . . ." annual [except 1978], *Library Journal*, December 1 issue, 1967–1994.

"Airlie Conference." *College & Research Libraries* 24 (July 1963): 337–338.

Ambrose, Lodilla. "The Orrington Lunt Library." *Library Journal* 19 (October 1894): 338–340.

Anschutz, C. W. "Library of Wittenberg College." *The Cycle, Published by the Junior Class of Wittenberg College* 1 (June 1892): 31–32.

Architectural Forum 88 (January 1948): 134–135.

Architectural Forum 97 (September 1952): 120–127.

Arnest, Barbara M. "Historic Coburn Library Still Serves CC." *Colorado College Magazine*, Winter 1960.

Bailey, J. Russell. "Mr. Architect, Listen." *Library Journal* 90 (December 1, 1965): 5147–5151.

Bishop, William Warner. "The Historic Development of Library Buildings." *Library Buildings for Library Service*, 1–11. (Chicago: American Library Association, 1947).

———. "New Library Building of the University of Michigan." *Library Journal* 44 (October 1919): 637.

Bonk, Sharon C. "Temples of Knowledge." *Milestones to the Present; Papers from Library History Seminar V*, 53–72. (Syracuse, N.Y.: Gaylord Professional Publications, 1978).

Burchard, John E. "Buildings and Architecture." *College & Research Libraries* 7 (January 1946): 78–79.

———. "Postwar Library Buildings." *College & Research Libraries* 7 (April 1946): 118–126.

Clark, George T. "The New Library Building at Leland Stanford Junior University." *Library Journal* 44 (November 1919): 716–717.

Clayton, Howard. "The American College Library, 1800–1860." *Journal of Library History* 3 (1968), 120–137.

College & Research Libraries, Volumes 1–55, 1939–1994.

Connolly, S. J., Brendan. "The Fixed-Function Library." *Wilson Library Bulletin* 44 (April 1970): 858–860.

Coolidge, Charles A. "History of Libraries." *Harvard University Architectural Quarterly* 2 (September 1913): 1–14.

Eastman, W. R. "Library Buildings." *Library Journal* 26 (Waukesha Conference, 1901): 38–43.

Ellsworth, Ralph. "Academic Library Buildings in the United States." *Advances in Librarianship* 3 (1972): 119–136.

———. "The College and University Library as a Building Type." *American Institute of Architects Journal* 11 (May 1965): 69–72.

Fletcher, William I. "Library Buildings." *Library Journal* 14 (January–February 1889): 39–40.

Foster, William E. "A.L.A. Report on Library Buildings." *Library Journal* 23 (Chautauqua Conference 1898): 13–17.

Fuhlrott, Rolf. "Bibliotheken unter der Erde." *ABI-Technik* 5 (1985, Nr. 1): 1–13.

———. "Underground Libraries." *College & Research Libraries* 47 (May 1986): 238–262.

Garrett, Joe B. "The Carpeted Library." *The Library Environment: Aspects of Interior Planning*, 57–59. (Chicago: American Library Association, 1965).

Ginter, Laura. "Building Billings." *Vermont* (Winter 1984): 2–7.

Goldberger, Paul. "Form and Procession." *Architectural Forum* 138 (January–February 1973): 45.

Goodrich, Nathaniel L. "University of Texas Library." *Library Journal* 37 (June 1912): 325–326.

Gould, Carl. "The American University and Its Library Problem." *Architectural Forum* 44 (June 1926): 361–366.

Green, Bernard R. "Library Buildings and Book Stacks." *Library Journal* 31 (Narragansett Pier Conference 1906): 52–56.

Hamlin, A. D. F. "The Views of a Consulting Architect." *Library Journal* 31 (Narragansett Pier Conference 1906): 57–62.

Harris, George W. "The New Library Building of Cornell University." *Library Journal* 14 (April 1889): 121–24.

Haselden, Clyde L. "Lafayette in Sequence." *Library Journal* 88 (December 1, 1963): 4577–4579.

Hill, Frank P. "Library Buildings—Some Preliminaries." *Library Journal* 24 (October 1899): 563–569.

"History of Marietta College Library," *Marietta College Olio* 33 (March, April 1905): 81–84, 99–100.

Holley, Edward G. "Academic Libraries in 1876." *College & Research Libraries* 37 (January 1976): 15–47.

Huber, W. L. "The Doe Memorial Library, University of California." *Engineering Record* 62 (August 10, 1910): 241.

"Huntington Memorial Library of Hampton Institute." *Library Journal* 28 (May 1903): 241–243.

"Institute for College Library Building Consultants." *College & Research Libraries* 25 (September 1964): 424–425.

Jesse, William H. "New Library Buildings: Some Strengths and Weaknesses." *Library Journal* 89 (December 1, 1964): 4700–4704.

"John M. Johansen Declares Himself." *Architectural Forum* 124 (January–February 1966): 64–67.

Jones, William G. "Academic Library Planning: Rationality, Imagination, and Field Theory in the Work of Walter Netsch—A Case Study." *College & Research Libraries* 51 (May 1990): 207–220.

Kaser, David. "American Academic Library Building, 1870–1890." *Journal of Library History* 21 (Winter 1986): 60–71.

———. "Andrew Carnegie and the Black College Libraries." *For the Good of the Order: Essays in Honor of Edward G. Holley*, 119–133. (Greenwich, Conn.: JAI Press, 1994).

———. "19th-Century Academic Library Buildings." *College & Research Libraries News* 48 (September 1987): 476–478.

———. "Rise and Demise of the Multi-Tier Structural Stack." *Trends in International Librarianship*, 33–41. (Karachi: Royal Book Company, 1991).

———. "Twenty-Five Years of Academic Library Building Planning." *College & Research Libraries* 45 (July 1984): 268–281.

———. "The 'User-Friendly' Academic Library Building." *Journal of Information, Communication and Library Science* 1 (Summer 1995): 9–16.

Keally, Francis. "An Architect's View of Library Planning." *Library Journal* 88 (December 1, 1963): 4521–4525.

Keogh, Andrew. "The Sterling Memorial Library." *Library Journal* 56 (June 15, 1931): 529–533.

Lane, William C. "The New Harvard Library." *Library Journal* 38 (May 1913): 267–270.

Larned, J. N. "Report on Library Architecture." *Library Journal* 12 (September–October 1887): 377–381.

Libraries, Volumes 1–36, 1896–1931.

"Library Buildings." *Library Journal* 14 (January-February 1889): 39–40.

Library Journal, Volumes 1–118, 1876–1994.

Little, George T. "A Library Building for a Small College." *Library Journal* 28 (June 1903): 290–292.

Macdonald, Angus Snead. "A Library of the Future." *Overbiblioteker Wilhelm Munthe pa Femtirsdagen 20. Oktober 1933*, 168–184. (Oslo: Grøndahl, 1933).

Maloney, John W. "Modular Library Under Construction." *Architectural Record* 104 (July 1948): 102–109.

Mason, Ellsworth. "Back to the Cave, or, Some Buildings I Have Known." *Library Journal* 94 (December 1, 1969): 4353–4357.

———. "The Development of Library Lighting." *Advances in Library Administration and Organization* 10: 129–144. (Greenwich, Conn.: JAI Press, 1992).

———. "Writing a Building Program." *Library Journal* 91 (December 1, 1966): 5838–5844.

Mauran, John L. "The Relation of the Architect to the Librarian." *Library Journal* 26 (Waukesha Conference 1901): 43–46.

McDonald, John P. "Campus Contemporary." *Library Journal* 87 (November 1, 1962): 4376–4379.

Meggett, Arthur. "The James B. Colgate Library." *Philobiblon* (February 1964) pp. 1–9.

Mierow, Charles C. "The Library Building for a Liberal Arts College." *Association of American Colleges Bulletin* 14 (April 1928): 198–215.

Mills, Jessie C. "A Catalog of Misfortunes." *Library Journal* 92 (December 1, 1967): 4341–4643.

Muller, Robert H. "College and University Library Buildings, 1929–1949." *College & Research Libraries* 12 (January 1951): 261–265.

———. "College Library Buildings Self-Appraised." *College & Research Libraries* 9 (July 1948): 221–226.

———. "Future Library Building Trends among Colleges and Universities." *College & Research Libraries* 12 (January 1951): 33–36.

Munthe, Wilhelm. "Modern American Library Buildings." *Library Association Record* 3d ser II (1932): 286–287.

"National-Library Building.—The Proposed Plan." *Library Journal* 6 (April 1881): 77–81.

"Netsch, Walter A(ndrew Jr.)." *Contemporary Architects*, 585–586. (N.Y.: St. Martin's Press, 1980).

Neutra, Richard J. "Centerpiece of a Library." *Library Journal* 89 (December 1, 1964): 4695–4699.

"Northwestern University Library." *Architectural Record* 148 (July 1970): 89–96.

O'Connor, Robert B. "Problems of Modern Materials," *Planning a Library Building*, 30- 34. (Chicago: American Library Association, 1955).

"Octagon for Marywood." *Library Journal* 93 (December 1968): 4513.

Oehlerts, Donald E. "American Library Architecture and the World's Columbian Exposition." *Milestones to the Present; Papers from Library History Seminar V*, 73–79. (Syracuse, N.Y.: Gaylord Professional Publications, 1978).

———. "Sources for the Study of American Library Architecture." *Journal of Library History* 11 (January 1976): 68–78.

Orne, Jerrold. "The Renaissance of Academic Library Building 1967–1971." *Library Journal* 96 (December 1, 1971): 3947–3967.

Patton, Normand S. "Architects and Librarians." *Library Journal* 14 (St. Louis Conference 1889): 159–161.

Phinney, Herman K. "Rah for Sibley!" *Rochester Alumni Review* 11 (February–March 1933): 55–57.

Poole, William F. "The Construction of Library Buildings." *Library Journal* 6 (April 1881): 69–77.

———. "Progress of Library Architecture." *Library Journal* 7 (Cincinnati Conference 1882): 130–136.

———. "Small Library Buildings." *Library Journal* 10 (Lake George Conference, 1885): 250–256.

"Progress of Library Architecture." *Library Journal* 7 (July–August 1882): 130–136.

Putnam, Herbert. "The Planning of Libraries." *Architectural Quarterly of Harvard University* II (September 1913): 15–28.

Raney, M. Llewellyn. "Gilman Hall—The New Library of the Johns Hopkins University." *Library Journal* 38 (November 1913): 607–612.

"Report on Library Architecture." *Library Journal* 12 (September–October 1887): 379.

Retan, F. S. "Colgate Library Building." *Madisonensis* 21 (May 18, 1889): 209–212.

Reynolds, Helen Margaret. "University Library Buildings in the United States 1890–1939." *College & Research Libraries* 14 (April 1953): 149–157.

Rogers, A. Robert. "Systems Building: A Solution to the Cost Squeeze." *Library Journal* 94 (December 1, 1969): 4360–4363.

Rouse, Roscoe, Jr. "The Library Buildings Award Program of the American Institute of Architects and the American Library Association." *Advances in Library Administration and Organization*, 8:241–252. (Greenwich, Conn.: JAI Press, 1989).

"Small Library Buildings." *Library Journal* 10 (September–October 1885): 250–256.

Soule, Charles C. "Points of Agreement among Librarians as to Library Architecture." *Library Journal* 16 (San Francisco Conference 1891): 17–19.

Stallings, H. D. "College and University Library Buildings: Results of a Questionnaire." *College & Research Libraries* 13 (July 1952): 212–214.

Stanford, Edward B. "Federal Aid for Academic Library Construction." *Library Journal* 99 (January 15, 1974): 112–115.

Stanley, Hiram M. "University Library Buildings." *Library Journal* 14 (St. Louis Conference 1889): 264–265.

Tilton, Edward L. "Architecture of Small Libraries." *Public Libraries* 17 (1912): 40–44.

———. "College Library Planning." *American School and University* (1933): 225–229.

———. "Scientific Library Planning." *Library Journal* 37 (September 1912): 497–501.

Toan, Danforth W. "Libraries." *Encyclopedia of Architecture, Design, Engineering & Construction.* 3:220–268. (N.Y.: John Wiley & Sons, 1989).

Toombs, Ken E. "The Evolution of Academic Architecture." *Journal of Library Administration* 17 (4, 1992): 25–36.

Towne, Jackson E. "Charles Kendall Adams and the First University Library Building." *Michigan History* 37 (1953): 129–144.

Utley, H. M. "Report on Library Architecture." *Library Journal* 15 (Fabyan House Conference 1890): 12–14.

Van Name, Addison. "Report on Architecture." *Library Journal* 14 (St. Louis Conference 1889): 162–163.

———. "Report on Library Architecture." *Library Journal* 14 (May–June 1889): 167–168.

Van Slyck, Abigail A. " 'The Utmost Amount of Effectiv (*sic*) Accommodation': Andrew Carnegie and the Reform of the American Library." *Journal of the Society of Architectural Historians* 1 (December 1991): 359–383.

Vinton, Frederick. "Hints for Improved Library Economy." *Library Journal* 2 (October 1877) 53–54.

"Walter A. Netsch." *Interiors* 130 (November 1970): 110–115.

West, Theresa H. "Report on Library Architecture." *Library Journal* 19 (Lake Placid Conference 1894): 96–106.

Willard, Ashton R. "College Libraries in the United States." *New England Magazine* ns17 (December 1897): 433.

Williams, Talcott. "Plans for the Library Building of the University of Pennsylvania." *Library Journal* 13 (August 1888): 237–242.

Winsor, Justin. "Library Buildings." *Public Libraries in the United States. . . . Part I,* 464–475. (Washington, D.C., Government Printing Office, 1876).

"Ye Architect and Ye Librarian." *Library Journal* 13 (November 1888): 338.

Index

acoustical problems in libraries,
140–41, 144
Adams, Charles Kendall, 34, 37
additions to library buildings,
156–57
Adelphi College, 145
Agnes Scott College, 113
AIA/ALA library building awards,
137
air treatment in libraries, 110, 113,
116, 140, 144, 153
Airlie House, 124
Alabama A & M University, 68
Albany Library School, 35
Albion College, 80
Allegheny College, 80
Allyn, Lawrence Holford, 101
alternatives to new construction,
155
American Architect, 47–49
American factory style, 97
American Institute of Architects,
31, 137
American Library Association, 31,
45–50, 88, 98, 120, 122, 137, 159
American University, 158
Americans with Disabilities Act,
115
Amherst College 3, 9, 19–20, 48,
122
Andrews, G. W., 67
Andrews, Jacques & Rantoul, 54
Anglo-American Code, 107
Architects Collaborative, 147
Architectural Record, 114

Arizona, University of, 99, 101, 111
Arkansas, University of, 99
Asheville-Biltmore College, 122,
144
Association of College and Re-
search Libraries, 120
Astor Library, 46
Atlanta University. *See* Clark At-
lanta University
atria, use of in libraries, 47, 49, 139–
41, 144. *See also* interior and exte-
rior courts
Atwood & Nash, 101
Augustana College, 147
Austin, Henry, 19, 21
Austin Peay State University, 123

Bailey, J. Russell, 117, 147
Bakewell & Brown, 96
Baldwin-Wallace College, 55
Ball State University, 145
Baltimore, University of, 122
Bard College, 55
Barnwell, Robert W., 13
Bates College, 80, 147
Bauhaus movement, 130, 134
Baylor University, 80
Beloit College, 66, 50
below-grade library construction,
152–53, 162
Benedict College, 68, 77, 146–47
Benson, Mary, 55
Bertram, James, 66–69, 71–73,
76–77
Bibliothèque Mazarine, 2

Bibliothèque Nationale, 34, 107
Bibliothèque Ste. Geneviève, 36, 91, 107
Biddle University. *See* Johnson C. Smith University
Billings, Hammett, 19
Birkerts, Gunnar, 151, 153
Bishop, William Warner, 97
Bluffton College, 100
Bodleian Library, 2
Boll, John J., 2, 16
Bond, Richard, 16, 19, 26n3
bookstacks, 109; bookstack locations, 99, 102; multitier stacks, 64, 67, 72, 78, 85, 95, 97, 102, 105, 107–11, 115–56, 126; stack towers, 100, 104, 111, 136, 149. *See also* compaction of library materials
Boston Athenæum, 46, 48
Boston College, 147
Boston Public Library, 24, 60, 91
Boston University, 122
Bowdoin College, 79–80, 122
Bradley University, 114
Breuer, Marcel, 144
Brigham Young University, 130
Brooklyn College, 99
Brown, Hugh M., 71
Brown University, 8, 14, 17, 32–33, 38, 41, 46, 78, 85, 87, 115, 122, 144, 147, 149
Bryn Mawr College, 79–80
Bucklin, James C., 8
Buffalo Library, 47
building shapes, 137–38; octagonal, 17–18, 20, 24–25, 32–33, 139; rectangular, 2–3, 130, 134, 138; round, 5–6, 17, 20, 24–25, 38, 58–59, 138–39; triangular, 139. *See also* shelving arrangements in libraries; radial shelves
Bulfinch, Charles, 14
Bumstead, Horace, 68

Burgh, Thomas, 3
Burton, Ernest DeWitt, 88
Butler University, 80, 122, 141–42, 146
Byers, Edna Hanley, 113, 118

Cadwallader, Morris, 19
California-Berkeley, University of, 38, 91–92, 94–95, 97–98, 101–2, 110, 115
California-Los Angeles, University of, 99–100
California-San Diego, University of, 125, 139, 146, 150
Cameron, Donald F., 114
Carleton College, 80, 83–84
Carnegie, Andrew, 63–73, 76–79, 81, 118
carpet, use of in libraries. *See* floor covering in libraries
Carroll, F. L., 80
Carson, Charles L., 39
Center for Research Libraries, 158
Centre College, 9, 19–20, 39
Chabot College, 139
Chandler, George L., 103
Charleston, College of, 9, 19–20, 92
Cheyney State University, 70
Chicago, University of, 87–90, 95, 135, 139, 141, 148
Chicago Public Library, 45
Cincinnati, University of, 80
Civil War, effect of on libraries, 19, 45, 60n1, 86, 96
Claflin College, 60, 64, 146
Clark Atlanta University, 68–69, 99
Clark University, 79–80, 135, 141, 143–45
Clark, J. G., 80
Classical Revival style, 4, 10, 14–15, 18–20, 22, 57, 65, 67–68, 70–71, 74, 77–78, 91
Clemson University, 140, 147

Colgate University, 35–36, 52, 113, 130, 134, 144, 162
Colgate, James B., 36
College & Research Libraries, 114, 119
Colorado, University of, 112, 114, 120
Colorado College, 54, 140
Columbia University, 31, 58–59, 63, 74, 85, 87, 99, 101, 104, 115, 138
Columbian Exposition. *See* World's Columbian Exposition
compact shelving. *See* compaction of library materials
compaction of library materials, 116, 157–58
computers, use of in libraries. *See* electronic technology in libraries
Conference on Libraries and Automation, 124
consultants. *See* library building consultants
Converse College, 78, 147
Cooperative Committee on Library Building Plans, 112–14, 117, 119–20, 130, 131
Cornell College, 66
Cornell University, 31, 35–38, 51, 87, 93, 115, 120, 146
Corpus Christi, University of, 139
costs of library construction, 155
Council on Library Resources, 124
Councill, W. H., 68
Countway Medical Library, 141
Cram & Ferguson, 101
Cravath, Paul D., 69
Cret, Paul, 104, 149
Cutter, Charles Ammi, 48

Daly, Leo A., 133
Dancy, John C., 70
Dartmouth College, 33–34, 51, 100–101
Davis, Alexander Jackson, 18–19, 22

Davis, Raymond Cazallis, 34
Delessert, Benjamin, 6, 18, 25
Delta State University, 141
Denison University, 38
Denver, University of, 147
Dewey, Melvil, 31, 35
Dickinson College, 39
Doane College, 56
Dodds, Harold W., 112
Doe, Charles Franklin, 91
Dogan, M. W., 72
Drake University, 100
Drew University, 42, 100
Drexel University, 139
Duke, J. B., 80
Duke University, 80, 114
D'Youville College, 158

Earlham College, 122
earthquakes, damage to libraries, 20, 85, 96
École des Beaux Arts, 31, 55–56
Edison, Thomas, 61
Educational Facilities Laboratories, Inc., 120, 125
Eggers & Higgins, 150
electric lights. *See* library lighting
electronic technology in libraries, 124–25, 159, 163
electronic texts. *See* electronic technology in libraries
Ellsworth, Ralph, 112, 114, 119–20, 130, 136, 139
Emory & Henry College, 147
Emory University, 56–57, 74, 100–101, 147
Emporia, College of, 66

federal funding of library construction, 117–18, 155–56
field theory of design, 135, 139
fire, damage to libraries, 8, 14, 20, 30, 39, 51, 57, 68–69, 71, 112

Fisk University, 66, 69–70, 125, 145, 149
fixed-function buildings, 85, 110–11, 129, 134, 156
Fletcher, William Isaac, 48–49
floor covering in libraries, 113, 121–22, 126, 128n23
Florida A. & M. University, 71
Florida Southern College, 138, 154n14
fluorescent lights. *See* library lighting
Ford Foundation, 120
Forsyth, Layton Hicks, 101
Franklin and Marshall College, 55
Franklin College, 80
Frick, H. C., 80
Furman University, 78
Furness, Frank, 35
Fussler, Herman, 118

Gassette, Lettie, 80
George Peabody College, 77
Georgia, University of, 80, 113
Georgia Institute of Technology, 140
Georgian style, 39, 90, 100, 130
Gerould, James Thayer, 118
Gibbs, James, 5
Gilbert, Cass, 95, 102
Githens, Alfred, 113
glass, use of in libraries, 35–36, 91, 109, 145–46
Goler, W. H., 70
Gordon & Kaelber, 101
Gothic Revival style, 3–5, 10, 15, 19, 21, 23, 25, 35, 48, 50, 79, 89, 100, 104, 130, 153
Gould, Jay, 59
Great Depression, effect of on library construction, 104
Grinnell College, 39, 75, 78, 140, 146
group study rooms, 122–23

Grove City College, 66
Guild, Reuben, 32

Hadley, Arthur T., 64
Hallett & Rawson, 75
Hamilton College, 19, 21, 24, 141
Hampden-Sydney College, 147
Hampton University, 64, 69, 80
Hanley, Edna Ruth. *See* Byers, Edna Hanley
Hanover College, 80, 145
Hardin-Simmons College, 114, 129
Harvard University, 7–9, 14–15, 19, 30–31, 34, 46, 51, 87, 95–96, 108, 113–15, 140, 148, 152
Haverford College, 19, 21
heat, effect on books, 47
Heidelberg College, 50, 139, 143
Hellmuth Obata & Kassabaum, 147
Hendricks, Mrs. E. S., 80
Hendrix College, 152–53
Hibbs, Henry, 101
high-rise library buildings, 148–49, 152
Higher Education Facilities Act, 117
Hill, J., 80
Hiram College, 80
Hobart and William Smith Colleges, 39
Hofstra University, 120, 123, 149
Hollins College, 80
Holy Cross, College of the, 100–101
Howard University, 73, 76, 100–101
Howard, John Galen, 102
Hubbard, T. H., 80
Huntington, Collis P., 64
Huntington, Mrs. C. P., 80
Hutton, Addison, 32, 56

Illinois, University of, 54, 99–101, 115, 152–53, 162
Illinois, University of, at Chicago, 135

Illinois Wesleyan University, 141
Indiana State University, 80
Indiana University, 50–51, 80, 114–15, 120, 145–46, 148, 150
interior and exterior courts, 116, 139–41. *See also* atria, use of in libraries
interlibrary loan, 159
International style, 130, 139
Iowa, University of, 114, 132
iron, use of in library construction, 25, 30, 32, 34, 104

Jefferson, Thomas, 5, 8, 14, 57
Jennings, Arthur B., 54
Jesse, William, 120
Jewett, Charles Coffin, 17–18, 21, 24, 32
Johansen, John M., 135, 143
John Crerar Library, 149
Johns Hopkins University, 30, 87, 89–90, 95–96, 152
Johnson, Philip, 135, 141, 152
Johnson C. Smith University, 72, 77
Johnston, C. H., 101
Judson College, 78

Kahn, Albert, 97
Kansas, University of, 51, 54–55, 99–102
Kaser, David, 120
Keffer & Jones, 132
Kenyon College, 39
Kilham, Walter H., Jr., 113. *See also* O'Connor & Kilham
King's College Chapel, Cambridge, 16, 26n3
Knoxville College, 73
Koch, Theodore, 113
Kuhlman, A. F., 113

LaBrouste, Henri, 34, 107–8, 116
Lafayette College, 80, 122, 137
Lake Forest College, 80

Larned, Joseph N., 47
Larson, Jens, 101
LaSalle University, 132, 147
Latrobe, Benjamin, 14, 18
Layton Hicks & Forsyth, 103
Le Vau, Louis, 2
Lehigh University, 32–34, 39, 46, 56, 92, 141, 144
LeMoyne College (TN), 137
Library Administration and Management Association, 120
library building consultants, 113–14, 117–21
Library Buildings and Equipment Institute, 120, 122
Library Company of Philadelphia, 2
Library Journal, 46, 48, 119
library lighting, 31, 110, 112–13, 116, 122, 144–45, 153
Library of Congress, 14, 24, 47, 60, 104, 107, 124, 163
Library Technology Project, 122
Lieber, Francis, 13
Lincoln University (PA), 56, 64
Livingstone College, 70, 75
Louisiana State University, 8, 80, 130
Louisville, University of, 113, 133–34
Lucker, Jay, 120
Lyles Bissett Carlisle & Wolfe, 147
Lyman & Place, 101

Macalester College, 147, 151
Macdonald, Angus Snead, 111–12, 115–16, 147
MacLean, George E., 86
Maginnis & Walsh, 101
Maine, University of, 78
Maloney, John W., 114
Marietta College, 19, 21, 50
Marymount College, 139
Marywood College, 126, 139

Mason, Ellsworth, 120
Massachusetts, University of, 148–49
Massachusetts Institute of Technology, 31, 65, 113–14, 120, 140, 148–49
McAdams, Nancy, 121
McGranahan, R. W., 73
McIver & Cohagen, 101
McKim, Charles Follen, 57–58, 91, 135. See also McKim, Mead & White
McKim, Mead & White, 74
Memphis State University, 149
Mercer University, 78
Meredith College, 117, 147
Merrill, J. G., 66, 69
Merrimack College, 147
Metcalf, Keyes D., 114, 119–20, 138, 145–46
mezzanines, use of in libraries, 140
Miami, University of, 137
Miami University, 78
Michigan, University of, 34–36, 51, 54, 87, 97–98, 115, 153, 158
microfilming of library materials, 159
Middlebury College, 80
Miller, Robert, 114
Miller, William H., 37
Mills, Robert, 14, 19, 22
Mills College, 39
Milwaukee-Downer College, 80
Minnesota, University of, 99, 101, 148, 161
Mississippi, University of, 42
Missouri, University of, 114
modular construction, 107, 111–17, 129, 136, 142, 156, 164
Montana, University of, 99, 101
monumentality in library buildings, 144–45
Morrill Act, 29, 71, 152
Morris Brown College, 69

Mount Holyoke College, 19, 21, 78–79
multitier structural stack. See bookstacks: multitier stacks
Murphy & Mackey, 136, 142

National Science Foundation, 124
Nebraska, University of, 55, 86, 101
Neilson, J. Crawford, 39, 41
Netsch, Walter, 135, 139
Nevada Southern University, 139
New Brunswick Theological Seminary, 26n11
New York Mercantile Library, 149
New York Public Library, 36, 100
New York University, 59, 63, 125, 135, 138, 141, 145, 148
Newman, H. S., 134, 144
North Carolina, University of, 8–9, 18–19, 22, 87, 99–101, 113–14, 120, 148
North Dakota State University, 114
Northeastern University, 147
Northern Iowa, University of, 123
Northwestern University, 56, 99–101, 113, 123, 135, 139, 148
Notre Dame, University of, 123, 148–49

Oberlin College, 39, 78, 147
O'Connor, Robert B., 134. See also O'Connor & Kilham
O'Connor & Kilham, 133
Ohio State University, 81
Ohio Wesleyan University, 9, 19–20, 56–57
Oklahoma, University of, 66, 99–101, 103
Olivet College, 54
Online Computer Library Center, 107
Oral Roberts University, 139, 146
Oregon, University of, 100–101
Orne, Jerrold, 120

Osburn, A. C., 68
Otis, William A., 56
Otterbein College, 78

Palladio, Andrea, 10
Pantheon, 5
Parker, Ralph, 114
Parthenon, 55
Patton, Normand S., 49, 54, 80. *See also* Patton & Miller
Patton, S. M., 57, 74
Patton & Miller, 53
Peabody, George, 80
Peabody Library, 46, 141
Pennsylvania, University of, 35, 87, 115, 144
Pennsylvania State University, 66, 78
Pereira, William J., 139, 150
Peru State University, 60, 80
philanthropists, libraries funded by, 36, 55, 57, 59, 63–78, 80–81, 91, 89, 95, 131
Pittsburgh, University of, 123
Platt, Charles A., 101
Pomona College, 78
Poole, William Frederick, 45–48
postmodern style, 134
Potter, Edward T., 38, 40
Potter, William A., 19
Powell, Benjamin E., 114
Princeton Theological Seminary, 26n2
Princeton University, 19, 24–25, 32–33, 112–14, 130
Providence College, 141, 144
Purdue University, 50
Putnam, Herbert, 76

Quick, Edwin A., 36, 52

Radcliffe Camera, 5
Ramée, Joseph Jacques, 38
Randolph-Macon College, 147

Raney, M. Llewellyn, 89
Reid, A. S., 80
Reis, W. E., 80
Renaissance style, 50, 55–57, 59, 64, 78, 86, 95, 100
Rice University, 113, 141
Richards Bauer, 143
Richardson, Henry Hobson, 33, 36, 39, 48–50, 52, 54–55, 96
Ricker, Nathan C., 54
Roanoke College, 38
Rochester, University of, 38, 99–101, 104
Rochester Institute of Technology, 146
Rockefeller, John D., 89
Rockefeller Foundation, 114
Rogers, James Gamble, 101, 104
Romanesque Revival style, 19, 24, 33, 35–36, 38–39, 42, 50–53, 55, 61n11, 79, 96, 100
Rosary College, 144–45
Rush, Charles, 114
Russell, Archimedes, 35
Rutgers University, 80, 114
Ryder & Harris, 19

Saint Augustine's College, 55, 64
Saint John's University (MN), 122, 144, 152
Saint Lawrence University, 19, 21, 40
Saint Louis University, 130, 133, 140
Saint Mary's College (IN), 141, 145
Saint Mary's Dominican College, 144
Saint Meinrad College, 152
Saint Michael's College, 139
Saint Olaf College, 80
Saint Paul's Cathedral, 2
Saint Peter's College, 139
Saint Stephen's College. *See* Bard College

Saint Thomas College (MN), 130
Sanders, D. J., 72
Sangamon State University, 139, 145
Sarah Lawrence College, 145, 147
Scarritt College, 130, 145, 160
Scott, Emmet J., 72
Scripps Institute of Oceanography, 152
seating configurations in libraries, 126
seminar style of instruction, 13, 29–30, 85–91, 95–97, 108
shelving arrangements in libraries: perimeter shelves, 2, 6, 20, 110; radial shelves, 5–6, 21, 24–25, 62, 68, 138–39; transverse shelves, 3–4, 6, 16, 18, 20. See also bookstacks
Shepley, Henry R., 113. See also Shepley Bulfinch Richardson & Abbott; Shepley Rutan & Coolidge
Shepley Bulfinch Richardson & Abbott, 147, 151
Shepley Rutan & Coolidge, 70, 85, 88
Sibley, Hiram, 38
Simpson College, 141
Smithmeyer, J. L., 47
smoking rooms, 113
Sommer, Robert, 126
Soule, Charles C., 50
South, University of the, 38, 130
South Carolina, University of, 9, 13, 19, 22, 46, 85, 137, 147, 160
South Carolina State College, 147
Southern California, University of, 100–101
Southern Illinois University, 79, 81, 140
Southern Illinois University at Edwardsville, 147
Southern Methodist University, 113

Spear, Charles V., 39
stacks. See bookstacks
Stanford, T. W., 80
Stanford University, 80, 85, 96–97, 105, 120, 141, 149
Starr, E., 80
State University of New York at Binghamton, 148
Staub, John F., 113
steel, use of in library construction, 30, 104
Steensland, H., 80
Stewart, B. F., 66
Stone, Edward Durell, 149
student society libraries, 16
Sullivan, Louis, 130
Swarthmore College, 78–79
Sykes, Henry A., 19
Syracuse University, 37, 51, 78

Taft, Howard, 76
Talbert, Horace, 67
Talladega College, 66–67, 73
Tate, Vernon, 114
Taylor, R. R., 65
Tefft, Thomas A., 17–19
telephone, use of in libraries, 61
Temple of Diana Propylea, 8
Temple University, 99–100
Tennessee, University of, 50, 120
Texas, University of, 93–95, 97, 102, 104, 121, 139, 148–49
Texas Christian University, 135
Thayer, Samuel J. F., 33
Thirkield, Wilbur P., 73
Thomas, Jr., Douglas H., 90
Thompson, E. C., 80
Thompson, Mrs. F. F., 80
Thompson, W. R., 80
Tilton, Edward L., 101
Tilton, Mrs. F. W., 80
Toronto, University of, 148
Tougaloo College, 151
Tower of the Winds, 17

Trinity College, Cambridge, 140
Trinity College, Dublin, 3
Trinity University (TX), 145
Trowbridge, Alexander B., 64
Trumbauer, Horace, 95–96
Tulane University, 80–81, 113
Turner, Paul, 138
Tuskegee Institute, 65–66, 72, 77

Union College, 6, 30, 38, 40, 93
United States Air Force Academy, 145
United States Military Academy, 8
Upham, Mrs. H. A. J., 80
Upper Iowa College, 66
Utah, University of, 99, 141
Utley, H. M., 50

Vail, William H., 57
Van Brunt, Henry, 34–37, 51
Van Wickle, A. S., 80
Van Wormer, A., 80
Vanderbilt University, 100–101, 113, 147, 152–53
Vassar College, 79–80, 85, 146, 161
Vermont, University of, 33, 51–52, 61n11
Vinton, Frederic, 24–25, 32
Virginia, University of, 5, 8, 57–58
Virginia Polytechnic Institute, 130
Virginia State Library, 121
Voorhees, R., 80

Walker, George C., 19
Walker, Ralph, 113
Walker, William A., 32
Walker & Gould, 41
Wallace, T. W., 70
Walsh, Robert, 121
Warner Burns Toan & Lundy, 147
Washington, Booker T., 64–68, 70, 72, 77
Washington, University of, 99–100, 141

Washington and Jefferson College, 80
Washington and Lee University, 39, 41, 78
Washington College (MD), 123
Washington Monument, 14
Washington State University, 114
Washington University, 136, 142, 147, 152
Weber, David C., 120
Wellesley College, 77, 85
Wells College, 135, 139, 145
Wesleyan University, 5, 19, 21, 46
West Virginia University, 79, 83n35
Western Illinois University, 139, 141, 147
Westminster College (PA), 100
White, Andrew Dickson, 36–38
White, Stanford, 57, 59, 83n35. See also Mckim, Mead & White
Whitfield, Henry D., 76. See also Whitfield & King
Whitfield & King, 71, 76
Widener, Harry Elkins, 95
Widener College, 139
Wilberforce University, 67
Wiley College, 72
William A. Potter, 24
Williams College, 9, 17–20, 24, 32
Wilson, Louis R., 113
Winsor, Justin, 34–35
Winthrop College, 78, 147
Wisconsin, University of, 79
Wisconsin-Parkside, University of, 147
Wittenberg College, 53–54
Wofford College, 147
Woollen, Evans, 152
Wooster, College of, 80
Worcester Polytechnic Institute, 139
Worcester State College, 139
World War I, effect on libraries, 104
World War II, effect on libraries,

110–14, 121, 129, 131, 138, 140, 155, 157
World's Columbian Exposition, 55–57, 74
Wren, Christopher, 2, 140
Wright State University, 139
Wright, Frank Lloyd, 138, 154n14

Yale University, 3–4, 8, 9, 14–16, 19, 21, 23, 25, 46, 64, 87, 101, 104, 149, 153
Yamasaki, Minoru, 142
Yost & Packard, 51
Young, Nathan P., 71

About the Author

David Kaser has consulted on the design of more than 220 college and university library buildings. Over the past thirty-seven years this work has taken him throughout North America and also to multiple assignments in Asia, Africa, and the Middle East. A practicing librarian with masters' degrees from Notre Dame and the University of Michigan, where he also earned the Ph.D. degree, Dr. Kaser is currently distinguished professor emeritus of library and information science at Indiana University.

Dr. Kaser has served as chair of the Buildings and Equipment Section of the American Library Association and was from 1989 to 1993 a member of the Standing Committee on Buildings of the International Federation of Library Associations and Institutions. He is a past president of the Association of College and Research Libraries and was for many years editor of the journal *College & Research Libraries*. Among other responsibilities, Dr. Kaser served as director of libraries at Vanderbilt University for eight years and at Cornell University for five.

A member of Phi Beta Kappa, a past president of Beta Phi Mu, and sometime Guggenheim Fellow, Dr. Kaser's fourteen previous books have appeared over such imprints as the University of Pennsylvania Press, Scarecrow Press, and the University Press of Virginia.